P9-DNL-731

Acclaim for Maureen Corrigan's

Leave Me Alone, I'm Reading

"A wonderful work that strikes a pitch-perfect balance between erudite literary criticism and common sense."   —*The Columbus Dispatch*

"A fine apology for bibliophilia. . . . [Corrigan] segues from perceptive discussion of novels by Austen, the Brontës and Anna Quindlen to her own life, including her journey to China to adopt a child. . . . Funny and insightful. . . . A celebration of the fellowship of book-worms."   —*San Jose Mercury News*

"This reflective and entertaining memoir is about more than just books. It's about being a daughter and an adoptive mother, a student and a teacher, a feminist and a skeptical Catholic—about being Mau-reen Corrigan. Learning about Maureen's life made me think about how my own life was shaped by books."
     —Terry Gross, host of NPR's *Fresh Air*

"Corrigan deals . . . with that intimate connection between reading and life, launching many of her critiques with personal anecdotes in a seamless blend of autobiography, literary criticism and essay."
     —*The Atlanta Journal-Constitution*

"What will most draw fellow bookworms in and delight them about Corrigan's book is her appreciation of how books can be like people— affecting you in ways you were not expecting, pushing you when you need the push, and forcing you to look at your own life differently. . . . [A] heart-felt journey through life and literature and its transects."
     —Gothamist.com

"If you wonder about the secret life of bookworms, this is the book that will open up the rich rewards of going around with your nose stuck in a book. . . . Delightful, absorbing, and engaging."
—Bobbie Ann Mason, author of *An Atomic Romance*

"[Corrigan is] an intelligent, unpretentious critic whose love of books—all kinds of books—comes across in both her radio reviews and her engaging new memoir. . . . Engrossing."
—*The Journal News* (Westchester County, New York)

"An educated and engaging discussion of some of the author's favorite books and how she thinks they've affected her life. . . . A thoughtfully assembled reading list . . . should inspire you to explore some of the books she mentions."   —*New York Post*

"Splendid. . . . Whether your taste runs to *Pride and Prejudice* or *The Maltese Falcon*, you will love *Leave Me Alone, I'm Reading*. It's the book for people who love books."
—Susan Isaacs, author of *Any Place I Hang My Hat*

"For anyone who regards a trip to the bookstore as an all-day event or who might judge new acquaintances by the number of volumes in their living rooms, *Leave Me Alone, I'm Reading* is a must read."
—*The Portland Tribune*

"A little gem."   —*Deseret News* (Salt Lake City)

"From the first page of the introduction to *Leave Me Alone, I'm Reading*, I knew I was in the hands of another book luster. I valued her insights into contemporary and classical literature and the connections she made to her own life, but I especially loved her enthusiasm for books and the act of reading."   —Nancy Pearl, author of
More Book Lust: Recommended Readings for Every Mood, Moment, and Reason

Maureen Corrigan

Leave Me Alone, I'm Reading

Maureen Corrigan is the book critic for NPR's *Fresh Air*. Her reviews and essays have appeared in *The New York Times*, *Newsday*, *The Nation*, *The Boston Globe*, *The Village Voice*, and other publications. Winner of an Edgar Award for criticism, Corrigan also regularly writes a mystery column for *The Washington Post* and teaches literature at Georgetown University. She lives in Washington, D.C., with her husband and daughter, both avid readers.

Leave Me Alone, I'm Reading

Leave Me Alone, I'm Reading

FINDING AND LOSING MYSELF IN BOOKS

Maureen Corrigan

VINTAGE BOOKS
A Division of Random House, Inc.
New York

FIRST VINTAGE BOOKS EDITION, DECEMBER 2006

Grateful acknowledgment is made to the following for permission to reprint previously published material:

Curtis Brown Ltd.: Four-line poem by Ogden Nash, copyright © 1954 by Ogden Nash. Reprinted by permission of Curtis Brown Ltd.

New Directions Publishing Corporation: Excerpt from "Not Waving but Drowning" from *Collected Poems of Stevie Smith*, copyright © 1972 by Stevie Smith. Reprinted by permission of New Directions Publishing Corporation.

The Library of Congress has cataloged the Random House edition as follows:
Corrigan, Maureen.
Leave me alone, I'm reading : finding and losing myself in books / Maureen Corrigan.
—1st ed.
cm.
1. Corrigan, Maureen—Books and reading. 2. Books and reading—
United States—Biography. I. Title.
Z1003.2.C67 2005
028'.9—dc22
2005042822

Vintage ISBN-10: 0-375-70903-7
Vintage ISBN-13: 978-0-375-70903-6

Book design by Dana Leigh Blanchette

www.vintagebooks.com

Printed in the United States of America
10 9 8 7 6 5 4 3

This book is dedicated to my father,
John Joseph Corrigan (1920–1997),
and to my husband, Richard Yeselson.

Two champion readers; two great dads

"Bet you didn't learn anything about foundations when you were in graduate school for English."

—remark made by basement-waterproofing contractor in November 2003 as he was writing out a $10,000 estimate for draining the leaky basement of my row house, where some 4,000 books are shelved

Contents

Introduction

It's not that I don't like people. It's just that when I'm in the company of others—even my nearest and dearest—there always comes a moment when I'd rather be reading a book.

And, for many hours of almost every day, that's what I'm doing. I have a great job—or, to be more accurate, cluster of jobs—for a bookworm. I read for a living. For the past sixteen years I've been the book critic for the NPR program *Fresh Air*. Just about every week, I read a new book and review it for *Fresh Air*'s approximately four and a half million listeners. I get paid to read, to think, to share opinions about literature. I also write a regular "Mysteries" column for *The Washington Post* and review books for other newspapers and journals.

"Do you ever get tired of reading?" people sometimes ask me—particularly people who've seen the inside of my house, where stacks of books are piled on the dining room table, the floor of my bedroom and study, even on the radiators in summertime. The truthful answer is "Rarely." There are those occasional stretches where I'll review three new novels in a row that are all about five hundred pages long and packed with nature descriptions and I push myself to finish these books out of professional duty rather than pleasure. But there's always another, possibly better book on the horizon that I'm curious about, another world to lose myself in. After more than a decade of weekly reviewing, during which, on average, I receive about fifty new books a week sent to my house by publishers hoping for a review on *Fresh Air,* I still feel an upsurge of curiosity every time I rip open another cardboard book box to look at the new title inside. There's always a chance that this new novel or work of nonfiction will be a book I'll love, a book that I'll pass on to friends and rave about on *Fresh Air;* a book that changes the way I "read" my own life. For the chance of finding such magic—as I do maybe ten times a year—I misspend hours of my life reading what turn out to be the wrong books: biographies promoting glib psychological keys to their subjects, or novels that go nowhere, or mysteries narrated by cats. No pain, no gain.

In addition to being a book critic, I'm a professor of literature (for the past sixteen years at Georgetown University). Again, a nice job for a compulsive reader, especially since it allows me to escape the relentless pressure of reading hot-off-the-press books and return, again and again, to familiar literary works—some classic, some personal favorites that haven't been anointed as "canonical." Years ago I wrote a Ph.D. dissertation on, among other figures, the twentieth-century British social critic and artist Eric Gill. Gill was a gifted coiner of aphorisms, and one in particular has always stayed with me: "The free man does what he likes in his working time and in his spare time what is required of him. The slave does what he is obliged to do in his working time and what he likes to do only when he is not at work." According to Gill's definition, through the grace of literature, I'm a "free man."

But here's a catch: I live an intensely bookish life during a resolutely nonliterary era. An absurdly small number of people in America care about what I or any other book critic has to say about the latest novel or work of nonfiction. Despite the proliferation of mega-bookstores and neighborhood reading groups, most Americans are indifferent to the lure of literature: in fact, according to a *Wall Street Journal* article of a few years ago, some 59 percent of Americans don't own a single book.

Not a cookbook or even the Bible. Just as I find that statistic incomprehensible, a lot of people consider what I do for a living fairly pointless, as the epigraph to this book demonstrates. All that reading and so little material reward. My own mother, who's always dazzled by my facility in answering questions in the literature category on *Jeopardy!* whenever we watch it together, keeps urging me to try to get on the show to make all those years spent reading finally pay off.

There's another downside to what I do: a critic makes enemies. I'm no Sheridan Whiteside, aka The Man Who Came to Dinner; I don't enjoy slamming other people's work. Indeed, there's always greater happiness all around in praising a book rather than in panning it: the author and publisher are delighted; my editor or producer feels good about devoting space to a book that merits it; and I, the reviewer, presumably have had a good-to-great experience reading a book that I can recommend to others. But if a book is lousy, I say so. Besides other, more noble reasons—such as integrity—I selfishly care about the quality of my own writing, and whenever I've attempted to be "nice" and make a book sound better than it is, my review sounds forced and wooden. As a consequence of the negative reviews I've written, I've lost freelance jobs (because an editor was either friends with or a fan of the writer) and been the target of angry authorial outbursts. I answered the phone in my office some years ago to hear a tearful voice say, "Professor Corrigan, you've ruined my life." The voice belonged to the author of a novel I had just given a thumbs-down to in *The Washington Post.* "Why?" was the title of a two-page cri de coeur e-mailed to me by a prominent newspaper columnist whose first book I'd positively reviewed but whose second I thought was poorly thought out. The sense of personal betrayal felt by that author was palpable.

I don't shrug off these incidents. Nor do I get pleasure from the attentions of the eccentric NPR listeners that I've attracted. One fellow has been sending me penciled postcards every couple of months or so for years, chiding me for pronunciation problems like my New Yorker's dentalized "*t*". Barbara Walters, he's assured me, had the same problem early in her career. I've also been treated to the sexual fantasies some listeners harbor about me, and I regularly receive piles of books as well as unpublished manuscripts that listeners want me to use my influence to get noticed. There well might be another *Ulysses* moldering away unseen in those piles, but I'll never have the time to find out. I'm always reading on deadline. I read every opportunity I can, and the pressure to grab those opportunities has grown more intense since the arrival of my daughter six years ago. I read and take notes on books I'm reviewing every day—as well as on vacations and all the major holidays. I read in the hours before dawn and while I proctor my students' exams and while I wait for an oil change or a doctor's appointment. Luckily, my job demands constant reading, otherwise I'd have to figure out some other excuse.

This, my own book, is my attempt to figure out some of the consequences of my prolonged exposure to books and to explore how reading has transformed my life, mostly for the better, sometimes for the worse. Because I read so widely and so much, I've recognized some rarely discussed themes—in particular, powerful ideas about womanhood and work—running through the subtexts of some of the most hallowed classic texts as well as some of the most devalued popular books. I want to share those insights—and their effect on my own life—with my readers. Think of this book as analogous in method to those marvelous mongrel texts written by M.F.K. Fisher or Laurie Colwin that combine recipes and revelations about food with autobiographical digressions. Some people live to eat; others of us live to read. In both instances, the particular hunger and the life are absolutely intertwined.

Hovering over all the ruminations about literature and life that follow is the cosmic question of why so many of us feel compelled to go through life with our noses stuck in a book. I'd like to propose a resolutely earnest answer—all the years I devoted to reading the Victorian Sages in graduate school have left their mark on my beliefs about literature. I think, consciously or not, what we readers do each time we open a book is to set off on a search for authenticity. We want to get closer to the heart of things, and sometimes even a few good sentences contained in an otherwise unexceptional book can crystallize vague feelings, fleeting physical sensations, or, sometimes, profound epiphanies. Good writing is writing that's on target; that captures, say, the smell of sizing on a just-sewn garment the way no other known grammatical scramble of words has before. (Ann Packer's recent wonderful debut novel, *The Dive from Clausen's Pier,* did just that.) Those are, unfailingly, the sentences that we reviewers quote in our reviews because they leap out and offer those cherished "Aha!" moments in reading. Little wonder that one of the most overused words in favorable reviews is the adjective *luminous.* Readers, professional or casual, are alert to passages in a book that illuminate what was previously shadowy and formless. In our daily lives, where we're bombarded by the fake and the trivial, reading serves as a way to stop, shut out the noise of the world, and try to grab hold of something real, no matter how small. Hence the enormous popularity of extreme-adventure tales that take their readers to the "last good places," like the top of Mount Everest or the middle of the ocean—places that are still unsullied, authentic. Detective fiction, another literary genre that I love and will talk about in this book, oftentimes weaves the search for authenticity into its plots. What I and a lot of other readers consider to be the greatest American detective-fiction tale of all time, Dashiell Hammett's 1930 novel, *The Maltese Falcon,* describes a fast-paced search for a bejeweled falcon that dates from the Middle Ages. When detective Sam Spade finally gets his hands on the bird, it turns out to be a fake. Spade, being made of tougher stuff than most of his shocked readers, takes his disappointment in stride and forges on. Detectives, like Spade, are close readers. They have to be to catch all the hidden clues. Spade's close reading throughout *The Maltese Falcon* as he searches for the authentic treasure mirrors our own activity as readers of the novel, as we search in Hammett's story for something authentic that will deepen our understanding of our own lives.

The roots of my own yearning to read are easy enough to trace. I was a shy kid, an only child who grew up in a two-bedroom walk-up apartment in Queens. Reading offered companionship as well as escape. It also gave me a way to be more like my dad, whom I adored. Every weeknight, after he came home from his job as a refrigeration mechanic and ate supper, my dad would go to his bedroom and read. Mostly, he read adventure novels about World War II. He had served first in the Merchant Marine and, then, after Pearl Harbor, in the Navy on a destroyer escort. Those Navy years were the most intense of my father's life, although he never said so. My dad belonged to that generation of men, forged by the Great Depression and World War II, whose unspoken motto was "The deeper the feeling, the fewer the words." He didn't talk a lot about the war, but I knew it haunted his memory because every night he cracked open a paperback (usually one with an embossed swastika on its cover) and sat smoking and reading. Near his chair was a framed photograph of his ship, the USS *Schmitt*. To read was to be like my dad and, maybe, to get a glimpse of his experience—to me, as wide and unfathomable as the sea.

In his youth my dad's reading tastes had been more eclectic. For one thing, he liked poetry. On a childhood expedition into his dresser, I once came across a wrinkled green pamphlet—the kind, I later learned, that used to be sold on newsstands. It was entitled *The Most Wonderful Collection of Famous Recitations Ever Written*. They were, too. Inside were funny and melodramatic poems by Robert Service, Rudyard Kipling, and other now-demoted bards. The titles alone would draw a reader in: "The Cremation of Sam McGee," "Casey at the Bat," "Laugh and the World Laughs with You," "Over the Hill to the Poorhouse," "Woodsman, Spare That Tree," "One Day of Turkey, Six Days of Hash." It even included a Shakespeare soliloquy, "All the World's a Stage." I used to hear stories from relatives about how, in his drinking days, my dad would stand up and recite Shakespeare at parties. When I was growing up, the sole evidence of my dad's former hamminess was the line "Sound and fury signifying nothing," which was one of his catchphrases, usually muttered when a politician appeared on television.

He liked Dickens, too. "That's a good one," he said to me when I brought home *A Tale of Two Cities* from grammar school. As a product of "the American Century," my dad also harbored a great love for American history, particularly the American Revolution. He regularly reread all the novels of F. Van Wyck Mason, took my mother and me on vacation pilgrimages to Valley Forge and Williamsburg, and held me spellbound as a small child, spinning out vivid tales of General Washington's soldiers fighting the British and dying in the snow. Without ever talking about it, my father understood how, through reading, a person's world could be immeasurably enlarged. Because he was happy to see an early love of reading taking hold of me, he even helped me commit my first Catholic-school act of insubordination. We second-graders at St. Raphael's Parochial School weren't allowed to bring our *Dick and Jane* readers home because the nuns didn't want us reading ahead. (Why? Don't ask. Stay in line.) Memory is hazy on the specifics, but I must have asked my dad for my own copy of the reader. I do remember the two of us going down to Macy's at Herald Square, which, back in the early 1960s, had a big book department, and my dad buying the reader for me. I finished all the stories weeks before we got to them in class, where I sat, bored, during reading period. So, instead of learning to sound out the words I already knew, I learned, firsthand, about the void that all devoted readers dread—the void that yawns just past the last page of whatever good book we're currently reading.

Luckily, given my jobs, I don't often have that problem. Still, to guard against that emptiness, I've planked over nearly every surface of the row house I now live in with my husband and daughter with piles of books and magazines. (They each have their own messy, sizeable collection of books and magazines, too.) The books are different and so is the style of furniture, but the basic decorating theme in my house is the same as that in my dad's old bedroom.

My mom, on the other hand, would rather try to talk to just about anybody—Minnie Mouse, Alan Greenspan—than read a book. She used to grow restless on those long-ago evenings when my dad and I would be lost in our separate fictional worlds. Because she knew better than to bother him, she'd invariably sidle up to me and complain that I was ruining my eyes by reading in the (perfectly adequate) light of the living room lamp, or she'd feel my head and tell me that I was "getting bumps" from too much reading. Sometimes I'd give in and watch TV with her for a while. But at some point I'd always pick up my book again, leaving her, as she'd complain, "all alone." My poor mother. How did she get stuck with the two of us reader-loners for company?

The necessary solitude of reading has something to do with my mom's disinclination; she also has a Mrs. Malaprop way with words that betrays her essential uneasiness with language. One Sunday morning she called, all excited because she thought she'd won the Lotto. "I'm going to buy you and Rich a condom!" she announced breathlessly. "Have some machos," she once urged us during a visit, offering a plate of chips and salsa. When I gave her a copy of the first theory-encrusted article I ever published in the academic journal *English Literature in*

Transition, she proudly told relatives that I had "written a story" for something called *English Literature in Translation.* Actually, she was right that time.

She was also eerily on the mark when she would tell people that I was teaching not at Haverford College but at "Rutherford College," a name that sounds like it came out of a Marx Brothers movie.

My mother had the bad luck to be a Depression-era child who had to leave high school early to work and help support her family. For a long time I've worn the small onyx "graduation" ring her older, already-working sister gave her to mark the transition. It reminds me of her courage in the face of limited options—the days spent hiding out at the Paramount Theater when she was supposed to be looking for work, the months spent at the hated factory jobs. It also reminds me to be grateful, especially on those gray mornings when I'm shuffling off to teach a class on a book, like Ann Petry's novel *The Street,* that I admire for its various strengths but don't particularly enjoy rereading. In the first awful year after my dad's death, I sometimes stupidly sought to ease my mother's grief by prescribing novels for her to read, good thick stories by Susan Isaacs and Maeve Binchy. And, slowly, my mother tried to read them. Maybe she sensed, as I did as a child, that reading was the way to be near my father.

Of course, it's a bit misleading to cast my parents as the Mr. Yin and Mrs. Yang of reading; for one thing, like most human beings, they sometimes acted unpredictably and switched roles. When I was a sophomore in college and recovering from a broken heart, it was my mother who urged my frugal father to help fund a literary escape for me—a month in Ireland in the company of a few chosen students and our beloved English professor. And I remember visiting my parents years later and turning on the TV set in the living room to watch a BBC production of a Shakespeare play. After about ten minutes, my father began sighing, drumming his fingers on his chair, and otherwise signaling that he found the actors and their orotund tones altogether too fluty; my mom pleaded, "Let her watch it"—even though neither the Brits in general nor Shakespeare in particular was her cup of tea. Like Lillian Hellman says in her lying-but-magnificent memoir, *Scoundrel Time,* "The traceries from what you were to what you became are always too raw and too simple."[1] Still, I'd say that the very different literary and anti-literary influences of my parents have shaped my life and career. As an English professor and book critic, I'm lucky enough to spend my working life reading, reading, and reading until, as my mother still warns, "my eyeballs will fall out." But the way I talk about books and try to get other people interested in them in the classroom, in print, and on National Public Radio may well owe more to her indifference than to my dad's passion.

A few years ago I was standing in front of my fall semester "Women's Autobiography" class (thirty-seven women and one lone male—either enlightened or desperate for a date). I was running down the syllabus with them and got to Gertrude Stein's *The Autobiography of Alice B. Toklas*. "It's a brilliant puzzle text that anticipates deconstructionist approaches to autobiography by half a century," I said. Noticing a couple of young women in the corner who looked like they were mentally mixing and matching their fall ensembles from Banana Republic, I decided to switch tactics. "In many ways, this is my favorite of all the autobiographies we're reading. It's an elegant goof! Stein lampoons the arrogance of all those guys who, for centuries, have been yammering on about 'me, me, me,' in their autobiographies." There, I got what I wanted: faint amusement on the faces of those two women. Now, for a moment, instead of mulling over cargo pants, they were admiring a weird book written by a woman they no doubt would have been appalled by in the flesh.

I absolutely want other people to love, or at least appreciate, the books I love. It doesn't take a Sam Spade or a Sigmund Freud to figure out why. "What's that story about?" my mother would sometimes ask. And so I'd tell her about *Rose in Bloom* or *Mrs. Wiggs of the Cabbage Patch* or, later, *The Great Gatsby*. If I made the story sound funny or tragic, did justice to the surprising twists and turns in the plot, and, most important of all, kept my summary short, I'd be rewarded with a light of interest in her eyes; if I waxed too intellectual about themes and symbols, I'd get blankness. My reading-averse mother surely has a lot to do with the fact that I make my living trying to get other people excited about books in the classroom, in newspaper book-review sections, and in four-minute reviews (keep it short) on NPR.

Years ago, my fellow *Fresh Air* commentators and I attended our one and only "voice workshop." The point was not to rid us of our various accents; fortunately, NPR seems to like regional twangs. Instead, the voice coach wanted to help us sound more natural, more "talky," as we read our pieces on the air. "Imagine, when you're in the studio recording, that you're in a room with a bunch of friends who are really interested in what you have to say," she suggested. I try to do that each week. I people the closet-sized studio I record in here in Washington with a crowd that nods enthusiastically at every insight, every bon mot, I utter. But somewhere in that crowd stands my mother, and she's bored. I've got to work harder—loosen up my diction, inject more energy into my voice—to make her see what's so wonderful about this book.

"Write what you know," the old saw advises, and what I know, with much more certitude than I know almost anything else, is the world of books and what it feels like to be a passionate reader. This is a book about books . . . but not only about books. I want to talk about the unexpected places books take us readers. By way of demonstration, I want to revisit some of the extraordinary places books have taken me— in my imagination and in my "real life"—as well as some of the characters, both fictive and flesh-and-blood, I've met along the way. I want to talk about how books can give us readers some understanding of the boundaries of our own identities and how they can make us less afraid of moving back and forth across those boundaries into other stories, other lives. I'm certain that they've done that for me.

I come from a short maternal line of shy women who've had to push themselves out of their shells. (A short line because I don't know anything about my ancestors beyond my grandparents.) My mother's mother, Helen Mrosz, got on an immigrant boat when she was seventeen and came to America, all alone. She had to—there was no work, no life for her back in turn-of-the-century Poland where her brothers would inherit the family farm. My mother, as I've already acknowledged, reluctantly left school at fourteen during the Depression to find work and help support her family. Both my mother and my grandmother were propelled by larger forces of history to leave their familiar worlds; I was booted out by books. There's the irony. Like so many bookworms, I was timid and introspective, and yet reading, my earliest refuge from the unknown world, made me want to venture out into it, instead of sticking with my own kind. My yearning to fit in, to hang back, hasn't been eradicated; it's a lifelong inclination born of nature and nurture and who knows what else. But a lot of the courage I've found to sometimes diverge off familiar paths I owe to reading, and I want to talk about some of those turning points in my life and their literary sources.

Many of the stories that have most profoundly affected me have come packaged in genre form—the word literary people give to books thought to be mass productions, unlike the "unique" genius of the Great Books. I especially want to look at men's and women's lives as they've been depicted in three mostly noncanonical categories of stories: the female extreme-adventure tale, the hard-boiled detective novel, and the Catholic-martyr narratives. These three literary genres are enormously popular, and I expect that some of the surprising and even subversive messages I've stumbled across in these books have resonated with many other readers, perhaps even changed their lives to a degree, as they have mine. But first, some definition is in order. The female extreme-adventure tale is the genre that I chiefly concentrate on throughout this book, and I want to clarify that I'm not talking about powder-puff versions of *The Perfect Storm* or *Into Thin Air*—two male accounts of endurance that, by the way, I loved reading. The classic female variant on the implicitly male extreme-adventure tale is, I think, a thriving literary genre that's long been overlooked because its power has traditionally derived from its suffer-and-be-silent modesty. And when I say long been overlooked, I mean for centuries, millennia even. If we identify Homer's Ulysses as the first male extreme-adventure hero in Western literature, then his wife, Penelope, qualifies as the first extreme-adventure heroine. While Ulysses was roaming the world, fighting the Cyclops and steeling himself against the Sirens, Penelope was also engaged in a life-and-death struggle, of sorts, with those greedy, repulsive suitors swarming all over the palace. Penelope doesn't boast or bellyache in Homer's account; instead, she hides her suffering and marshals her intelligence and emotional stamina to tolerate and eventually triumph. Penelope's narrative establishes the basic plot characteristics of the female extreme-adventure tale, as I'll go on to describe. These stories, up until very recently, have been about women who withstand psychological and sometimes physical torments over an extended period; they are usually played out in the secluded realms of the home, sometimes even within a woman's own body. Recognizing the existence of this hardy tradition of women's writing about private tests of endurance comforted me with the knowledge that I was in good company during a time when I was undergoing an extreme female adventure of my own.

Unlike the male extreme-adventure tale, which has remained pretty constant for the past two millennia, the female extreme-adventure tale has taken speedy advantage of the social changes wrought by the Second Women's Movement of the late 1960s to begin a major makeover that's still in progress. Classic features remain in evidence in the feminist extreme-adventure tale: the heroine herself, and certainly the secondary female characters, usually retain aspects of the Penelope ethos of suffer and be still—and busily scheme under cover of darkness. But now women characters under pressure not only bear their trials, they *act*. In *Black and Blue,* the bestselling 1998 novel by Anna Quindlen that first got me thinking about the existence of the female extreme-adventure tale, the heroine, Fran Benedetto, tolerates her policeman-husband's fists and curses for years. Then, one fateful morning, she runs off with her young son. Aided by a feminist rescue network, she settles in an anonymous suburb, gets a job, and changes her entire life—all the while looking anxiously over her shoulder. Contrast her story with some earlier, more hopeless literary portraits of abused wives, such as that of Helen Graham, the heroine of Anne Brontë's *The Tenant of Wildfell Hall,* or Mrs. Heathcliff (the poor deluded Isabella Linton) in Emily Brontë's *Wuthering Heights*. All three of the Brontë sisters were queens of the Victorian female-adventure tale, but, as I'll discuss in Chapter 1, the most massive crown of thorns goes to Charlotte.

These women had no realistic alternatives but to stay in place and endure. With the advent of the Second Women's Movement, however, other possibilities began to open up for women in literature as well as in life. Besieged, threatened, and overwhelmed female heroines no longer "just" carry their considerable burdens quietly. Some talk back, while others make use of their advanced educations and professional positions to wield some power in the world. Still others confront hazards physically, relying on self-defense training to kayo thugs with their feet and fists. A few, in the most dire of circumstances, shoot first and ask permission later. An important word about these rock-'em-sock-'em dames: I think the post-1960s female mystery novel—itself a hugely popular product of second-wave feminism—is a grandly utopian version of the female extreme-adventure tale. The gal gumshoes and pistol-packing lawyers in novels by Sue Grafton, Sara Paretsky, Lisa Scottoline, Liza Cody, and a host of other good women writers get to do what Jane Eyre and her long-suffering sisters couldn't even dream of doing: they get to fight back.

The underground tradition of the female extreme-adventure tale— a genre that has been remodeled but not razed by the social changes wrought by the Second Women's Movement—is one I'll focus on in the first chapter of this book, and will continue to trace, via its changing incarnations and near relations, throughout the chapters that follow. The female extreme-adventure tale is a genre whose possibilities fascinate me, perhaps in part because I've always been drawn to literature that preaches a stiff-upper-lip attitude toward life. In the middle of this book, I delve into the dark world of the hard-boiled detective novel. During the decades that I've been an avid detective-novel fan, I've also become more and more aware of surprising and complex views of work and family that these novels offer us. In the final section of this book, I revisit the beloved literature of my parochial-school girlhood, where secular saints like Marie Killilea of the bestselling autobiographical Karen books and Beany Malone of the eponymous girls series gave a recognizably Catholic spin to the ethos of female suffering in silence. Rereading these books as an adult, I was much more aware of the covert maneuvers through which their heroines managed to criticize the status quo and still keep their ladylike mantles in place. I think that, consciously or not, the sometimes seditious comments on conventional womanhood that these books offer contributed to their enormous popularity, particularly with women readers.

Because I didn't read all these books while hermetically sealed in a library carrel, I also want to talk about how life and art interrelate— specifically how what was happening to me at certain times in my life affected how I've read literature, as well as how books have affected how

I've "read" and, to a certain extent, shaped my life. I think all of us committed readers experience this kind of symbiotic relationship with books. Another way of explaining the organization of this book is to say that it charts three major literary and life journeys, journeys that I've taken with different uniforms on: the book critic, the teacher, and the student. In the first instance, a flip feminist digression I made in a book review turned out to be the magic words that cleared the trail into some of the uncharted territory that still exists, in boundless stretches, within all great books. In the second escapade, a genre that I'd known and loved for years introduced me to a dissolute distant relation and we ran off together. And, in the third and earliest literary outing, cherished books of my childhood that were supposed to be safe and saintly shanghaied me into a wickedly naughty realm of righteous anger and pride.

Books are wayward. You can begin a book assuming that you're entering one kind of world, getting one kind of message, only to find out that beneath that cover story lurks another kind of tale—or two, or three—altogether. Books can turn us readers around, mess with our directional signals, deposit us, drained and bewildered, on completely foreign shores. A forgettable book disappoints or merely meets our conscious expectations; unforgettable books take us to places we didn't even suspect existed, places we may not even have wanted to go. So many times I've started a book and, like my famous kinsman Douglas "Wrong-Way" Corrigan, who one July day in 1938 took off in his plane from Floyd Bennett Field in Brooklyn for California and wound up some two days later in Dublin, Ireland, I've found myself on a strange and faraway shore by story's end. There's no such thing as travel insurance when it comes to reading. Sure, the syllabi I draw up for the literature courses I teach may look like itineraries—and they certainly are intended to give the reassuring impression that reading is an orderly tour from one fixed point of interest to the next—but it's not so. We readers linger on particularly captivating language, get drawn into thickets of symbol patterns, or find ourselves stepping out of the book altogether to investigate its biographical or historical context. As I relearn, semester after semester, the route from *The Autobiography of Benjamin Franklin* to *The Autobiography of Alice B. Toklas* is never a straight line.

Nor is reading a risk-free activity. As elevating and enlightening as literature can be, prolonged travel in the alternative worlds of books can also make a reader more prone to fantasy thinking and estranged from his or her "real" life. In the company of my then preschool-aged daughter, I've watched a lot of children's programs on PBS and even sat through a few onstage extravaganzas featuring Snow White and the Three Little Pigs. These children's shows routinely offer a paean to reading, no doubt as a sop to educated middle-class parents who worry about the fact that their kids are sitting before the TV screen or in a darkened sports arena, zombified by the antics of, say, Winnie-the-Pooh in animated or costume form, instead of actually reading about his adventures in A. A. Milne's stories. What these songs and skits in praise of reading don't mention, however, is that the child who gets lost in a book can emerge from that experience a changeling.

Lots of great American writers have written about the initial walk into a public library that transformed their lives, but certainly Richard Wright's account in *Black Boy* is one of the most thrilling. Wright, of course, wasn't just handed that first Pandora's box of books; he had to snatch it across the color line by asking a semi-sympathetic white man for the loan of his library card. Here's an excerpt from Wright's description of first opening up and reading H. L. Mencken's *A Book of Prefaces:*

What strange world was this? I concluded the book with the conviction that I had somehow overlooked something terribly important in life. I had once tried to write, had once reveled in feeling, had let my crude imagination roam, but the impulse to dream had been slowly beaten out of me by experience. Now it surged up again and I hungered for books, new ways of looking and seeing. It was not a matter of believing or disbelieving what I read, but of feeling something new, of being affected by something that made the look of the world different.

As dawn broke I ate my pork and beans, feeling dopey, sleepy. I went to work, but the mood of the book would not die; it lingered, coloring everything I saw, heard, did. I now felt that I knew what the white men were feeling. Merely because I had read a book that

had spoken of how they lived and thought, I identified myself with
that book.[2]

My own less dramatic early transformations through literature turned
out to be—for me, personally—just as profound. "Yes'm." I remember
standing in the doorway of our kitchen and speaking that outmoded
phrase to my mother, in answer to a question she'd just asked. I must
have been about seven and had just finished reading some story where
all the children said "Yes'm" to their mothers. "What did you say?" asked
my baffled mother. I snapped back to my "old" self the next moment,
but constant reading kept pulling me away from the world of my childhood, the world of my parents. Reading the Nancy Drew books made
me emulate Nancy's patrician manners, circa 1935, and regular visits
via reading to her gracious home in leafy River Heights made me dissat-
isfied with our dark city apartment. Reading Joyce's *Portrait of the Artist
as a Young Man* as a junior in high school made me take myself and
my writing ambitions seriously enough that I signed up that summer
for a creative-writing course at the New School in Greenwich Village
—hippie-infested terra incognita for a Catholic girl from working-
class Sunnyside. (The teacher, as I remember, had another job, writing
quiz-show questions; if I'd been smarter, I would have taken note of
the fact that this published writer held down two day jobs to survive.)
Eventually, I left my parents' apartment and the close-knit community
I grew up in, half consciously lured away by the promise of books
and the wider, more intense life they seemed to offer. But not without
a cost.

For all readers, male and female, there is a discrepancy between the
possibilities offered by the world of the imagination and the possibilities
offered by real life. That's one of the reasons we read fiction: to fantasize
about what might be. But, until the social revolution of the Second
Women's Movement, that discrepancy, generally speaking, had been
more gaping for women readers. Because so many of fiction's heroes are,
well, heroes instead of heroines, women readers, out of pleasant necessity, have learned to step into the roomier footwear of the Deerslayer,
Beowulf, Ulysses, Ishmael, David Copperfield, and so on. These heroes
lead lives of on-the-road adventure, recklessness, and big dreams—all

played out in the public sphere. And therein lies the bad-boy allure of these tales. Victorian and turn-of-the-century patriarchs worried that middle-class female readers would get all stirred up by "questionable" literature—like romances and adventure sagas—and, for a time, live through their imaginations like men. They would squeeze back into their own overstuffed parlors with their heads full of mutinous androgynous possibilities.

Some of Western literature's greatest novelists, because they them-selves were also avid readers, chronicled the particular dangers that fan-tasy fiction posed to nineteenth-century women. Catherine Morland in Jane Austen's *Northanger Abbey* goes gaga over Gothic novels, to the extent that she imagines skeletons in every closet and mad monks in every alcove; she also almost reads herself out of a good marriage match. Gustave Flaubert's Madame Bovary reads herself into adultery and an early grave, so frustrated is she by the stultifying confines of her actual wifely existence. Of course, Bovary's cautionary tale is over-the-top: her "death by books" is a fate threatening only the most susceptible of female readers. The more humdrum consequence of heavy reading is that it encourages lots of already shy girls—as it certainly encouraged me—to be dreamy solitaries who would rather be alone with a book than mingle with friends and family. In terms of traditional gender roles, women are supposed to be chatty and warm—bridge builders. Women who read seriously, however, are temporary recluses, antisocial loners.

Louisa May Alcott's Jo March is certainly a contender for the most beloved heroine in Western literature. Nestled in the bosom of her soro-rial family, Jo, nevertheless, elects to spend hours isolated in the icy attic, scribbling away at her blood-and-thunder dramas. When she matures into a young lady, Jo makes a radical break from her dear mother, sisters, and neighbor, Laurie. She chooses to live alone in a faraway city, housed in a spinster's bed-sitter, trying to secure her literary reputation by writ-ing adult versions of her dramatic thrillers. She returns to the March manse eventually with that peculiar German professor, Mr. Bhaer, in tow (dubious marriage material at best, in the eyes of her solid New England family). Jo comes home, but she's a different person from the adolescent madwoman-in-training who first began nursing her aspira-tions in the attic. Jo's lengthy devotion to literature is to blame. Like every other bookwormish girl who's ever encountered and worshipped Jo in *Little Women,* I identify with her; more than that, I feel like the broad plot of my life follows hers. A love of books gloriously screwed us both up; rendered us intermittent hermits holed up in corners of our childhood homes; snatched us from our bemused families and pushed us into distant, lonely, and often ludicrous tests of ambition and resolve; and made the return journey home (in my case, also, accompanied by a "stranger" to the tribe) fraught with difficulty.

If reading is a journey, it's a dicey one. Books have lured me into tight jams, ego-shredding experiences, euphoric heights, and abysmal lows. Books have deeply enriched my life; they've also deluded me. Throughout this book, I'll talk about the adventure of reading as well as some of the misadventures that reading has led me into.

But before we set out, I need to address the long-term damage that attending graduate school in English can wreak on one's psyche. And the further toll that regular reviewing, relentlessly casting a cold eye on other people's books in search of cracks and fissures, has taken on my courage. My own internal book critic has already anticipated any snide remarks that might be offered by other reviewers about this book. I've even come up with the perfect one-word negative review of *Leave Me Alone, I'm Reading:* "Gladly."

When I was on the academic-job market, I interviewed for a position as assistant professor at Columbia University. I wanted that job. Other English graduate students I knew at the University of Pennsylvania were counting themselves lucky to be deported to places like North Dakota for teaching jobs; I wanted to return to New York. I walked into the conference room where the interview was being held and was greeted by the assembled Big Names of the Columbia English Department. Carolyn Heilbrun was the only other woman present and the only professor who smiled as she shook my hand. I immediately developed an eye tic. Things went downhill from there. Late in the interview, Steven Marcus roused himself and asked, in regard to my Ph.D. dissertation: "Ms. Corrigan, does this dissertation have *any* methodology?" I should have toughed it out and said, paraphrasing T. S. Eliot's famous remark about Aristotle: "Well, Professor, there is no method except to be very intelligent." Instead, I smiled my best Mrs. Miniver smile and tried to pass myself off as a "soft" Marxist (not exactly what Lenin had in mind). Of course, I didn't get the job. I'd failed the academic bear-baiting test: I backed down, tried to be nice, and lost face professionally.

One of the pleasures of writing autobiographically, however, is that you get to revise the past—as long as you're up-front about doing so. So, let's try it again. Does this *book* have any methodology? Not much of one. It explores some major literary subjects and features some unexpected themes and repeated allusions: Ira Einhorn—the notorious New Age hippie who was recently extradited to the United States and convicted of the 1977 murder of his girlfriend, Holly Maddux—makes appearances in three of its four chapters. I had no idea, before sitting down to write, that he was such a creepy presence in my life. Class, Catholicism, work, and my dad are big subjects, and dermatological problems caused by anxiety are mentioned more than once. I have a fondness for the genre of serial fiction—mysteries and series novels make up about half of the literary references here. I've also noticed that I use semicolons a lot. That punctuational rut is partly a consequence of the years I spent reading Victorian nonfictional prose writers such as Thomas Carlyle, John Ruskin, and William Morris, who were capable of raging on in page-length, semicolon-studded sentences about, say, the evils of the Industrial Revolution. But there's more to it than that. The semicolon is my psychological metaphor, my mascot. It's the punctuation mark that qualifies, hesitates, and ties together ideas and parts of a life that shoot off in different directions. I think my reliance on the semicolon signifies that I want to hold on to my background—honestly, without sentimentality or embarrassment—and yet, also transcend it. I come from, and still partly reside in, a world where most people, including my own parents, didn't, and still don't, read or hear what I have to say about books because they are oblivious to NPR, *The New York Times,* and all the other educated middle- and upper-class outlets where popular conversations about culture and literature take place. I now spend most of my time in a world where most people know who Stanley Fish is but have only the haziest notion of (and even less interest in) what a shop steward does.

How do you own what you've become without losing what you were—and want to keep on being, too? I'm an NPR contributor, college professor, feminist, leftist, person ambivalent about the constraints of family and community; I'm a child of the working class, a mother, a good daughter, a skeptical Catholic, a Queens booster, and a flag waver on the Fourth of July and other national holidays, even before September 11. (Why should the right own the flag?) Hence, that semicolon trying to link things that otherwise would spin off and settle into disparate categories.

The only conscious literary methodology lurking around here is this one: I've read all these books carefully and thought about them and what they have to do with life, including my life and the world around me. It's an old and venerable methodology, by the way, that seems to be enjoying a comeback. Formidable literary critics such as Frank Lentricchia and Harold Bloom have, in the past few years, cast off theory and resolved to wrestle with books bare-handed, mano a mano. I prefer the family metaphor. Like Wrong-Way Corrigan, I take off on a series of literary journeys and life adventures in this book. Also, like my notorious kinsman (who supposedly engineered that "mistake" of landing in Ireland instead of California), I've planned on arriving at some of the unlikely destinations in the following chapters. But every time I've reread the great books I discuss here, I've found new areas to explore; I imagine my readers will have similar experiences. We'll all be making some unscheduled stops, some emergency landings. Where we finally wind up is anybody's guess.

Leave Me Alone, I'm Reading

CHAPTER ONE

Ain't No Mountain High Enough:
Women's Extreme-Adventure Stories
(and One of My Own)

*A*mong the many dangers of being an obsessive reader is that you tend to mediate your life through books, filter your experiences through plots, so that the boundary between fiction and fact becomes porous. One evening, during the years I was living as a graduate student in Philadelphia, I was watching TV when a commercial for the local electric company came on. The commercial was promoting a program to help addled senior citizens keep track of their bills. On the screen was an elderly man sitting at a dining room table, staring at a pile of windowed envelopes. He looked a little bit like my dad, and sure enough, as the screen widened out to include the rest of the room, there was a big black-and-white photograph of my father as a toddler, dressed in a sailor suit, surrounded by his two older sisters and their parents. "Oh, there's the photograph," I thought to myself. I had a framed copy in my living room—all the Corrigans and their descendants have a copy of that photograph hanging somewhere in their homes. Aside from being a striking image—

my grandfather with his handlebar mustache staring soberly into the camera; my grandmother in a long dark dress with a lace collar, holding my dad on her lap; my two aunts, smiling, one in a First Communion dress—it was a picture occasioned by tragedy. My grandmother Margaret had been diagnosed with cancer, and she and my grandfather John had the photograph taken to help the children remember her. She died in 1925, when my father was five years old.

"Oh, there's the photograph." It took me at least a full minute to realize that the Corrigan-family photograph was on TV. I was like those American soldiers described in *Dispatches,* Michael Herr's great book about Vietnam, who, as they ran into enemy fire, shouted "Cover me!"—a line they'd absorbed from countless World War II movies. I, too, had gone to a lot of movies and watched too much TV. My fuzziness in distinguishing between reality and simulacrum was a postmodern condition shared by all of us who'd come of age in the culture of spectacle. But in my case, books were the worst troublemakers when it came to wreaking havoc with my head. From adolescence on, at least, I've read my life in terms of fiction, and so that evening, when I saw a personal object from my life turn up in a TV commercial, it seemed, at first, natural. (By the way, after calling the electric company's public-relations office, I learned that the photograph had been found in a secondhand-furniture store on Arch Street in Philadelphia. The location made sense. The one-two punch of my grandmother's death followed by the Great Depression a few years later knocked the Corrigan family down. House and car disappeared and my grandfather John, taking advantage of the first month's free rent offered by desperate landlords, moved with the children into a series of apartments in West Philadelphia. A lot of family treasures, like the photograph, were put into storage, never to be rescued.)

My Catholic girlhood, my school days, my first forays into dating, college and graduate school, tortured love affairs, jobs, teaching, marriage—all these events had been mirrored in, even anticipated by, the books I read. When I worked in a five-and-ten during the latter part of high school, I thought of myself as young David Copperfield wasting away in the blacking factory. When I found myself marooned, night after night, in a one-room graduate-school apartment that basically consisted of a bay window and some linoleum, I thought of myself as Tennyson's Lady of Shallot, trapped in glass. Jo March, Holden Caulfield, Lucky Jim, Nancy Drew, Elizabeth Bennet—I thought of myself, at one time or other, as all of them . . . and still do. But, then, at the age of forty-three, after at least three decades of understanding my life through literary analogues—indeed, sometimes shaping my life in the image of fiction—I arrived at a crucial moment that I couldn't "read" through books. To return to the "Wrong-Way" Corrigan metaphor, I felt as though I were flying blind. For years leading up to the moment I received that life-changing phone call from the adoption agency, I had been living a classic version of the female extreme-adventure tale—a veiled narrative that I had begun to recognize as an essential component of many women's stories, old and new. By the time that realization dawned, however, I was about to set out on another kind of adventure altogether.

The traditionally male extreme adventure has been *the* trend in nonfiction writing—apart from autobiographies—for roughly the past decade. I can make this pronouncement with confidence because I must get one or two new specimens of this kind of book delivered to my house every week. Jon Krakauer contributed to the increasing demand for this genre of saved-by-the-skin-of-his-teeth new journalism with his two bestsellers *Into the Wild* and *Into Thin Air*. Sebastien Junger's superb book, *The Perfect Storm,* is, perhaps, the apotheosis of this genre, which, as yet, shows no signs of waning popularity with he-man first-person sagas about polar explorations, solo round-the-world sails, rodeo riding, and firefighting steadily muscling their way into bookstores along with more scholarly works like Nathaniel Philbrick's award-winning *In the Heart of the Sea,* a true-life saga about the whale ship *Essex* that inspired Melville's better-known fictional extreme-adventure tale, *Moby-Dick.*

The traditional extreme-adventure story is a one-shot testosterone expenditure of physical courage that pits man against nature/man/himself, with man (the narrator usually) left standing, bloody but unbowed, amidst the wreckage of his fancy sporting gear. Scale the mountain; weather the storm at sea (or not); fight the war, the fire, the flood; carry out manifest destiny; be the first to fly over the ocean or to the moon;

climb down into volcanoes and Egyptian tombs; or simply learn to survive with the intestinal fortitude of a Crusoe, Kurtz, or Leatherstocking.

Granted, there have always been women, real and fictive, who've
grabbed the spotlight by playing boys' rough games by boys' rules.
These women enter the fray with gusto, but they never stray so far out
of the gender borders that they're dismissed as freaks. That most famous
of all woman warriors, Joan of Arc, would have really shaken things up
if she had led her armies in female dress; outfitted as an honorary male,
she reaffirmed the militaristic status quo—although even that sartorial
sleight of hand didn't save her from the stake. Harriet Tubman, "the
Mother of the Underground Railroad," made solo rescue missions to the
South every winter for a decade after she herself escaped from slavery.
Armed with a pistol and her nerves of steel, she led more than a hundred
slaves to freedom in Canada and then went on to serve as a Union spy
during the Civil War. Because her missions in both arenas were clandestine
and largely undocumented, the specific details of most of Tubman's
astonishing exploits have been lost to history. Aviatrixes Amelia Earhart
and Beryl Markham also wore men's clothes when they flew off to distant
horizons, but out of the cockpit they made sure they were photographed
in ladylike costumes. (The lithe Earhart never looked as ungainly as she
did in those trumpet skirts and heels she trussed herself up in for public
appearances.) Then there's my personal favorite female buccaneer, Nellie
Bly. I first learned about the turn-of-the-century "mother" of investigative stunt journalism by reading a juvenile biography of her that was
shelved (improbably) in the makeshift library at St. Raphael's School. I
remember being so excited to find out there was such a woman—a journalist who made her living by writing (like I dreamed of doing) who also
lived a life of adventure (like every kid dreams of doing). Bly first made a
name for herself by posing as a deranged immigrant woman and getting
herself committed to New York's infamous Blackwell's Island. Only her
editor knew of her exploit; if he had suffered, say, a fatal heart attack
while Bly was buried in Blackwell's, she might have spent the rest of her
life there.

But Bly was rescued, and her first-person account of the horrendous
treatment of Blackwell's inmates, some of whom were locked away simply because they couldn't speak English, predated Geraldo Rivera's ex-

posé of Willowbrook State School by some six decades. In 1889 Bly went on to best the record of Jules Verne's hero Phileas Fogg by traveling around the world in a breathless seventy-two days. The famous picture of her from that trip shows a pretty, wasp-waisted young woman, demurely outfitted in checked traveling skirt and jacket and carrying a carpetbag. Bly might have circled the globe unchaperoned, but she did so properly cloaked in the protective mantle of late-Victorian ladyhood.

Then there are the early-twentieth-century sports marvel Babe Didrikson Zaharias, and that blond and glamorous "just one of the boys" photographer Margaret Bourke-White. Other standouts are the African plantation owner Isak Dinesen and World War I nurse and outspoken women's rights advocate Vera Brittain, both of whose autobiographies (Brittain's mournful *Testament of Youth* particularly) inspired me when I discovered them in my early twenties. Strangely, in fiction as opposed to real life, female daredevils are scarcer; furthermore, the ones that do exist are almost exclusively the product of male writers' imaginations and their risk-taking is usually erotic in nature. In 1722, three years after he created the ur-survivor, Robinson Crusoe, Daniel Defoe gave readers Moll Flanders, whose picaresque adventures as a prostitute, society lady, thief, and convict he tried to pass off as a true-life autobiographical account. Flanders was a kind of eighteenth-century reincarnation of the Wife of Bath, Chaucer's immortal gap-toothed, much-married sensualist. Shakespeare's Cleopatra also insinuates herself into this hip-swiveling sorority of literary Mae Wests, as do, I suppose, William Makepeace Thackeray's Becky Sharp and Henry James's and Edith Wharton's bevy of more pallid social adventuresses such as Daisy Miller, Undine Spragg, Madame Merle, and Lily Bart.

The Brontë sisters' far less curvaceous creations—Jane Eyre, Catherine Earnshaw, Shirley—outrageously defy convention, but with the possible exception of Jane's flight from her aborted wedding to (the still-married) Rochester in which she stumbles through a storm on the moor, their physical adventures don't really qualify, in the traditional sense, as "extreme." Jane Austen's Catherine Morland, the impressionable young heroine of *Northanger Abbey,* wanders, every other page or so, into secret passages and ghostly chambers, but this Gothic novel is too much of a send-up, too much on the order of *Abbott and Costello Meet*

Frankenstein, to seriously qualify as an "adventure." In fact, with the exception of Nancy Drew, who was the initial creation of a man, Edward Stratemeyer, but whose series life and escapades were sustained throughout the next two decades by women writers, I can't think of very many other female-authored women of adventure in fiction—certainly not before the onset of the Second Women's Movement, and even then . . . who?

The thought of Nancy Drew reminds me that the two places where swashbucklers in skirts have long thrived have been in the "can't-get-no-respect" genres of juvenile and detective fiction. The juvenile-fiction connection makes sense: before the fall into adolescence, it's easier for girls to get away with acting as tomboys. There's Astrid Lindgren's fearless anarchist, Pippi Longstocking, Dorothy from L. Frank Baum's *The Wonderful Wizard of Oz,* Ludwig Bemelmans's Madeline, and the whole fairy-tale crowd of female high-wire acts—Little Red Riding Hood, Goldilocks, Fa Mu Lan—many of whom have been gussied up and diminished into girly-girls by Disney. Almost from its very inception, detective fiction has sanctioned curious women to gamble with their lives and enjoy the male thrills of exploring the unknown and hunting down prey. A relentless quest for fresh variations on the old formula certainly had something to do with the literary introduction of female detectives, especially in the pulp serials. Maybe the fact that most crime stories end up restoring and affirming the prevailing social order also gave mysteries more leeway to experiment with unconventionally daring heroines: to all appearances, at the end of these tales, everyone—victims, criminals, and detective—is put back in their proper place. With few exceptions, the careers of many turn-of-the-century female detectives ended in marriage.

The fact that many detecting women have been figured as "unawakened" adolescents like Nancy Drew or "over-the-hill" busybodies like Miss Marple has also made them less threatening to the status quo. Sure, there has always been the occasional married female snoopster—Agatha Christie's Tuppence (of the twinkly Tommy and Tuppence series) or Dashiell Hammett's Nora Charles (hitched to fellow boozehound Nick)—but they're deviations from the norm. Until feminism electroshocked the formula in the 1970s, the prevailing attitude toward female sleuths was most eloquently voiced by Sam Spade in *The Maltese Falcon.* Congratulating his secretary and part-time detecting partner, Effie Perine, on an assignment she's just completed, Spade rasps, "You're a damned good man, sister."[1] In other words, to be a credible detective, a woman had to become an honorary man.

I've loved reading about the exploits of many of these female adventurers, real and fictive, and relished the opportunity to (vicariously) compete, swagger, and spit alongside the boys, as they do. Maybe because I read so many new novels written by women and because I have a scholarly background in the nineteenth-century British novel—a genre in which women more than held their own with their male contemporaries—I began to think about the existence of a specifically female variant of the extreme-adventure tale. The female extreme-adventure tale, as I was beginning to discern it about eight years ago, was light on feats of derring-do and braggadocio, heavy on anxious waiting and endurance. The precarious situations described in these female extreme-adventure stories—childbirth, unwanted pregnancies, abortions (legal and illegal), abusive relationships, fatiguing caregiving—are ones that are faced almost exclusively by women. Their physical ordeals are augmented or even outweighed by heavy emotional burdens. Much space is devoted in these stories to the value of a woman quietly keeping her nerve through hours—sometimes years—of strain. And above all, it's the quotidian quality of their pain that separates the women from the boys. Blinding blizzards and numbing frostbite, such as Jon Krakauer describes, last for a few hours, maybe days, and then, one way or another, the nightmare is over. In contrast, the torments particular to women's extreme-adventure tales continue year after year. Climbing Everest looks like a snap compared with waking up every morning to, say, the enervating prospect of attending to an elderly invalid parent.

I was really struck by the idea of a "women's only" version of the extreme-adventure tale in the course of reviewing Anna Quindlen's 1998 novel, *Black and Blue,* for *The New York Times.* Around the same time, like millions of other readers, I'd caught extreme-adventure fever from reading Krakauer's books and *The Perfect Storm.* The contrasts between those books and Quindlen's novel were obvious: hers is what would be traditionally labeled a "small story"—the saga of a battered woman who finally decides to take her ten-year-old son and flee from the sporadic violent rages and tearful apologies of her policeman husband. *Black and Blue* opens on Fran Benedetto's suspenseful escape. Early one fateful morning, Fran chops off her long red hair with kitchen scissors, dyes it blond, and leaves with her son, Robert. Assisted by a member of an underground women's rescue network, they drive to Philadelphia's Thirtieth Street Station, and there they sit, waiting for another anonymous angel of deliverance to tell them what train to board to their new life. Fran and Robert eventually wind up in a garden apartment in Lake Plata, Florida, an American Nowheresville of strip malls and retirement complexes. Under an alias, Fran enrolls Robert in school and begins working as a home health-care aide. And she waits every day in fear that her husband will find them; she knows it's only a matter of time.

Fran's story never feels like a story; rather, it reads like a series of compelling dispatches from an extremely courageous and harrowing life. It evoked many of the same responses in me that those male skin-of-their-teeth survival (or not) stories did. So did Quindlen's first novel, *One True Thing*, which chronicled the everyday horrors a young woman braves in nursing her mother, who's dying of cancer. The heroines of Quindlen's female extreme adventures don't simply suffer silently and endure, as did most of their literary counterparts in the nineteenth century and earlier. Fran, in particular, comes to her own rescue by fleeing her abusive husband and creating a new life from scratch. Because of the changes wrought by the Second Women's Movement, Quindlen's characters (and their real-life equivalents) get to take action, talk back, and forge professional identities outside the private sphere of the home—*without* having to become male impersonators.

I loved the vicarious thrills of the passages where Quindlen's heroines get mad and get moving, but I found myself just as engrossed in the long, tense interludes where they simply have to endure. Thinking about the power of those narrative stretches made me think about earlier, prefeminist women's stories—stories of extreme emotional and sometimes physical adventure—where, because the social options are so much more limited, the heroines have no alternative but to tough things out, silently. These female extreme-adventure stories have never been awarded the medals for bravery that the men's stories garner; instead, they're commonly regarded as the literary equivalent of the women's movies or "weepies," like *Mildred Pierce* and *Imitation of Life,* that used to be so popular with female filmgoers in the 1940s into the '50s.

Why the gender discrepancy in value? Well, female high-risk stories usually get lost within the larger, more muscular dimensions of the male genre. As that metaphor suggests, there's a differing emphasis on physicality in male and female stories. The male adventure stories heave with exertion and bleed every few pages or so; women's feats tend to be less Herculean and more Sisyphean in nature. Just like the mythical Sisyphus, who was doomed to push a boulder up a mountain, only to have the boulder roll down again and the process repeat itself over and over for eternity, many female "adventurers"—in literature and real life— face unremitting daily strains like tending families, children, elderly relatives, or the sick or the disabled. The most famous female adventure tale of them all featuring a handicapped child and a teacher's day-in, day-out fight for her independence is that of Annie Sullivan, "The Miracle Worker," and her extraordinary, "buried alive" student, Helen Keller. *The Miracle Worker,* as most stories in this specialized subgenre do, concludes on a note of triumph: after years of toil by herself and Sullivan, Helen is prepared to enter the workaday world. But ending, as they do, on the achievement of "normalcy," these tales of endurance are much less flashy and spine-tingling than their male counterparts, which typically feature superhuman feats of achievement.

If stories about women plugging away, day after day, sound more like a literary call to conscience than a pleasure to read, stories about caring for the elderly—or stories of the lives of old people and their struggles— have even less of the potential-bestseller aura about them. Getting old and infirm is way down on anyone's list of favorite fantasies, and this fact is reflected in how few novels, short stories, or poems have tackled the subject. Yet, I think that aging and its attendant challenges and miseries are very much the stuff of real-life female extreme adventures as well as of a small group of novels and memoirs. Some not-quite-dead-yet Great Men have written about their declining years, but statistically, women far outlive men. Male reflections of old age—such as Tennyson's "Ulysses" and "Tithonus" and W. B. Yeats's masterpiece, "Byzantium"—

tend to dwell on the loss of sexual potency. A downer, certainly, but there are other kinds of losses that must be braved, quietly, by the many women who tend their husbands through their last illnesses and then find themselves alone at the end of their own lives.

A couple of years after my father died, I took my mother, who was visiting me in Washington, to a local senior club in an effort to get her connected to other retirees in our area. "Bring a partner and dance," read the advertisement in our neighborhood newspaper. Like a lot of other adult daughters I know, I was now my widowed mom's designated partner. We arrived at the social center and found that the club consisted of three beautifully turned-out women and one old man who had charge of playing what he called the "Victrola" and dancing, in turn, with each of the ladies. Female-with-female dancing was not done. The fact that this amiable old fellow was in such demand just gives further evidence of the essential unfairness of life when it comes to gender differences. My mom shyly danced a polka with this obliging man ("I thought he was going to keel over," she whispered to me afterward), and then she and I made some excuse and fled—to have a drink at a nearby bar/restaurant. I remember thinking that day that I wouldn't have the guts for what might lie ahead in my old age—searching for friends, maybe for another partner; dancing in the face of approaching death. Certainly that neighborhood Fred Astaire has his own story to tell, but he's far outnumbered by all those patiently waiting Ginger Rogerses, who dance the same steps he does—but backward and wearing heels.

The solo entry of women into the "extreme" landscape of widowhood and the attendant feelings of diminution or even invisibility is a tough subject only a few brave literary women have tackled. There's Barbara Pym's dour novel *Quartet in Autumn,* about four oldsters—two women, two men—who work in the same office, attempting to fend off retirement. Significantly, early in the story, one of these women—an avid novel reader named Letty—thinks about the fiction selection in her local library: "If she hoped to find [a novel] which reflected her own sort of life she had come to realize that the position of an unmarried, unattached, ageing woman is of no interest whatever to the writer of modern fiction."[2] When it was published, Pym's novel was inevitably compared to one of the few others that have turned a cold eye on the subject of female aging, Muriel Spark's rather sinister *Memento Mori*. In contrast, Agatha Christie wrote what is essentially an old-cat fairy tale in her Miss Marple series, which turned the invisibility of old women into an advantage for her master detective. Ditto for Christie's American predecessor, Anna Katherine Green, in her 1897 mystery, *That Affair Next Door*, which introduced her snoopy spinster detective, Amelia Butterworth. Autobiographical writers like M.F.K. Fisher, in a few posthumously published essays, and Kate Simon, in her last memoir, *Etchings in an Hourglass,* wrote bitter, vivid accounts of the disrespect and loneliness they experienced as elderly women dining and traveling solo. I asked a former editor and friend of mine who lives in New York and who likes to play literary parlor games to poll her wide circle of acquaintances for titles. So far, they've come up with *A Lost Lady* by Willa Cather and Simone de Beauvoir's *Adieux: A Farewell to Sartre.* Almost every player started off by mentioning Barbara Pym's *Quartet in Autumn.*

If aging isn't a sexy topic for literature, neither is caring for the old and sick; yet that's a job—I'd call it an extreme emotional, and sometimes even physical, adventure—that still primarily falls to women. When I was growing up in Sunnyside, it seemed as though every large apartment house contained at least one apartment tenanted by an elderly woman and her single adult daughter. Although I grew up and moved away, some of my cohorts remained behind to live at home, work in "the city," and take care of their aging parents. The three-story apartment building next to the one I grew up in was owned by a Ukrainian couple with one daughter, Christine. They were hardworking people and devout Catholics. Since Christine was several years older than I, we played together only occasionally, but our mothers were friendly, talking to each other in a patchwork of Polish and Ukrainian. While Christine was in medical school, her mother died. Even after she became a doctor, Christine lived at home with her father in the small two-bedroom apartment that was a mirror image of our own. For the last several years of his life, her father was paralyzed; he needed Christine's help to perform all the basic bodily functions. On several occasions he stopped breathing and Christine, using her medical skills, resuscitated him. For years she didn't work outside the home at all; she just took care of her father—spelled occasionally by health-care aides and by the parish priest, who visited several times a week to administer Holy Communion. Nowadays, Christine works at a New York hospital and lives in that same apartment by herself. Word around the neighborhood is that she's leaving the apartment house and all her savings to the local parish church when she dies.

Christine's story is an extreme example of an extreme female adventure in caring for the elderly. Most of the friends I have these days would dismiss her decision to remain with her dying father as an exercise in Catholic masochism. I feel both identification and dread when I think about her. I understand her decision as partly the consequence of, yes, being a good Catholic girl but also being an only child (and, particularly, an only daughter) and, on top of all that, being the transplanted offshoot of an Old World culture in which the family always came first. Christine's self-sacrifice reproaches and terrifies me—terrifies because I can almost see myself swaying a little too close to the edge of that particular chasm into which many good, dutiful daughters have fallen. Almost, but not quite. When my mother was diagnosed with breast cancer early in my graduate-school years, I traveled every weekend up to New York for months to help her through the ordeal, but I refused to take a leave of absence from school, which is what she asked me to do. I felt, rightly or wrongly, that I would never get back into that graduate-school world if I left it; that I would lose my fellowship and drift into becoming another one of those adult daughters living at home, one day taking care of her parents. And, even though Jane Austen, Emily Dickinson, the Brontës, and plenty of other literary women were adult caretaking daughters living at home who still managed to find time to write in between changing the bed linen and cooking supper, I knew that no *Pride and Prejudice*s—or even book reviews—would be written in my parents' apartment in Sunnyside.

So, to my low-grade-but-still-extant shame, I shrank from that particular female extreme adventure. But lots of women, literary and civilian, haven't and still don't. Because caretaking is such an unappealing and enervating adventure to write about, it's hard, once again, to find whole novels or memoirs devoted to the subject. Accounts of the deadening ordeal, however, are sometimes tucked into the corners of larger narratives written by women. In one of the early chapters of Charlotte Brontë's *Villette,* for example, the novel's young heroine, Lucy Snowe, reluctantly agrees to become the companion of a Miss Marchmont, an elderly single woman of means who's crippled by rheumatism. What other options, after all, does the orphaned Lucy have? Even so, she hesitates to commit herself to a life of self-denial spent in Miss Marchmont's sickroom. Her description of her time there—in between the declarations of devotion to the compelling Miss Marchmont—reads like an extreme adventure in keeping her nerves steady and her panic tamped down while she's entering a sensory deprivation chamber:

> Two hot, close rooms thus became my world; and a crippled old woman my mistress, my friend, my all. Her service was my duty— her pain, my suffering—her relief, my hope—her anger, my punishment—her regard, my reward. I forgot that there were fields, woods, rivers, seas, an everchanging sky outside the steam-dimmed lattice of this sick-chamber; I was almost content to forget it. All within me became narrowed to my lot.[3]

Miss Marchmont conveniently expires and releases Lucy from her prison, but the numbed Lucy says she would have "crawled on"[4] with Miss Marchmont for twenty years if fate had decreed otherwise. That verb choice is significant, I think, because it intensifies the impression that this whole chapter creates of caretaking as an underground life— one that threatens to break the health and spirit of the caretaker herself.

Nice girls don't whine and Lucy is a nice girl, so her description of her time spent nursing Miss Marchmont is mournful rather than complaining. By social necessity, I think, the complaints or even cries of female desperation in literature have been encoded. And few writers have been better at transmitting subversive messages about the extreme adventures of womanhood through an enigma code of deceptively childlike vocabulary and black humor than one of my all-time favorite twentieth-century poets, the still-underappreciated Stevie Smith. Because Stevie's writings and her life contain so many contradictions, labels always fall short. Toss out the interpretation and she arches backward at the crucial moment. Her peculiar poems are simple, complete with lines that rhyme, rhythms borrowed from the nursery and hymnal, and illustrations—in the tradition of William Blake and James Thurber—composed of loopy doodles. But a host of classical, literary, historical, and theological references lurks beneath the naïveté.

Stevie herself affected childishness; to call her "Ms. Smith" would be to address the adult she only sometimes pretended to be. By most accounts, she was a startlingly plain woman who cultivated a preschool image with her Buster Brown fringe and homemade smocks. She lived from age six till her death at sixty-nine in the same house in the dowdy London suburb of Palmers Green. For many of those years, she nursed her beloved maiden aunt, Margaret Annie Spear, whom she immortalized in her poetry as "the Lion of Hull" or, simply, her "Lion Aunt." Before illness and old age set in, Lion Aunt cosseted Stevie. She warmed Stevie's bedtime glass of milk every night and was fiercely proud of her niece the poet—although her own appreciation of art extended only to the parish theatricals. Perhaps that tone deafness to poetry was a good thing, because if Lion Aunt had been a perspicacious reader, she might have sensed the insurrectionist messages expressed through the notoriously wicked wit of Smith's work.

Stevie's off-kilter poetry abounds with the inappropriate laughter of the Wise Child, splitting her sides over life, death, the existence of a benevolent God, and the wish of every "normal" woman to be a mother. Many of her poems' titles sound like snatches of conversation Stevie presumably overheard while marketing in Palmers Green: "Was He Married?"; "I Could Let Tom Go—but What About the Children?"; "Do Take Muriel Out"; "Emily Writes Such a Good Letter." Were the poems merely send-ups of suburban culture, they'd be boorish; instead, they ramble from their familiar points of origin into secluded zones of erudition and pathos.

Her most famous poem, the macabre masterpiece "Not Waving but Drowning," which she wrote in April 1953, has been read as an existential commentary on human isolation. That's what Stevie would have called the "smug-pug" or "smartie" reading. The poem describes the ludicrous, life-threatening situation of a drowning man whose frantic signals for help are misinterpreted by the smiling crowd on shore as cheerful greetings. I think, however, if you don't allow yourself to be dis-

tracted by the sex of the drowning victim (a cover?), the poem also can
be read as a vivid dramatization of the solitary, weighty situation of good
"daughterly" caretakers like Stevie herself:

> *Nobody heard him, the dead man,*
> *But still he lay moaning:*
> *I was much further out than you thought*
> *And not waving but drowning*
>
> *Poor chap, he always loved larking*
> *And now he's dead*
> *It must have been too cold for him his heart gave way*
> *They said.*
>
> *Oh, no no no, it was too cold always*
> *(Still the dead one lay moaning)*
> *I was much too far out all my life*
> *And not waving but drowning.*

I imagine Stevie returning every night from her secretarial job (she
worked for more than thirty years as a private secretary to an aristocratic
publisher) to that house in Palmers Green. She waves and smiles at the
neighbors—puts a good face on—as she walks up to the door, enters,
and once again takes up the slow nightly routine of being a companion
and, eventually, nurse to her elderly aunt. Throughout her life, Stevie
was susceptible to "drowning" in depression. Not surprisingly, given her
overburdened routine, many of her poems restlessly reenact a fantasy of
escape: the spinster whose wind-propelled hat lifts her away to a desert
island; the typist who leaps, during lunch break, into a Turner painting;
the poet who longs for Coleridge's "Porlock Person" to interrupt her
thoughts and carry her out of life. Stevie herself would have been an
ideal reader for all those male extreme-adventure tales that are currently
so popular—although I can't quite imagine her reading *Into Thin Air*
and the rest of that thrilling but undeniably self-aggrandizing and
sweaty canon without chortling.

Do the women's writings I've just surveyed constitute high-risk "adventure" tales? Certainly they did to the women—real and fictive—who lived them. But the impediments to their recognition as adventure literature are obvious. As I've said, most of these female extreme adventures in child rearing or caretaking aren't glamorous. Then there's the problem of location, location, location—three words that are as crucial in literature as they are in real estate. I think a lot of women's extreme-adventure stories have been categorized as something else—melodrama, tales of sentiment—because the women involved meet their challenges inside a parlor, kitchen, or bedroom, rather than outside on some blasted and barren ice floe or wide, empty sea. There's also a difference in what exactly is being risked: men usually gamble with their lives; lots of women, too, face physical risks, but more typically the emphasis in their stories is on the threatened loss of their sanity and their sense of self. The struggles described in this literature are often internal and psychological, rather than life-and-death contests in Technicolor. And there's another odd fact that emerges once you begin to look at these male and female extreme-adventure tales in aggregate: men tend to seek adventure in packs, while women are isolated by their trials. Ironically, for all the feminist lit-crit theorizing about how women form their identities and experience their lives in community, the female extreme-adventure tale is imbued with a deep sense of seclusion—no wonder the extreme-adventure heroine fears a loss of sanity. Even Crusoe had Friday for company, and Stanley his Livingston. But the girls go it alone.

By now, Reader, you've probably thought of some real and fictive exceptions to this theory of mine—and so have I. John Bayley's memoir *Elegy for Iris,* about caring for his wife, Iris Murdoch through her struggle with Alzheimer's; Philip Roth's extraordinary memoir *Patrimony,* about nursing his aged father in his last illnesses. Just as women sometimes live out male adventure plots, these men endured and recorded an adventure that's more traditionally female.

"Reader"—that cozy form of direct address beloved of the nineteenth-century novel and most closely identified with the famous ending of *Jane Eyre*—flew into my head a second ago because, just as soon as I began reflecting on the essential ingredient of solitude in women's adventure tales, I thought of Charlotte Brontë, the author of the two most encompassing and traumatic female extreme-adventure tales of all time.

All three of the literary Brontë sisters were poets of solitude—not surprising, given their childhood in that parsonage out there on the moors; the early deaths of their mother and the two eldest sisters; and the dubious guidance of their volatile father, Patrick. Anne and Emily certainly captured the call of the wild and lonely in their novels, but Charlotte was the sister who ventured the deepest in exploring the terrors of utter isolation. I'm not talking about just the physical experience of being all by your lonesome; no, Charlotte Brontë shoves her readers into the dark prison house of self and throws away the key. In *Jane Eyre,* she relents and finally opens the door; by the time of writing *Villette,* Brontë had grown more courageous as a writer, or maybe more merciless. In that novel, which is almost unbearable to read, she lets the key to the cell slip through her fingers and sink into the void. Brontë rivals her American literary soul mate, Edgar Allan Poe, in treating readers to the vicarious horrors of being buried alive, of sensing the walls slowly closing in, of being bounded on all sides by icebergs towering out of a frozen sea, like those miserable crewmen on the *Endurance,* Ernest Shackleton's doomed ship.

In both *Jane Eyre* and *Villette,* this waking nightmare is gendered: it's one that only women suffer. The sensitive and intelligent—but undeniably plain—heroines of those amazing novels describe for us a particularly traumatic version of a female extreme adventure that is by no means restricted to the nineteenth century but whose terrors have faded somewhat for contemporary women thanks to the saving social interventions of the First and Second Women's Movements. I'm talking here about the extreme female adventure of the marriage market. Fortitude, wits, and, above all, keeping one's nerves steady in an isolated, time-sensitive contest: these are the defining features of the marriage-market extreme adventures that are reenacted, fictively, in the parlors and pump rooms of so many nineteenth-century British and American novels written mostly by women. (Henry James, of course, is the great male master of this subject.) If a young woman didn't successfully come through the ordeal, she could expect a death-in-life future of second-class citizenship as a female dependent—years spent outside the home as a governess or

companion or immured inside the family manse caring for elderly relations; playing the stern or doting aunt to hordes of nieces and nephews;
and, quite possibly, at the end of her life being turned out of the ances-
tral pile when her father died and the male heir claimed his inheritance.[5]
To me, as a semi-active, semi-autonomous feminist reader, the most
chilling aspect of the nineteenth-century marriage-market extreme adventure for women was that the "contestants" had to remain, at least out-
wardly, still. To be observed plotting or maneuvering an eligible man of
means into your clutches would be to forfeit the game—and one's
demure claims to ladyhood—at the outset. In Edith Wharton's *House of
Mirth,* scheming, or being seen scheming, was what destroyed Lily Bart.

Whenever I read accounts in nineteenth-century novels of young
female characters reining themselves in and waiting breathlessly for a
male partner to take notice of them, I think of that scene in the middle
of the first James Bond movie, *Dr. No.* Bond, played definitively by Sean
Connery, is asleep in his Caribbean-island hotel room when something
on his leg—a tickle? a soft tentacle?—awakens him in the dead of night.
He spies a roundish lump moving up under the white sheet that covers
his leg. Instantly, Bond knows that in order to save his life he must
remain absolutely still. The lump moves up, out from under the sheet,
and onto his chest. Bond sees that it's a tarantula. The tarantula moves
onto his neck, his cheek. Bond remains still. At last, the tarantula crawls
off the bed and Bond leaps up and squashes it. To save their lives in the
extreme adventure of the premodern marriage market, women had no
choice but to remain, like Bond, immobile while their lives hung in the
balance.

Even *Pride and Prejudice,* that sunniest, most beloved nineteenth-
century novel about courtship and marriage, is rimmed with dark shadows—fearsome alternative tales of the horrors that would befall women
who marry unwisely or not at all. The marriage of the Bennet parents is
itself a catastrophic case study in the consequences of marrying in haste
(a mistake that the Bennets' boy-crazy third daughter, Lydia, is geneti-
cally programmed to repeat, running off, as she does, with that charming and shallow soldier of fortune, Colonel Wickham). Here's part of a
passage where the all-knowing wry narrator of *Pride and Prejudice*
"reads" Elizabeth's mind on the subject of her parents' marriage:

Had Elizabeth's opinions been all drawn from her own family, she could not have formed a very pleasing picture of conjugal felicity or domestic comfort. Her father, captivated by youth and beauty, and that appearance of good humor, which youth and beauty generally give, had married a woman whose weak understanding and illiberal mind put an end to all real affection for her. Respect, esteem, and confidence, had vanished for ever; and all his views of domestic happiness were overthrown. But Mr. Bennet was not of a disposition to seek comfort for the disappointment which his own imprudence had brought on, in any of those pleasures which too often console the unfortunate for their folly or their vice. He was fond of the country and of books; and from these tastes had arisen his principal enjoyments.[6]

Mr. Bennet is a man, so he can remove himself from his family for long stretches of time. Indeed, throughout *Pride and Prejudice,* he's described as hibernating in his study; in other words, he uses reading as a means of escape. His marriage is a disappointment, but it is not his destiny. That's why his detached amusement at his wife's overly obvious attempts to engineer a "good match" for their daughters comes off as a bit sadistic: he can afford to laugh; it's left to the inept Mrs. Bennet to shove her daughters into the lifeboat of a respectable marriage—even though she herself, at least subconsciously, knows how leaky such a marriage can be. But not to marry is a fate worse than death. Certainly that's the fear fueling the grotesque marital surrender of Elizabeth Bennet's best friend, Charlotte Lucas. Charlotte's panicky decision to wed the smug and sexually unappetizing Mr. Collins could have so easily been Elizabeth's own that it reads like a noir alternative to it. Mr. Collins first proposes to Elizabeth, and then, when she declines his offer, within a few short days he turns around and proposes to Charlotte, who accepts him. Elizabeth is stunned by what she perceives as her girlfriend's "humiliation."[7] But the dowdy Charlotte doesn't possess Elizabeth's signature advantages of a "fine pair of eyes" and a witty tongue. She's not likely to receive other offers. Unlike Mr. Bennet, Charlotte walks into this dreadful marriage with eyes open, armored in pragmatism. "I am not romantic you know," Charlotte tells Elizabeth. "I never was. I ask only a comfortable home; and considering Mr. Collins's character, connections, and situation in life, I am convinced that my chance of happiness with him is as fair, as most people can boast on entering the marriage state."[8]

One can almost hear in that speech the creak of the coffin lid closing. Alas, poor Charlotte, we knew her well. And, in fact, Charlotte does become diminished, growing quieter and more deferential, after her marriage. But will "fine eyes" and a talent for clever repartee be enough to rescue Elizabeth from a different, solitary kind of social entombment? Some months later when Elizabeth pays a visit to the now married Charlotte, she's patronized and pitied by Mr. Collins, who, in his moronic way, embodies the prevailing view toward superfluous single women. *Creak.* The scariest part of *Pride and Prejudice* is that section where Elizabeth and her beautiful older sister, Jane, are walled up in their house, all hopes for a union with Darcy and Bingley (Jane's inamorato) lost. (I do, by the way, mean to use that adjective *scary,* even though it doesn't seem to accord with the overall tone of *Pride and Prejudice.* Austen, after all, was a great reader of Gothic novels, and she even wrote one herself: *Northanger Abbey.* Because of the life-and-death dramas that are publicly enacted in them, those bright rooms at Longbourn are as fearsome, in their way, as the creepiest Gothic dungeon.) And the absolutely scariest pages within that long suspenseful section are those where Elizabeth at last encounters Darcy again: first, in the parlor of the Bennets' house, Longbourn (when he and Bingley come to pay a visit after their strange absence), and then, in the dining room of that house a few evenings later. Like Bond, Elizabeth—arguably the most spirited, the most resourceful, and the most confident heroine in all of nineteenth-century literature—can only hold her breath and wait during these decisive meetings whose outcome will determine whether she "lives" or "dies." The emotional power of these drawn-out passages is cumulative, but even in this snippet from the second meeting, a reader can see how very painful—and imperative—it is for Elizabeth to maintain her position of passivity:

> Anxious and uneasy, the period which passed in the drawing-room, before the gentlemen came, was wearisome and dull to a degree that almost made her uncivil. She looked forward to their entrance,

as the point on which all her chance of pleasure for the evening must depend.

"If he does not come to me, *then*," said she, "I shall give him up for ever."[9]

Darcy doesn't come to Elizabeth *then*. Austen wants to make her readers squirm a bit longer. And we really would squirm if, the first time we read *Pride and Prejudice,* we weren't reassured by our teachers or parents that "Jane Austen is a comic writer" or "*Pride and Prejudice* is a great love story." Imagine not knowing how this novel will turn out and reading those scenes that describe Elizabeth's almost unendurable waiting. The whole fate of her life—indeed, whether she'll even have what many of her peers would regard as a life—rests on whether this man Darcy looks at her; whether his gaze lingers; and whether he, once again, likes what he sees enough to airlift Elizabeth up and out of the limbo of Longbourn and off to the Cinderella's castle of Pemberley.

Jane Austen *is* a comic writer, and *Pride and Prejudice is* a great love story. The terror of the marriage-market extreme-adventure scenes that abound in *Pride and Prejudice,* as in all of Austen's other novels, is contained by her wit and her fondness for qualified happy endings. (The exception, of course, is her last novel, *Persuasion,* where the witty worldview slipped away, although the qualified happy ending hung on by its fingernails.) Austen is like the smart-ass Army private from Brooklyn who's a stock character in virtually every World War II movie ever made. He takes in the carnage around him, but he's tough: he reflexively cracks jokes to keep fear at bay. Maybe, because he grew up on the streets of Brooklyn, this guy never had high expectations of humanity in the first place. To extend this analogy, Charlotte Brontë is like the idealistic young kid, also a staple of the cinematic Army platoon, who breaks down because the horror, the horror, of war is too much to bear. Brontë and her heroines never take a single ironic step back from their situations. If there's a funny moment in *Jane Eyre* and *Villette,* I've missed it, repeatedly. Jane Eyre and Lucy Snowe have no defense mechanisms; indeed, it's almost as if they have no skin. Their first-person narratives are frostbitten to the core. Both heroines recount their individual frantic attempts to escape from subzero existential solitude into the warmth of a sheltering marriage. The deadening cold of their Shackletonian slogs across the ice and snow of polar emptiness toward the elusive fires of human companionship permeates their voices, as well as their souls.

The opening pages of *Jane Eyre* warn us that we're in for a rough trip across stark terrain. Indeed, chronology aside, those pages could have been cribbed from Shackleton's own journal. The novel begins on a gloomy scene where the ten-year-old orphan, Jane Eyre, is whiling away the long hours of a wet November afternoon by looking at an illustrated volume called Bewick's *History of British Birds*. She stares raptly at these paintings of lone sea-fowl who inhabit "the bleak shores" of

> the Arctic Zone, and those . . . regions of dreary space—that reservoir of frost and snow, where firm fields of ice, the accumulation of centuries of winters, glazed in Alpine heights above heights. . . . Of these death-white realms [Jane tells us] I formed an idea of my own: shadowy, like all the half-comprehended notions that float dim through children's brains, but strangely impressive.[10]

Brontë suggests here that Jane's fascination with the blankness of the godforsaken Arctic region is the same fascination she displays a few pages on when she stares into a looking glass. Jane is transfixed by the book's geographical representation of her own emotionally frozen personal circumstances: orphaned, friendless, without hope.

Jane fears being alone in the world, and her fear stirs up the very thing she most dreads. As she's reading, her concentration is shattered by the taunts of her older cousin John Reed. Jane is unjustly punished for talking back to this thug by being locked away in the supposedly haunted "red-room." As night casts its dark shadows into that moldy chamber, Jane ruminates on her outcast status as a dependent in her widowed aunt's family: "I was a discord in Gateshead Hall; I was like nobody there; I had nothing in harmony with Mrs. Reed or her children, . . . If they did not love me, in fact, as little did I love them."[11] Jane's terrifying and precocious awareness of what promises to be her extended sentence to emotional solitary confinement climaxes when she glimpses a ghostly gleam in the room. Because fortitude is one of the womanly virtues celebrated by the female extreme-adventure tale, I think it's significant that Jane tells us at this crucial point in the narrative that: "*endurance* broke down; I rushed to the door and shook the lock in desperate effort. Steps came running along the outer passage; the key turned, Bessie and Abbot entered. [italics mine]"[12] But the nurse and the lady's maid know which side their bread is buttered on, and they desert Jane to the cruel ministrations of her Aunt Reed, who promptly thrusts her into the red-room again and locks the door. At last, Jane (temporarily) escapes her prison via the tried-and-true method of Gothic heroines from Ann Radcliffe's Emily de St. Aubert, star of the 1794 trendsetter *The Mysteries of Udolpho,* to the unnamed mousy narrator of Daphne du Maurier's *Rebecca:* she faints.

Devoted readers of *Jane Eyre* know the torments of spirit and tests of strength that follow, all of them having to do with Jane's struggle to escape her own chill loneliness. Jane is eventually cast out of the Reed mansion and packed away to Lowood, a boarding school of dubious quality. There her hopes for the rescue of companionship are briefly satisfied—and horribly dashed—first, by her friendship with schoolmate Helen Burns, and then, by her adulatory apprenticeship with a teacher, Miss Temple. Helen approaches Jane after Jane has been publicly and unfairly branded as a liar by the ogre who runs Lowood, Mr. Brocklehurst. She tries to inspire Jane with an "Invictus"-like pep talk on the virtues of self-love. Here's a bit of their dialogue:

"If all the world hated you, and believed you wicked, while your own conscience approved you, and absolved you from guilt, you would not be without friends."

"No; I know I should think well of myself; but that is not enough: if others don't love me, I would rather die than live— I cannot bear to be solitary and hated, Helen. Look here; to gain some real affection from you, or Miss Temple, or any other whom I truly love, I would willingly submit to have the bone of my arm broken, or to let a bull toss me, or to stand behind a kicking horse, and let it dash its hoof at my chest—"[13]

Poor Jane sounds a little like what contemporary pop psychology has branded as one of those "women who love too much." Stripped of its elegance, Helen's response to Jane's emotional vulnerability is to tell her to "buck up," and the rest of the novel can be read as a kind of a basic-training manual in which Jane's spirit hardens as she endures the twin rigors of tragedy and tedium until she finally learns to embrace her solitude—at which point, in this novel that's essentially a Gothic fairy tale, Jane is rewarded with a soul mate in the shape of a reformed and blinded (and therefore, symbolically, less potent) Mr. Rochester.

But I get ahead of Jane's ordeal by ice here. One of the many amazing things about *Jane Eyre* is how unflinching it is in the many trials it administers to its heroine. After delivering her advice to Jane, Helen contracts the swamp fever that periodically infests Lowood. One night she and Jane cuddle up in their "little crib" together and slumber, until Miss Temple comes upon the pair at dawn—Jane's arms tightly wrapped around Helen's cold corpse. In all of nineteenth-century fiction is there any more appalling image of the elemental human need for closeness, for warmth, cosmically denied? Then, a few pages on, in a much less traumatic episode, Miss Temple abruptly marries the Rev. Mr. Nasmyth and the numbed Jane tells us she spent the half-holiday the school grants in honor of the nuptials "in solitude."[14]

That solitude hardens when Jane moves to Thornfield to begin her life as a governess—the ultimate in lonely occupations for an educated woman in the nineteenth century. Jane's pupil, Adèle, is charming but narcissistic—the kind of child who constantly insists that adults "Look at me!" as she twirls and toe-dances around the parlor. No company for Jane there. Thornfield's elderly housekeeper, Mrs. Fairfax, is pleasant but pedestrian, the type of person who talks a lot about the weather. The other inhabitant of Thornfield on hand to welcome Jane (in a manner of speaking) is Bertha Rochester, the master's first wife, who has degenerated into a madwoman locked away in the attic. "While I paced softly on," Jane tells us, recalling her tour of the upper rooms of the mansion house on her second day in residence, "the last sound I expected to hear in so still a region, a laugh, struck my ear. It was a curious laugh; distinct, formal, mirthless. I stopped: the sound ceased, only for an instant; it began again, louder. . . . It passed off in a clamorous peal that seemed to wake an echo in every lonely chamber."[15]

The weird figure of the first Mrs. Rochester has inspired a lot of brilliant critical readings, first among them, a chapter in Sandra Gilbert and Susan Gubar's pioneering book on the female Gothic called, in tribute to Bertha's centrality, *The Madwoman in the Attic.* Gilbert and Gubar see Bertha as a demonic double for Jane—a woman who destructively vents the anger that Jane herself has been struggling to repress ever since that wild tantrum in the red-room. As we learn by reading between the lines of Rochester's eventual confession to Jane about his marriage, Bertha initially caught his eye because of her exotic sexual allure. Thus Bertha also serves as an erotic mirror image for Jane, who's much more conventionally ladylike in this regard. No question these prevalent theories about Bertha are right, but I think she also embodies the dangers that can befall a woman who can't translate herself, can't make her truest self clear to those around her. That's the reading of Bertha dramatized by a novel I otherwise don't like: Jean Rhys's turgid "prequel," *Wide Sargasso Sea.* Rhys focuses on Bertha's "otherness" (she is of Creole descent and was raised in the West Indies), rather than her inherited madness, as the ominous impediment to a blissful union with the young Mr. Rochester. The sex is good; they just can't talk afterward.

To be linked for the rest of your life to a man who doesn't "get you": so many women's stories dwell on this particular nightmare. To name two: Kate Simon's *Bronx Primitive*—a nuanced memoir of growing up in the teens and twenties in New York City—contains a chapter called "Fifth Floor," which catalogues all the "crazy ladies" who dwelled in Simon's tenement. The crazy ladies are mostly immigrant women who've been disoriented by their transplant to the New World and whose husbands demonstrate a tone-deaf impatience with their anxieties. In Maxine Hong Kingston's book *The Woman Warrior* (critical debate continues over whether this is a novel or a fanciful autobiography), similar stories about immigrant crazy ladies abound, along with a mesmerizing tale about a woman in China who wears a headdress that encloses her in mirrors, and whose failure to communicate with her fellow villagers results in her death by stoning. In *Jane Eyre,* I think that cautionary vision of utter emotional isolation, as much as the bars and chains of Bertha's actual physical imprisonment, is what really terrifies Jane after her bungled wedding ceremony to Mr. Rochester and sends her running out of Thornfield and into the wilderness. It's tricky to support this interpretation, because the cries from the heart about how lonely that first, star-crossed marriage was emanate from Mr. Rochester as he tries to explain himself to a devastated Jane: "I found her nature wholly alien to mine. . . . I found that I could not pass a single evening, nor even a single hour of the day with her in comfort; that kindly conversation could not be sustained between us. . . . I tried to devour my repentance and disgust in secret; I repressed the deep antipathy I felt."[16]

Our sympathies lie with Mr. Rochester, except that he's not only misled but also "misread" Jane, and that's a very bad omen for their future together. Right after Jane accepted his proposal, Mr. Rochester swept her off on a shopping expedition where he tried to dress her up in rainbow silks. No clotheshorse, Jane consents to a gray wedding gown. That Mr. Rochester even imagines, after their canceled wedding ceremony, that she's the kind of woman who might agree to an "unholy" union indicates how wide of the mark his understanding of her is. So, Jane flees. But she has no one or nowhere to flee to. She winds up losing herself in a landscape almost as hostile to life as the Arctic one described in the novel's first chapter.

By referencing that Arctic landscape, *Jane Eyre* consciously opened with an homage to male extreme adventures (after all, male explorers braved those polar climes to catalogue those birds) and signaled that, as a novel, it would be a female variant on those traditional tales. It's significant, after all, that Jane, not her loutish male cousin, John Reed, is fascinated by those illustrations of far-off places. Furthermore, *Jane Eyre* is a standout in the canon of female extreme-adventure tales of the nineteenth century because, in a short but powerful digression from its main "woman's story" about the torments of solitude and the struggle for psychic and economic salvation through marriage, it veers off into a conventional male physical-adventure narrative. I can't think of another nineteenth-century female adventure tale that dares this kind of gender-role reversal, in which the hero, Mr. Rochester, stays home and "stands and waits," while the heroine dashes off into the wilderness, camps out, and fights the elements.

When Jane eludes Mr. Rochester's illicit embrace and sneaks out of Thornfield in the dead of night, she skirts hedges, gets her shoes wet, and sleeps fitfully on the damp, brambly heath. She loses all her money and, starving, forces herself to beg and barter for food. Like other modest female adventurers, Jane is reluctant to boast of her exploits. Of her third day on the road, she only tersely tells us:

> Do not ask me, reader, to give a minute account of that day; as before, I sought work; as before, I was repulsed; as before, I starved; but once did food pass my lips. At the door of a cottage was a little girl about to throw a mess of cold porridge into a pig trough.
> "Will you give me that?" I asked.
> She stared at me. "Mother!" she exclaimed; "there is a woman wants me to give her this porridge."
> "Well, lass," replied a voice within, "give it her if she's a beggar. T' pig doesn't want it."[17]

This singular section of *Jane Eyre* reads like a Special Forces training manual. Like the typical male extreme-adventure tale, it's heavy on physical challenges and discomforts, which take place in a wild, out-doorsy setting. It's also an adventure of short duration. At the close of day three, Jane follows a light in the gloaming and discovers Moor House, where she's taken in by the kindly Rivers sisters and eventually embarks on another extreme adventure—this one female—when she takes a job teaching village girls in the local school: "It was truly hard work at first. . . . Wholly untaught, with faculties quite torpid, they seemed to me hopelessly dull; and, at first sight, all dull alike."[18] She also resists the aloof advances of the brother of the house, St. John Rivers, who's looking for a pliant dray horse of a wife to help him shoulder the burden of his anticipated missionary work. Thanks, but no thanks. Jane has learned that there is a fate more terrible than solitude: it's solitude in the company of a husband who essentially misunderstands you.

Then, Brontë relents. She gives Jane that waking vision where she hears Mr. Rochester's plaintive voice. Jane dashes back to her now widowed intended (recall that Bertha died in the fire that she herself maliciously set at Thornfield) and finds that Mr. Rochester has been punished for his earlier blindness to her true character by literal blindness. That affliction lifts after a few years of empathetic married life.

I've gone on at length about *Jane Eyre* because, as a female extreme-adventure tale, it pulls out all the stops—even, as I've said, digressing into a traditionally male adventure-tale plot that sends its physically delicate heroine off on an obstacle course where she climbs crags and competes with pigs for food. In its ruthless exploration of the female soul in solitary, no other nineteenth-century novel written by a woman bests *Jane Eyre*—except, of course, the last novel that Charlotte Brontë wrote: *Villette*.

Villette functions as an excruciatingly relentless version of a female extreme-adventure tale. One reason for the brevity of my tribute to *Villette*, Brontë's greatest novel, is that it scares me too much. I love it, I'm awed by it, but I don't want to spend extended periods in its world. About ten years ago I visited Emily Dickinson's house in Amherst, Massachusetts. In the company of a guide and a small group of Dickinson admirers, I toured the parlor and dining room; then I climbed up the staircase to Dickinson's bedroom. Her bed, her bureau, her night table, even one of her famous white dresses—they're all there. You never know how these kinds of places are going to affect you; I've toured plenty of great writers' houses that have felt as impersonal as museums. But I started to tear up when I stepped into Dickinson's bedroom: something about its smallness and the defiant intensity of the woman who lived so much of her life within its walls shook me. I wouldn't want to be in Dickinson's house after dark. Whether ghosts roam those rooms or not, the atmosphere of the old homestead is too charged for my psychic comfort. I feel something similar about *Villette*. It's a novel that so haunted my imagination after I first read it, I knew I would be compelled to pay short return visits to it every few years or so—during daylight hours. If I stay too long inside, however, night falls and I'm trapped. Better to stop in briefly and then scurry out and cross myself as I run off down the street.

Villette summons up the uncanny in its very first sentences. Whereas in *Jane Eyre* we readers get background information on how Jane became a dependent orphan, *Villette* volunteers no such biographical detail on Lucy Snowe. Like Kaspar Hauser, she's just there—a child who's profoundly alone because she seems self-created. This tale of extreme emotional deprivation proceeds with the inevitability of a nightmare. As I mentioned earlier, the teenaged Lucy takes a job as a companion to an elderly woman. After Miss Marchmont dies, Lucy is forced again to shift for herself and winds up as an English teacher/governess at a girl's boarding school in the mythical city of Villette. The school is run by the autocratic and sinister Madame Beck, who spies on her charges and her staff. Such is the "intimacy" the world of Villette offers Lucy.

The section of the novel that I want to anoint as the ultimate, the Olympian, the sine qua non of women's rough expeditions into the dark interior realms of the self occurs in the very last chapter of Volume 1, when Lucy is left behind at the school while everyone else, students and teachers, takes off for "The Long Vacation." Well, not completely alone. A servant is in shadowy residence, and Lucy has the care of "a poor deformed and imbecile pupil, a sort of crétin whom her stepmother in a distant province would not allow to return home."[19] The cretin is mute and her bodily needs nauseate Lucy ("there were personal attentions to be rendered which required the nerve of a hospital nurse; my resolution was so tried, it sometimes fell dead-sick"[20]). But even this poor soul turns out to have an aunt, a "kind old woman"[21] who shows up and takes her away for the remainder of the vacation. Critics have discussed the cretin as a kind of horrific double for Lucy, much as the apparition of a nun who roams the school also represents a mirror image of her aloneness. Lucy regards her as barely human, but once she's gone, Lucy is entirely cast out of proximity to other breathing bodies.

That's when she has a breakdown the depths of which twentieth-century literary "madwomen" like Sylvia Plath's Esther Greenwood in *The Bell Jar* and Elizabeth Wurtzel in *Prozac Nation* only prosaically skim. While wandering restlessly around the city of Villette, Lucy tortures herself by imagining the vacation gaiety her colleagues and students are enjoying. Inevitably, her health breaks down: "a day and night of peculiarly agonizing depression were succeeded by physical illness."[22] Sleep eludes Lucy as she's marooned in her single bed in a long dormitory room, whose white-sheeted cots look like "specters."[23] When sleep finally does come, it comes "in anger"[24]—with gruesome dreams that wring "my whole frame with unknown anguish; to confer a nameless experience that had the hue, the mien, the terror, the very tone of a visitation from eternity."[25] The descriptions in this section are as superheated as if Brontë were describing a military battle—a psychic "Charge of the Light Brigade" in which Lucy's sanity struggles to withstand an onslaught of self-generated horrors:

> Quite unendurable was the pitiless and haughty voice in which Death challenged me to engage his unknown terrors. When I tried to pray I could only utter these words:—
> "From my youth up Thy terrors have I suffered with a troubled mind."
> Most true was it.[26]

The turning point of this terrible contest with solitude comes when Lucy, "weak and shaking,"[27] dresses herself and desperately staggers out of the school, which she now thinks of as a prehistoric cairn, crushing her flailing body beneath it. She deliriously reasons that she can escape the "insufferable thought of being no more loved, no more owned"[28] if she can walk outside the city and reach one of the surrounding hilltops where she can breathe more freely. Along the way, she stops in a Roman Catholic church, where she seeks the comfort of human communication by entering a confessional and blurting out her torments to a priest. In her paranoid state, Lucy interprets the priest's sympathetic interest in her as a Romanist ploy to capture her Protestant soul, and she inwardly shudders as he makes an appointment to meet at his rectory the following morning. ("As soon should I have thought of walking into a Babylonish furnace.")[29] Then Lucy strays into an old, unfamiliar part of the city, gets lost within its "network of turns unknown,"[30] and lacks the nerve to ask directions of the strangers she passes. A furious storm breaks, bringing with it torrents of rain like sea spray. "The Long Vacation" concludes with a description of that storm, in which Lucy loses her struggle to, in the famous words of E. M. Forster, "only connect": "I suddenly felt colder where before I was cold, and more powerless where before I was weak. I tried to reach the porch of a great building near, but the mass of frontage and the giant-spire turned black and vanished from my eyes. Instead of sinking on the steps as I intended, I seemed to pitch headlong down an abyss. I remember no more."[31]

This is the first of the two "perfect storms" in the novel; the second occurs on its very last, cryptic pages, when the ship carrying Lucy's intended, Paul Emanuel, is lost in a storm of biblical dimensions that "roared frenzied for seven days."[32] In this first tempest, it's Lucy herself who goes overboard—as does the language of this entire "Long Vacation" chapter. We're told, in the first paragraphs of Volume 2, that Lucy, through a supreme effort, returns to life, although, like Jane Eyre in her earlier "outward bound" adventure, Lucy is typically ladylike in her reluctance to go into boastful detail about her struggle. ("Where my soul went during that swoon I cannot tell."[33]) The intense physical and mental pain generated by Lucy's reentrance into the material world is curtly but vividly described in a few short sentences: "The returning sense of sight came upon me, red, as if it swam in blood; suspended hearing rushed back loud, like thunder; consciousness revived in fear: I sat up appalled, wondering into what region, amongst what strange beings I was waking."[34]

Many critics have commented on the eerie "proleptic" voice of *Villette*'s narrator—the voice (also heard in some of Emily Dickinson's sepulchral poems such as "Because I Could Not Stop for Death") of someone speaking from beyond the grave. The loss of Paul Emanuel in the second storm finishes Lucy off, so that by the time she begins her retrospective tale, she is a dead woman talking. To fight her way back once from the underworld of the unloved, the solitary, the inconsequential, demanded a superhuman effort. The novel ends where it does because Lucy simply can't summon the will or the strength to fight her way back twice. I said earlier that Charlotte Brontë's serious and intelligent heroines almost seem to have no skin—so sensitive is their acuity, so raw and vulnerable are they in a fictional world populated by the self-interested and the cold-blooded. But thinking of skin metaphors makes me think of the incredible phrase Toni Morrison used to describe the existential solitude of her ghostly heroine in *Beloved*. On the penultimate page of that magnificent historical novel/female extreme-adventure story (which, like *Jane Eyre*, is distinguished by the fact that it subjects its heroine to both physical and emotional ordeals), Morrison says of Beloved that her "loneliness [was] wrapped tight like skin."[35] Jane

Eyre and Lucy Snowe also endure a loneliness "wrapped tight like skin"; in Lucy's case, those bindings constrict her to the point of strangulation.

We read literature for a lot of reasons, but two of the most compelling ones are to get out of ourselves and our own life stories and—equally important—to find ourselves by understanding our own life stories more clearly in the context of others'. Thinking about this "shadow genre" of female extreme-adventure tales made me realize that for roughly five years, from the time I turned thirty-nine to the age of forty-three, I had been living what constituted a classic prefeminist extreme-adventure narrative. Call Part 1 of it "The Infertility Saga." When my husband, Rich, and I decided that some high-tech medical intervention might be needed in order to help us attain our much desired goal of being parents, we entered the anxious and costly world of the clinically infertile. For the next few years we both went through painful surgical procedures and, subsequently, endured the monthly roller-coaster ride of Metrodin shots—a drug that promotes hyperovulation and that, as one forthright article I'd read about the treatment warned, makes your ovaries feel like bowling balls. Once a month I willed myself to be in a serene state of mind as the artificial-insemination ritual took place in my doctor's office. Then Rich and I waited. We waited much as Elizabeth Bennet waits in that drawing room for Darcy to choose her. We waited to know our fate—would this be the month we'd have a chance to become parents, or not? Three times I became pregnant, and three times I had early miscarriages. Each time, after a lull, the whole tense drama would start up again.

The isolation of an infertility ordeal is not anywhere near as awful as the ordeals of many women who've lost children after birth or after adoptions have fallen through. (Ruth Reichl's *Comfort Me with Apples*, the sequel to her first, wonderful memoir, *Tender at the Bone*, contains just such a horror story.) Nor did I go through anything close to the different kinds of extreme-adventure ordeals endured by Lucy Snowe or Jane Eyre. After all, I had a loving partner to hold on to during the bleakest days, and friends, and even a compassionate, talkative doctor. I also had work that I loved and that gave me a sense of control—I often "put myself back together" after setbacks during this time by writing reviews or teaching classes. But the fact that the drama of infertility—as well as pregnancy and miscarriage—was played out within the darkness of my own body gave an isolated quality to the whole experience. Every week I lectured to classes and recorded reviews, and nobody, outside of a few intimates and medical professionals, knew what was happening. It's not the kind of extreme adventure you share with people.

I'd call Part 2 of my traditional female extreme adventure "The Adoption Saga." More sad and anxious waiting, more feelings of power-lessness and confusion as both Rich and I felt that forces outside our control held our lives in the balance. But this time there was an unimag-inably happy ending. Sometime in the winter of 1998, we decided that we would try to adopt a baby from China. My dad had passed away by then; my mother's response when we told her of our decision was a howl of disbelief: "China! And what is that baby going to think when she grows up!" ("Well, she'll probably be as embarrassed by us as most kids are, at least temporarily, of their parents," I thought to myself. Admit-tedly, as parent material, Rich and I are on the oldish, oddish side but not as grotesque as some parents we've met.) To her credit, my mother later gave us money toward the adoption. All the while worrying. After all, I was, once again, doing such a strange thing by the standards of the world I'd grown up in.

By the time I'd committed to the adoption idea, I was used to worry-ing, disapproval, and sadness. Rich and I had gone through all those years of infertility treatments. After my third miscarriage, I proposed adoption. Rich hesitated. Then he proposed adoption from China. I hesitated. I'd read Pearl Buck, Maxine Hong Kingston, and Amy Tan. For some reason I now forget (probably to sneer at godless commu-nism), I'd also read Mao's Little Red Book in the world-history class I'd taken in Catholic high school. I knew how to ask for "hot water" in Mandarin because the father of my lifelong friend Mary Ellen Maher had served in the Air Force in China during World War II and he'd taught us neighborhood kids some phrases. Growing up in Queens, I'd never heard of anyone venturing into New York's Chinatown for dinner; we all stayed close to home with the Sun Luck Sunnyside on Queens Boulevard, where chicken chow mein and pepper steak were the stan-

dard fare. As an adult, I thought myself something of a minor gour-
mand for ordering mu shu chicken and hot-and-sour soup at Chinese
restaurants. That's it. I had just one Chinese American friend, and I
knew embarrassingly little (beyond the big names like Sun Yatsen and
Mao, of course) about Chinese politics and culture. What a perfect candidate to be the mother of a Chinese baby! But throughout the years I'd
been teaching, I had loved and disliked students of all races, ethnic
backgrounds, and income brackets. That experience, together with the
wider experience that reading had given me—of feeling at ease in other
worlds, other lives—gave me the necessary psychic shove to say yes to
adopting a baby from China.

Rich and I arrived at the mutual decision to adopt after going to
countless information sessions held by adoption organizations and local
agencies. Since neither of us are joiners, these meetings were usually an
ordeal. Many nights we would rush home from work, drive out to some
chilly church basement in Virginia, affix our name tags, and introduce
ourselves. "I'm Fred Jones, and this is my wife, Patty." Adoptionville, as
we first found it, seemed to be a suburb of Normative World: everyone
was married, with the wife absorbed under the husband's last name;
almost everyone was white; and they all "appeared" to be Republican
and Christian—the way Rich "appeared" to be a Jewish leftist. "What
agency do the lesbian Zoroastrian socialists use?" I remember Rich asking one night as we got lost driving home from yet another bleak Virginia suburb. Whichever one it is, we never found it. We listened to
social workers and parents talk about the process in speeches heavy on
extraneous detail. Most people don't know how to talk in front of other
people (keep it short and entertaining; don't proselytize). We were a cap-
tive audience for those folks who preached against abortion rights as
they framed the adoption of their children in conservative religious
terms. One night we listened (for hours?) to a friendly guy in a Promise
Keepers T-shirt give us an endless blow-by-blow account of adopting his
son from Russia. The whole time he spoke, his wife sat by his side; she
didn't open her mouth once. At an "open house" held by one adoption
agency we considered, the director, who was dressed in a Teddy bear
sweater, promised us yearning parents-to-be that she would find for us
all "the children we should have had." She described how she searched

for—and found!—a musically inclined toddler in a Russian orphanage who was "the perfect fit" for his guitar-playing adoptive father. Ordinarily, Rich and I tried to be on good behavior at these meetings; we were, after all, attempting to present ourselves as sturdy parent material. But at this particularly daffy meeting I couldn't restrain myself. "A biological child doesn't necessarily have the same looks or tastes or talents as her parents," I commented, thinking of my own mother's aversion to reading. *"YES it does!"* declared the director, who then pinned me down with her eyes for the next ten minutes as she described in disturbing detail the other "perfect fits" she had engineered. Rich and I snuck out at the bathroom break.

We chose the adoption agency we did because it was the only one that didn't present a Hallmark-card image of parenthood by adoption. The social worker who spoke at that open house mentioned that a baby recently brought home from China was diagnosed with hepatitis B. Ironically, that confession of "imperfection" reassured us. After all, parenthood is a crapshoot. Why should adopted kids have to be perfect or any more immune from disease, learning disabilities, or personality problems than biological kids? Even at that relatively sensible meeting, though, the treacle seeped in. Wrapping up the (always endlessly meandering) question-and-answer period, the social worker wheeled out a VCR and said: "I want to show you a video and play you a song one of our adoptive fathers wrote." What followed was a four-hundred-hour film of Happy Adoptive Families cavorting under Christmas trees accompanied by a soundtrack of this well-meaning Kenny Loggins imitator warbling a ballad. "I had no one, then I found you, son . . ." Film and song finally ended and the lights went up. People in the audience were audibly sniffling—which I understood, because everyone in that room had, like us, been through the wringer of infertility. Then Rich—who, like Jane Austen, handles fear and anxiety through comedy—piped up: "I guess being a terrible musician doesn't preclude you from being an adoptive father." Nobody but me laughed; the social worker looked confused. We called and signed on with that agency the next day, hoping the social worker hadn't been able to read our name tags.

I sound cynical, but you try sitting, hungry and tired, for hours on a folding chair as some stranger—uninvited—makes you listen to his songs or imparts to you her Philosophy of Life, or gives you a detailed travelogue of his trip to Vladivostock. And all the while you're stuck there, an anxious voice—your own—is whispering in your head: "It will never happen. I'll never be anybody's mother. This effort will end as the fallopian-tube test, the laparoscopy, the shots, and the sonograms did. With no baby." Later, talking with the women in our adoption travel group, I sensed that few of them had really believed in their heart of hearts that the longed-for baby would ever materialize. One of those women had had five miscarriages; another, who mysteriously dropped out of the group before we left for China, had lost a baby shortly after birth. All the time Rich and I were in China, I continued to worry, in a low-level way, that someone would take my new daughter away from me. When you've been through all the loss that most people suffer in order to reach the decision to adopt, you armor yourself in doubt.

Next came the interviews with a social worker. Clean the house! Toss out the Roach Motels! This was no joke. Rich and I had hastily moved into a two-bedroom apartment in our building to meet the standard adoption requirement of a separate bedroom for the child-to-be. The apartment turned out to be infested with roaches and water bugs so big you could saddle them. Then there was the paperwork. Someone later told me that the Chinese believe that the more important a transaction, the more seals the paperwork ratifying that transaction should have. I guess this speaks well of the official Chinese attitude toward overseas adoption because our documents—birth certificates, employment veri-fication, doctors' reports, personal testimonies by friends—had to be notarized and certified by the city and state. All those large red-and-gold seals perversely made our paperwork look fake—like forgeries generated by the Marx Brothers' Republic of Freedonia. For six months I waited in limbo for the FBI to clear my fingerprints. Usually the process takes a few weeks. Why the holdup? Every so often I'd call the FBI in Washing-ton, and they'd always tell me that all fingerprints were examined in the central clearing bunker in Nebraska and that number was unavailable to the public. So I'd wait and worry some more. Was my pinko NPR con-nection to blame?

Worst of all was dealing with the D.C. local government. "Kafka-esque" is an overused literary modifier, but in this case it's the fitting one. One morning I took our D.C. "police clearances" down to a city office to have them notarized. The functionary there informed me that these were the wrong kind of clearances; we needed a different form for overseas scrutiny. "We're only open till noon," drawled the functionary (it was then 11:05), "so you'll have to hurry over to Police Headquarters and come back." I sprinted a couple of blocks over to Police Headquarters, got on line with a lot of mean-looking (recently released?) people awaiting their police clearances, and, when I finally reached the window, explained the error to the clerk. "Honey," she said with a smirk. "These clearances aren't any good anyway. They were done in March. Police clearances in D.C. are only valid for a few months."

I felt so beaten down by the city bureaucracy—and by the hoop-jumping effort to become a parent—that I tried to burn off my frustration that day by walking all the way home, about three miles. I had tears in my eyes for much of that walk. Just above Dupont Circle, I passed a townhouse that I'd never seen before. Next to its front door was a plaque that said something about the house being the home of Eleanor and Franklin Roosevelt when he was secretary of the navy. I had recently read the first volume of Blanche Wiesen Cook's magnificent biography of Eleanor. "Think about Eleanor and all she went through," I told myself. "Her tragic childhood, her homeliness, Franklin's affair with Lucy Mercer, the ungrateful children (no, cancel that thought!), the nastiness of her political enemies." Eleanor-channeling helped to a point, but thinking of her also reminded me of all those fiercely independent "odd women" I had known while teaching, years before, at Bryn Mawr College, and thinking of them made me frightened because, like them, I seemed destined to be childless.

We left for China in early June 1999. One afternoon three months earlier I had picked up the phone and the adoption-agency social worker had said, "Maureen, I have news of your daughter." *My daughter.* I don't think any words anyone will ever speak to me will be so simultaneously unreal, frightening, and magical. Our trip was delayed a couple of weeks by the American military's inadvertent bombing in May of the Chinese embassy in Belgrade. We'd received Molly's wallet-sized "placement" picture the day after that life-changing phone call. Immediately after the bombing, China suspended overseas adoptions—temporarily, it turned out, but I didn't know that at the time. I was so scared we were going to lose her—not just a hypothetical baby anymore but *her*. Her name was Yangchun Chao, which translated as "spring morning," according to our one Chinese American friend. She was eight and a half months old when the picture was taken, and she had beautiful dark eyes, a little frown line on her forehead, and a pouty, down-turned mouth. Someone had dressed her in red (the Chinese color of good luck, we later found out). She was the daughter we didn't know we had been waiting for all those years, but we had.

That's when I felt as though the covers closed on my own female extreme-adventure story and another kind of adventure began, one that I didn't recognize from any of the thousands of books I'd read. For ten days I was beyond the radar of books, beyond all known stories—at least those known to me.

But that doesn't mean we didn't bring books along on this momentous journey. Before we left for Beijing, my friends in the English Department at Georgetown University threw us a shower. Books! Books! Lots of books! This would be a very well read and very underdressed baby. Then we took off, burdened by way too many suitcases and, what felt so very strange, a stroller. We also packed a duffle bag's worth of books. Plenty of how-to picture books on diapering and feeding, because neither Rich nor I had ever cared for a baby before, as well as recreational reading. We didn't know that you don't read much when you're sharing your hotel room with a ten-and-a-half-month-old baby.

In Beijing, we hooked up with some other about-to-be parents and, for three days, did some sightseeing and shopping. It sounds frivolous and it was, but after all those years of infertility anxiety and on the eve of all the responsibilities of parenthood, it was fun to run around Beijing being tourists. On our last day there, we were even escorted by our very own "personal shopper," a gorgeous Chinese American former student of mine named Jenny Fan, who took us to the best stalls to scoop up black-market Timberland sandals and Prada wallets.

The giddy consumption came to an end that evening, when we boarded a plane for Guangzhou (formerly Canton) in the far south of China where the American consulate is located and where all adoptions by Americans are processed. Early the next morning we were taken with our group—four other adopting couples and one single mom-to-be and her sister—to the Bureau of Adoptions. There we were interviewed via our translator and completed the Chinese adoption forms. Rich held the line up for a good half hour by insisting on truthfully answering the bureaucratic question "What do you do for a living?" Apparently, there's no phrase in Chinese for "labor-union researcher." "Union! Workers banding together!" Rich kept repeating to our translator. "C'mon, this is a Communist country. I fight for workers' rights—you people under- stand that!" Rich, well aware that China's state-run unions were a sham, was clearly enjoying throwing China's professed values back in the face of his interlocutors, something he enjoys doing with the American gov- ernment, too. But his timing was lousy. Confusion ensued on the part of the Chinese, and irritation grew on the part of our fellow soon-to-be parents. "Just say you're a teacher," hissed one man from Maryland. Rich's work identity eventually became blanded down to the innocuous "researcher," and we finally boarded a van for what would turn out to be an eight-hour drive still further south to Yangchun, where Molly's orphanage was located, a city close, relatively speaking, to China's bor- der with Vietnam. A few minutes out of Guangzhou, our van was hit by a car, necessitating a hurry-up-and-wait detour to a garage. Lots of downtime for reading, right? No. This was one of the few times in my life when I could have reached for a book and didn't. I was too petrified.

During part of that ride to Yangchun, we traveled on narrow dirt roads, through a tropical landscape filled with rice paddies and volcanic outcroppings and water buffaloes. People in bare feet and conical straw hats stopped and stared at our van as we drove by. Occasionally, the countryside was punctuated by small cities of new, uniformly dilapi- dated three-story concrete buildings faced in white bathroom tile where, as night fell, people in rooms open to the street gathered around the blue light of television sets. "The twelfth century meets *Blade Runner,*" I thought to myself, looking out at this strange landscape; the only real reference I had for what I was seeing was the nightly news footage of the Vietnam War when I was growing up and some of the descriptive pas- sages in Dr. Tom Dooley's memoirs that I had been assigned in parochial school. Most of the other soon-to-be parents chatted with one another and sporadically aimed their video cameras out the window.

Rich got into a political "debate" with one prospective father sitting in front of us who opined to our Chinese translator that "all Americans are against Clinton's war in Yugoslavia." That guy turned out later on not to be all that bad; maybe talking was just his way of coping with the fear of the impending unknown. Mine was to get quieter and quieter as an hours'-long out-of-body experience commenced. "What the hell are we doing?" I remember thinking to myself.

We arrived at nighttime at the Yangchun hotel (a real full-service hotel, as one of our group later quipped, since it featured a bordello on the third floor—which I stumbled into—and also provided the "delivery room" for our babies on the fifth).

I'll never forget the first stunned moments with Molly, the joy at hearing her very first laugh that night when we tickled her belly with our noses, the anxious days that followed when she would not eat because she missed the orphanage, and the "tough love" of the amazing orphanage director, Mrs. Yu, who force-fed her, talked to her in the local dialect, and held her for hours, to make sure she would be strong enough to leave for her new life. I could tell you, in detail, about that time, but those memories are semi-private, as much Molly's emotional property as mine, since they constitute her story. Suffice to say, we were thrilled and happy. Besides, isn't this supposed to be a book about books?

What about those books I said I packed for this trip—the most important trip of my life? Something uplifting and maternal, you'd think, the literary equivalent of a Mary Cassatt painting. Maybe Anne Lamott's *Operating Instructions: A Journal of My Son's First Year,* or *Little Women,* or that family classic, *Cheaper by the Dozen*? Or maybe, to exorcise some of my worst fears about how I would (or wouldn't) shape up as a mother, I could have brought along Sue Miller's *The Good Mother,* or even Charlotte Perkins Gilman's *The Yellow Wallpaper.* (Though not hormonal in origin, post-adoption terrors have some similarities to postpartum depression.) Maybe, to gain some understanding of the unfamiliar situation I found myself in, I could have brought along a memoir about adoption in general or a book about recent Chinese history.[36] Or, thinking in the most expansive terms, I might have at least packed a book that celebrates the happy possibilities of life: maybe one of Laurie Colwin's novels or short-story collections, or Jeannette Haien's wondrous novel *Matters of Chance* (which is partly about the thrill of adoption), or perhaps my favorite literary fairy tale, *Pride and Prejudice*. Nope, I didn't take anything like those books with me as I set out on the trip that would change my life forever. Instead, on the fourteen-hour plane ride to China, during the jet-lagged downtime spent in hotel rooms in Beijing and Guangzhou, and even in the quiet moments when my lovely new baby daughter napped under mosquito netting in her crib at the Golden Roc Hotel in Yangchun, I had my nose buried in a true-crime paperback called *The Unicorn's Secret: Murder in the Age of Aquarius* by *Philadelphia Inquirer* investigative reporter Steve Levy.

The Unicorn's Secret is about the notorious Ira Einhorn murder case, which I first learned about when I entered graduate school in 1977 at the University of Pennsylvania. Einhorn had been an undergraduate and graduate student at Penn during the 1960s, and as a prominent figure in Philadelphia's New Left and burgeoning New Age circles, he remained a fixture on campus well into the seventies. By virtue of his gift for intellectual patter and self-promotion, Einhorn numbered politicians, corporate executives, clergy, academics, and fellow counterculture icons such as Abbie Hoffman and Jerry Rubin among his friends. Overweight and not particularly cute, Einhorn also managed, by dint of his outsized personality, to be a highly successful roué; in 1972, his roving eye alighted on Holly Maddux, a pretty blond Bryn Mawr student from Texas. Soon the two were living together. Maddux disappeared late in the summer of 1977 (just as I was moving down to Philadelphia from New York), and although the police suspected that Einhorn was involved, they couldn't put the pieces together. Then, in 1979, a Philadelphia police detective, working on a lead developed by a private investigator hired by Maddux's distraught family, gained access to Einhorn's West Philadelphia apartment and decided to open a trunk out on the enclosed sunporch. Maddux's remains were inside.

Einhorn protested his innocence (one of his claims was that the CIA planted the ghastly trunk in his apartment), and many of his influential friends supported him. Arlen Specter signed on as his defense attorney and managed to get him out on an unusually low bail. Einhorn promptly skipped the country, resurfacing in 1997 in France, where, still proclaiming his innocence, he was arrested. Einhorn had been convicted, in absentia, some years before of Maddux's murder, and he was finally extradited to the United States in 2001 by French authorities. In October 2002 he was tried in person and convicted by a Philadelphia jury. By the way, Einhorn, who had been living the good life in a charming château, is married to a woman he met while on the run—a woman who was fully aware of the murder charges during their life together and still declares his innocence. Einhorn's case proves, once again, that while lots of wonderful heterosexual women I know seem destined to live out their lives without romantic partners, a man—even one who chops up his girlfriend and hides her in a trunk in his apartment for eighteen months—inevitably seems to find an adoring mate.

At this most extraordinary time in my life, what was I doing reading this well-researched tale about a sociopath whose crimes could have been scripted by that other notorious sometime Philadelphian Edgar Allan Poe? If the social worker who'd sincerely grilled Rich and me to determine our fitness as adoptive parents could have seen this paperback (with a photo of a mad-eyed Einhorn on the cover) perched on the hotel night table *near the crib!,* she surely would have pressed the alert button and had our exit visas and additional adoption paperwork frozen.

I've thought sporadically about this incongruous choice of reading, and I think I understand some of the reasons why I packed *The Unicorn's Secret* along with the diapers and stuffed animals. I think I was in self-protective denial after all those years of trying to have a baby and failing; I don't think I really quite believed there would be a baby waiting for us at the end of this journey. My first sensation upon stepping into the hotel room and seeing Molly in the arms of her caregiver that night in Yangchun was that of her "thereness," as Gertrude Stein might have said. Molly was a devout wish made flesh. Her physicality was overwhelming to me, and I had a first impression of her as being very big, even though she was, and still is, on the small side. Rich and I, along with most of our companions on this trip, had been burned by fate: we all had our stories of loss. I think that by choosing such an inappropriate book to take along, I was subconsciously steeling myself for an anticipated letdown.

When situations are emotionally overwhelming, in order to get through them people like me who reflexively turn to books for comfort will sometimes choose a book that's an escape from the crisis at hand. Looked at this way, *The Unicorn's Secret* is the tonal double of the novels by Susan Isaacs and Maeve Binchy that I read during my father's final hospital stay. I escaped into Binchy's 1950s Ireland and Isaacs's gutsy, funny wartime New York—places where the endings would be at least semi-happy. (I'm referring to *Shining Through,* Isaacs's wonderful novel about a working-class, half-Jewish legal secretary from Queens named Linda Voss who eventually becomes an undercover OSS agent in Nazi Germany. Isaacs, whom I've referred to in a review as "Jane Austen with a schmear" is one of our great underappreciated contemporary writers. She consistently celebrates female spunk and heroism without any of the gynocentric mysticism that sometimes intrudes on, say, Toni Morrison's novels. But because Isaacs works in the low-rent genres of mystery and suspense, she's been relegated to the outer borough of "genre fiction.") China, adoption, motherhood—it was all too much. I didn't want to read books about any of these subjects; I needed a book as far away from them as possible. The story of Ivy League maniac Ira Einhorn fit the bill.

Perhaps there are some life experiences that are simply beyond books. By that I mean not that those experiences are quintessentially "unique" but that they're so intensely personal, so crucial, that reading other people's literary approximations of them is frustrating, even painful, rather than helpful. Rose Lewis's children's book *I Love You Like Crazy Cakes* is annoying to me because her experience of adopting from China isn't mine. Lewis probably didn't intend her book to be representative, but right now it is among *the* select children's books about Chinese adoptions, so when I read it I become impatient. Other adoptive parents I know also have that complaint about it—it isn't representative of their experience. For years I avoided reading Mary Gordon's novels because I feared they would either approximate the Catholic-girl experience in a close-but-no-cigar kind of way or that they would mirror my own life so faithfully they would wipe out any need for me to write about it. When I did finally read *Final Payments,* I was relieved: Gordon nails the Catholic self-abnegation attitude, but the outer circumstances of her Catholic world in this and the other novels of hers that I've read make her experience sufficiently different for me to read in peace.

Those first life-altering days spent with Molly in her native city of Yangchun will always be sui generis experience in my life. But with forays into the female extreme adventures of infertility and the adoption process so recently behind me, I couldn't help but be aware that some aspects of the trip to China fit the traditional rough-and-rugged standards of the traditional male extreme adventure. Albeit, our group was cosseted in an up-to-date van that was stuffed to overflowing with Perego strollers, L.L. Bean diaper bags, and squirt bottles of waterless antibacterial soap, but state-of-the-art equipment doesn't cancel out the extremity of the adventure. If it did, then the high-tech climbing gear that Krakauer's crew lugged up Mount Everest in *Into Thin Air* and the sonar rig on the *Andrea Gale* described in *A Perfect Storm* would have disqualified those stories. Until the China trip, my high-risk adventures always had been emotional or intellectual, certainly not physical. When I was growing up, girls were not encouraged to be athletic. Of course, as a New York City kid, I played slap ball and hopscotch and jump rope on the streets every day after school. Phys ed at my Catholic high school was a stationary subject: I remember mornings spent sitting on the bleachers dressed in, I kid you not, yellow bloomers and taking written exams on the rules of basketball and golf. Title IX, guaranteeing girls equal access to athletic facilities, was passed during my last year of college at Fordham University in the Bronx, so no sports teams for me. I've always walked a lot, but apart from working, irregular enrollment in aerobics classes, and, these days, happily running around the playground, I've spent much of my adult life curled up on a piece of upholstered furniture, reading.

Sometimes I took what I consider risks in pursuing my love of reading: applying to Ivy League Ph.D. programs in English and then suffering through the trial of being a graduate student at the University of Pennsylvania; steeling myself to send book-review clips and then make "cold calls" to strange newspaper editors. (When I sent a bunch of clips from *The Village Voice* to *Fresh Air*'s executive producer, Danny Miller, he courageously took the initiative of calling me and saying "No thanks. We think you're too academic for the show." Fatefully, he changed his mind after I wrote a ribald exposé of my stint as a grader for the Educational Testing Service for the *Voice*.) The goal of all these exploits, however, always involved a chair and a book.

I do think my weekly deadlines for *Fresh Air* constitute an intellectual subset of the extreme adventure. As a comfort hound, I hate rousing myself from bed at 4 A.M., but I do so at least once a week to write my reviews. Physical discomfort aside, I like writing on deadline. My brain usually snaps to attention under pressure, and I get some of my best ideas when I'm concentrating against the clock. I also like immediate gratification. There's a rush that comes when I've found the right phrase to capture a complex point about a book, and I e-mail in the finished piece, and it's filed—*boom!*—on time. Sometimes, given the hectic schedule of *Fresh Air*, I finish reading a book at night, write the review before dawn, edit it with my producer, Phyllis Myers, early that morning, record it a little later, and hear it air that afternoon. Life on the edge, right?

Occasionally, though, this whirlwind pace knocks me flat on my face. Like my mother, I tend to mangle names. I've recorded reviews in which I've referred to a book, even a book that I love, by two different titles or I've committed dumb grammar mistakes—and the gaffe has slipped through the batlike ears of Phyllis, but not those of the listeners of National Public Radio. The worst on-air mistake I ever made was when I confused my old Jewish literary leftists, referring to Irving Howe when I meant to refer to Alfred Kazin. *Oy vey,* the listener mail on that one was nasty.

But back to China and the traditional extreme-adventure plot I was living out. As we rode that fateful day from Guangzhou to Yangchun in the gathering darkness along rutted lanes that seemed barely wide enough for a pair of water buffaloes, our young Chinese driver would stop every twenty minutes or so, take out his map, and consult anxiously with our translator, a shy, efficient, and altogether lovely woman whose English name was Nicole. Nicole had made this trip at least a few times before, but even she seemed confused by the random geography of abrupt forks in the road and crumbling twenty-block cities whose pavements ended in rice paddies. Once we found Yangchun and settled in with our daughters, our group meals featured grasslike steamed vegetables and mystery meat—one variety of which turned out to be a dish called, roughly, "snake on a stick." "Tastes like chicken," pronounced the intrepid Rich as I fantasized about a latte. Despite the Cokes, bottled waters, and beers we steadily chugalugged in lieu of drinking the contaminated tap water throughout China, he and I sweated off about six pounds each in the nearly two weeks we spent there. On our second full day in Yangchun, Mrs. Yu took three families, ours included, to the local hospital. Two of the baby girls had fevers, and Molly had stubbornly refused to eat or drink anything since the night she had been placed in our arms. (What a trauma that must have been for her. We didn't look or sound or smell like anyone she had ever met, and we had probably not yet conveyed to her confidently enough that we were now the two most important people in her life. As someone from our adoption agency said to us before we left, "You may have been waiting for your daughter for a long time, but she has not been waiting for *you*.") The reigning theory was that maybe she, too, was coming down with a bug.

To Western eyes, the hospital was a run-down place; all of its windows were open to the stifling heat and the omnipresent mosquitoes. A doctor entered the room where our group was gathered and approached Molly, who was now crying. As Nicole translated her symptoms, the doctor made a stern hand gesture to Molly that instantly translated into the order "Be strong." Then he took a tongue depressor out of his pocket, looked down her throat, and tossed the used depressor out the window. I looked out the window and saw a random dumping ground of depressors, bandages, and paper. We were given some medicine for Molly in case a fever developed, and the two other screaming babies were given IVs in their foreheads to reduce their temperatures. The decision to allow the doctor to insert those IVs was excruciating for those parents, for we all had been forewarned of the Chinese practice of reusing needles. But the babies had high fevers and Nicole assured their parents it was okay, and so they went ahead.

At the height of this anxious procedure, one of the fathers—who must have weighed more than three hundred pounds and who had been attracting crowds of starers since we arrived in Yangchun—began pacing out in the corridor and stepped on a floor tile, which cracked, loudly. All the hospital personnel came running to point their fingers and laugh at the poor guy, who, fortunately, had a gracious sense of humor. The crack broke the tension, the babies' fevers broke, and on day four, Molly began eating as we left Yangchun on the now even more jam-packed van. At last, after a flight from China filled with crying, pooping babies and punctuated by a four-hour delay in Detroit, Rich, Molly, and I arrived home, extreme adventure ended.

As journalist and fellow adoptive mother Karin Evans comments in her substantive and moving book, *The Lost Daughters of China*, many Americans who've adopted their children from China have come to believe in the idea of a "red thread"—the Chinese notion that, from birth, all of us are connected to those we will love by an invisible red thread. That's certainly how Rich and I feel about Molly, the daughter of our hearts and souls who came to us in a way we never could have imagined a decade ago. One of the many slogans prospective adoptive parents learn at information meetings is that adoption, for most of us, is a "second choice," not "second-best." That's one feel-good slogan that's absolutely true. It's also true that most of the time adoption isn't on our minds as a family; it's a word that describes how our family was formed, not how we relate to one another. But inevitably people make comments, particularly about transracial families like ours or, as a friend of mine who's the white mother of three African American children calls us all, "rainbow families." One autumn afternoon I was carrying one-year-old Molly past the bleachers of a neighborhood softball field while a game was in progress. A man's voice rang out: "Hey! Is she from China?" I unthinkingly answered, "Yes!" and looked up. A bleacherful of white faces stared down at us, but no one identified himself as the questioner. I felt as though Molly and I had been turned into curiosities by that bored crowd. I wish I had had the presence of mind to shout back, "Where are you all from?"

"Is she adopted?" asked a waitress in a café where four-year-old Molly and I were eating. "Yes," I answered, and she demanded of Molly, "Do you love your mother?" Would she have asked that of a biological child? A friend of mine, also Caucasian and the mother of two girls born in China, had a particularly bizarre experience in the women's changing room of a hotel swimming pool here in Washington, D.C. As this friend, Elizabeth, described the incident to me, she and her older daughter, Isabel, who'd just turned four, were stripping out of their bathing suits when a very large naked woman planted herself before them and demanded, "Are her parents *dead*?" Elizabeth tried to move Isabel into the shower, but the woman followed, barking the question over and over. Finally, just to shut this person up and protect Isabel as best she could, Elizabeth muttered, "We don't know." It's futile to point out to such people that, in fact, the adoptive child has two sets of "real" parents. Like the conservative Indian family Nell Freudenberger writes about in the title story of her recent debut short-story collection, *Lucky Girls,* many of the people who stare at or question "rainbow families" such as mine are folks who "believe that people, like the drapes and the sofa, should match."[37] The best Dorothy Parker–like riposte to nosy questions about adoption was uttered by a friend of a friend of mine on a New York City bus. This white mother and her Chinese baby daughter were riding up Madison Avenue when an older woman got on, sat down across from them, and barked out: "Is her father Chinese?" "I don't know," the mother replied. "It was dark."

I've been out of New York too long: I've lost some of my speed as a comeback artist. Anyway, writing, not speaking, has always been my medium. But I'm trying to get better, to not be so Catholic-girl accommodating, to protect my daughter from the idle inquiries and offensive remarks of strangers. And I try to focus on the wonderful encounters we've had with strangers who approach us to tell me about their grown-up adopted kids or with people who are just happy to see us together. When Molly was still a baby, we were approached by a man cleaning tables in McDonald's, and he summed up our situation: "You are beautiful!" he said, waving his hands around us and speaking in a strong Hispanic accent. "You wanted to be mother and she needed mother. You are beautiful." Some days more beautiful than others, perhaps, but that generous stranger was right. We found each other, and that's a miracle I will never get over.

Maybe I worry too much about protecting Molly. She's already survived one female extreme adventure in her life—anybody who knows anything about the situation of abandoned infant girls in China will know that. And her ordeal was preceded by the unknown sufferings of her Chinese parents. Molly also made it through those first few days with Rich and me, when we didn't know how to feed her or change her properly or make her relax with us enough to eat or drink. She's got a strong innate sense of self and a good sense of humor; she'll probably make her way just fine in the world. Already though, I'm trying to give her the talisman of some good books, good stories to help her forge her way through life. "Read, read, read," Molly chants as she sits beside me in bed; I'm reading whatever I'm reviewing that week; she's "reading" the pictures in *Curious George*. For a long time, one of her favorite books was *Emily* by Michael Bedard, a magical story about a young girl's visit to Emily Dickinson. There we are in bed, two peas in a pod, "reading" together. Who says there's no such thing as fate?

Fate and effort and will. Oftentimes, women's extreme-adventure tales have put forward an approved "cover story" that emphasizes their heroines' deliverance from solitude or disaster through an act of chance or charity by others. Think of that supernatural voice that calls out to Jane and "saves" her from the folly of a marriage to the glacial St. John Rivers. The version of my own grandmother's coming-to-America story, which was passed down to me as a sort of cautionary tale, illustrates this self-deprecating mode of presenting women's adventures.

At the age of seventeen, in, as close as I can estimate, 1905, my mother's mother, Helen Mrosz, boarded a boat all by herself and sailed from Poland to New York. (Where in Poland? My mother isn't sure. My mother doesn't even know the first name of her mother's mother. As the late great *Village Voice* writer Paul Cowan beautifully put it in his extended-family autobiography, *An Orphan in History,* "Millions of immigrant families . . . left the economically and culturally confining Old World towns where they were raised, and paid for the freedom and prosperity this country offered with their pasts."[38]) Grandma Helen sailed across in steerage, where, as the story goes, everybody was vomiting, constantly. Grandma spoke only Polish, and she was supposed to have been met on the New York docks by some relatives from Yonkers. But, for a reason never explained, those relatives never showed up. I imagine my teenaged grandmother waiting at the docks, her back to the ocean. She's survived the ordeal of the passage and the Ellis Island examiners; now the whole inscrutable country stretches out before her.

"Imagine what could have happened to her," my mother always says with a sigh at this point in the story. But what actually did happen was that Grandma had attracted the notice of a nice Jewish doctor and his wife (Jewish! The melting pot was already at work!). They had come across on the same boat and, seeing her stranded on the dock, they asked if she would come and keep house for them in New Rochelle. I'm told she learned to make good potato latkes and chicken soup. She never saw her parents or siblings again; sometimes she would have nightmares about a dog baring its teeth, nightmares that would always precede the arrival of a letter from Poland, announcing someone's death. Grandma Helen herself died when I was seven, so I mostly remember her as a nice old lady who, much to my wondering eyes, put her teeth in a glass of water every night.

My grandmother, it seems, was rescued by a twist of fate—just as Rochester's voice "rescues" Jane. Around the time I began thinking of women's adventure tales, I began to revise Grandma's adventure story for myself and make it into one more respectful of the strength she surely possessed—even if she herself didn't know she did. Grandma got on that boat alone—another solo female adventurer. She left her mother, an unspecified number of brothers, and one sister behind, but she made herself do it. She was sick to her stomach throughout the entire passage, but she held on. When she landed in New York, she was terrified, but she had enough sense—and, yes, luck—to go with people who looked as though they wouldn't mistreat her. Then she outlived one abusive husband and, for the rest of her active life, cared for a second invalided by heart disease, as she raised her two daughters and largely supported the family by cleaning offices and houses day and night. That's the alternative, more celebratory female adventure narrative lurking under the authorized, anxiety-ridden coming-to-America cover story. I think that many traditional female adventure narratives are cloaked by this overlay of fear beneath which lies a less sanctioned story about female desire, courage, and, often, qualified triumph. Maybe, together, they constitute the "true" story. I'm sure Grandma Helen would never have viewed her own life this way; by all accounts, she was a shy woman with a kind heart.

She was also one of the hundreds of thousands of immigrant women, from the end of the last century to the present, who began working the instant they arrived in this country and, thus, never learned how to read. The distance that stretches between the world she knew and mine—filled with books—is so vast that to me it's like Grandma Helen's first glimpse of the New York skyline. Incomprehensible.

"Books, what a jolly company they are"

$\mathcal{T}$he line is from Siegfried Sassoon's great 1918 poem, "Repression of War Experience," and it's meant to be taken, at best, ambivalently. The poem is written in the form of a dramatic monologue, and its narrator is a World War I vet suffering from shell shock. He's been shipped away to a rest home in the English countryside, but judging from his off-kilter observations, his prognosis looks bleak. The vet sees ghosts out in the wet darkness of the nearby forest and hears the thud of the big guns, booming, booming in the distance. Presumably, he's sitting in a library as he speaks, because he turns for comfort to the shelves of books nearby. Unfortunately, their black, white, brown, and green spines remind him of his once straight-backed comrades marching off to their deaths. Shaken, the narrator tries to get a grip on his nerves by reassuring himself that "all the wisdom of the world / Is waiting for you on those shelves," but it's a claim that rings hollow. Book learning didn't save a generation of young Oxbridge students from dying in the trenches, along with their shabbily educated working-class countrymen. Indeed, some of those books—filled with tales of chivalric adventure and noble sacrifice—misled their impressionable readers into their wartime deaths.

I can't imagine living in rooms without books, but like Sassoon's narrator, I also think the comfort books offer is qualified. All those voices, all those thoughts, all those reminders of how much there is to read and how little time there is to read it. Mentally and physically, books can be oppressive, even hazardous. Three years ago, my mildly hypochondriacal husband stuck a couple of heavy medical texts he'd been consulting on top of a row of books in a bookcase, rather than expending the effort to reshelve them. Later that evening, I bumped into that bookcase and the textbooks fell on top of my right foot—*snap!*—thus providing a dramatization of the literary term "irony." X rays have been taken, and nothing appears to be broken, but my big toe aches and I sometimes experience shooting pains in my arch when I walk barefoot. Question 10 on the medical-insurance reimbursement forms I have to fill out asks: "Cause of injury?" I could truthfully answer, "Assault by books."

When I was in graduate school, I lived in a succession of tiny apartments where the major furnishing motif was books. Piles of coffee-table books on nineteenth-century art and architecture literally formed the coffee table; paperback novels on hanging shelves gave color to the drab off-white walls; and solid anthologies of Victorian prose and poetry bolstered the mattress of my daybed. It was reassuring when I was living alone to have all those familiar presences in the room with me; it was also a little scary. Maybe I was turning into an eccentric whose apartment had become a macrocosmic metaphor for her own fevered mind. I know a fair number of people—some friends or acquaintances, some relatives—who would have wrinkled their noses at those cramped apartments smelling of paper. These people—let's call them the Bounderbys—see books only as commodities. (A refresher: Mr. Bounderby is the "eyes on the bottom line" businessman whom Dickens lampoons in *Hard Times*. One advantage of a grad-school degree in English is that you can insult people more elegantly.) "I like bigger books because you get more for your money," a Bounderby once half jokingly confided in me. "I read 'em and I toss 'em," another Bounderby announced when

I was visiting her book-free home. Books just don't register with this crowd. They think I lack common sense; I think they lack a part of their souls.

But I don't always feel so superior to the Bounderbys. The last time my husband and I moved—from a two-bedroom apartment to a nearby three-bedroom row house, the little house of my dreams, complete with a porch, perfect for reading on breezy afternoons—we had to buy and pack up some 150 boxes from the moving company to accommodate our three thousand odd books. The movers, three nice big guys, started at 8:30 A.M. and worked till 9:00 P.M. All because of the books. We certainly didn't have much furniture. "The only job worse than this I ever worked," said one of the guys, "was a lawyer's house; he had all those big law books." Some of our books went upstairs into the smallest bedroom, christened "the study." Most of them wound up in a big room in the basement that we mistakenly assumed was dry. Five years have gone by since we moved into our house, and about twenty boxes of books still remain to be squeezed into the bookshelves shoved up against the basement walls. It's the first time in my adult life that I'm not living with books lining the walls of every room, and it's nice to have a psychic break from them, some space that isn't taken up by other people's thoughts and fantasies. My daughter wants a playroom in the basement like her little neighborhood friends have. As soon as we clear out the remaining boxes, we can do some remodeling. (A chip off the old block, she naturally wants *her* Madeline, Arthur, and Junie B. Jones books shelved in a reading nook down there, next to the armless Barbies and dried-up Play-Doh containers.) But those overloaded bookshelves teeter-totter. We'll need to hire a handyman to drill holes in the cement walls and anchor the bookcases with wires and bolts. Otherwise, there might well be another, much more horrific book accident—this time involving a child, a training-wheel bicycle, and a wobbling bookcase.

The Bounderbys would be disgusted. So much money spent to move all those books! And we wound up just throwing away a lot of those empty cardboard book boxes we paid for, since we resolved never to move again. Those books are cluttering up good income-generating space. There's a bathroom down there, so the basement could be rented out. But for me and my husband—two people who met because of their shared love of reading—that basement is the messy, book-lined foundation of our lives together.

My dad didn't live long enough to see me fulfill the American Dream of home ownership. We bought our row house the autumn after he died. After Rich and I learned our bid on the house had been accepted, I called a close friend and heard myself excitedly describe the house to her as "shipshape." That's a term my dad might have used, but I don't think I'd ever spoken it before. As an old Navy man, my dad would have lamented the semipermanent chaos of boxes and paper in our basement, but he would have loved all those books. In the years following my marriage, whenever my dad visited the apartment Rich and I lived in, he would run his hands over the volumes shelved in our living room, dining room, and tiny galley kitchen. Even books on literary theory or eighteenth-century novels that he'd have no interest in got a pat, sometimes even an automatic thumbing through. Book lovers always have to touch books.

When I began to help my mother clear out the apartment in Queens she and my dad lived in for almost thirty years, I found out that he, too, was a pack rat, just a much tidier one than my husband. He'd saved all the letters, bound up in black electrical tape, that my mother had sent him during World War II; all his W-2 earnings statements dating back to the 1960s; the receipts for most of the appliances, large and small, he and my mother had bought throughout five decades of marriage. (The most thrilling find in the latter category was the title for our 1964 Rambler, a beloved big blue box of a car that my dad would exhume from the garage every weekend to take us on long drives to the beach or to Washington Irving's house in Westchester or Teddy Roosevelt's house in Oyster Bay on Long Island. I think my dad paid something like four thousand dollars for that car in 1964, but of course, I've already misplaced the title in the paper chaos of my own house.) In his bedroom were the boxes for many of the newer appliances. I'd always assumed he'd saved those boxes in case anything went wrong and he'd have to send the microwave or table fan back to the manufacturer. In his later years, my dad would have been too debilitated by dialysis to break

up the boxes and carry them downstairs to the apartment house's recy-
cling can.

When I opened the topmost box in one of these bedroom piles in
order to begin the drudgery of breaking them up, I found a surprise.
Books. Books, books, books. That box was filled with books; so were the
boxes below that one and the boxes beside and under his bed. My dad
had kept hardcovers and even proof copies of the mysteries and World
War II adventure tales I'd given him. There were well-worn paperbacks
of Revolutionary War novels by E. Van Wyck Mason and Kenneth
Roberts, as well as the Horatio Hornblower books and the 87th Precinct
novels by Ed McBain; there were hardcovers he'd bought at secondhand
stores. My dad had mentioned to me a few times that when he liked a
book, he would read it over and over again. Obviously. By keeping those
books close by, he made sure that he could always reread a good story.

So, what am I going to do with all those books? I've donated some to
the library; but otherwise, our basement collection of books on world
history and politics and modern American and European literature is
being augmented by titles like *Seizing the Enigma* by David Kahn, *Con-
voy of Fear* by Philip McCutchan, *Fall from Grace* by Larry Collins, and
Torpedo Junction by Robert Casey. I'm reading my way through some of
them; so far, they're all good stories, and I've even read the Larry Collins
novel twice. (It's a terrific World War II suspense story featuring a female
spy.) They're in piles on the floor, next to the cherished Nancy Drew
novels that my dad saved for me after I "outgrew" them in adolescence.
My dad's books make the basement a still more hazardous place for
my daughter to play. They're also upright memorials to the wonderful
grandfather she'll only get to know now through stories.

CHAPTER TWO

Tales of Toil: What John Ruskin and
Sam Spade Taught Me About
Working for a Living

*L*ike Grandma Helen, who left Poland for America in the early years of the twentieth century, I packed my bags as a young woman and left family, friends, and native culture to seek a new life. Except that I boarded an Amtrak train in New York City and got off in Philadelphia. Grandma Helen's epic journey was motivated by poverty and by the stories she'd heard about America; mine was inspired by an over-whelming—and overwhelmingly naïve—love of literature. At age twenty-one, I had been admitted to the Ph.D. program in English at the University of Pennsylvania. One of the big life questions that sometimes gnaws at me at three in the morning is whether or not entering that program was a Major Wrong Turning. "You earned a Ph.D. and read widely," murmurs the angel sitting on the pillow by my right ear. "You spent your youth walled up in a library," taunts the devil on my left. "You could have joined the Peace Corps or sailed around the world." (The devil has read far too many male extreme-adventure tales.) Mistake or not, I did it, and so, like the young Grandma Helen, I, too, stepped into a foreign land where I didn't speak the language. I adapted, as most immigrants do, and eventually found a way to make a meaningful working life for myself through reading. But not in the way I originally thought I would. Once again, books took me off course. Just as I think decades of avid reading are indirectly responsible for opening up my mind and heart to the idea of adopting my daughter from China, I think my discovery of and consuming love affair with detective fiction midway through graduate school steered me away from a career as a scholar. In both cases, books made me see myself differently and gave me a wider sense of possibilities.

But I had to pay a price for the self-knowledge I gained in graduate school: the price was *being* in graduate school. I think of those years as my time served as a character immured in a Gothic novel. To give you a sense of how weird—indeed sometimes even sinister—this world of graduate school was, let's journey back to the autumn of 1977. It's four o'clock on a Friday afternoon, and I'm standing in a small cluster of first-year graduate students who've been invited to the weekly "Sherry Hour" hosted by Penn's English Department. The dark lounge in Bennett Hall where the gathering takes place resembles, to my delight, a shabby drawing room out of an Agatha Christie mystery. I'm quietly crowing to myself: I've gotten a fellowship into an Ivy League graduate school, and I'm on my way toward achieving my dream of becoming an English professor. A few years of classes, a dissertation (basically a very long term paper, no problem), and I'll have my Ph.D. Then I'll be in the same rarified realm as the English professors I idolized as an undergraduate at Fordham University. Here I am already sipping sherry, for heaven's sake! I don't like it, but I'll learn to and . . . wait a minute. Professor X, who's holding court at the center of our little group, is saying something. I've been assigned to be his teaching assistant, so I'd better listen. Professor X knocks back another glass (what is this, his fourth?), stares over our heads at a spot on the wall, and mutters an oracular verdict: "None of you will ever come close to Ira Einhorn. He was the most brilliant student the department ever had."

Granted, those inspiring words were spoken before Holly Maddux's body was actually discovered in a trunk in Einhorn's apartment, but in the fall of 1977, Einhorn was widely regarded as the chief suspect in her disappearance. I should have gleaned two things from Professor X's pronouncement—and then I should have grabbed my book bag, run down to nearby Thirtieth Street Station, and hopped on the first train back to New York. First, I should have realized that I had landed in a little pond still very much patrolled by big male fish. Sure, it was the late seventies and the Second Women's Movement was thriving and Penn even had a prominent feminist scholar on its faculty (even if she dressed like Stevie Nicks and whispered animatedly to herself), but only male graduate students gained access to the select inner networking circles where they went out drinking, played racquetball, and, presumably, argued urgent matters of weighty intellectual portent with their mentors. We women could sleep with the faculty (that old story) and otherwise abase ourselves—I knew one nonsmoking woman who always had a book of matches at the ready in case her mentor wanted to light up—but in terms of intellectual community, we were mostly out in the cold. As Einhorn's grisly tale eventually revealed, a woman could even be murdered and stuffed in a trunk, but if her boyfriend was "brilliant," he was the one who would be mourned for having his promising career ruined; she was just an undistinguished student who had taken six years to graduate from Bryn Mawr.

That's the other thing the Einhorn tribute should have clued me in to: gender aside, the thing that mattered most in this elite new world of mine was brainpower—or, at least, the projection of brainpower. Being a decent, truthful, charitable person—none of those traditional Judeo-Christian virtues counted. Wit, verbal adroitness, a substantive intellectual background (or at least the illusion of one), and condescension toward one's mental inferiors were the marks of distinction here. Theory, with its bizarre vocabulary of literary encryption, was just beginning to take root at Penn and other top graduate schools across the land.

I was a pretty good close reader, so why didn't I read the writing on the wall at that Penn Sherry Hour? Simple: I was blinded by desire. I longed for a community of fellow readers—people who, like me, wanted to read and talk about books all the time. Instead, what I mostly found in graduate school were some oddly assorted bookworms, each of us already isolated in our own anxiously declared literary "fields," and a few ruthless careerists who, cannily assessing the shrinking academic job market, did things like razor out articles on reserve at the library for the master's exam we were all required to take. I was imperfectly armored against the masculine bias of graduate school by all my years of practicing what literary scholar Nancy K. Miller has called a "learned androgyny"—that is, the ability to effect a sex-change operation of the imagination, an ability I, along with millions of other female readers, had developed over decades of reading books mostly featuring male heroes and antiheroes. With the courage of the deluded, I assumed that I could easily step into a man's profession because I so easily stepped into men's stories in literature.

By the time I wised up, it felt too late to make a change. While I worked at a bunch of part-time jobs, taught literature at colleges in the area, and, most happily, began writing book reviews for *The Village Voice,* I stayed officially registered as a graduate student at Penn for almost a decade. I stayed there out of inertia, because Penn was giving me a free financial ride, and because retreating home to Queens seemed like a defeat. And I stayed out of love, because even after a few ego-shredding years as a graduate student, I still couldn't imagine a better line of work than to be an English professor, always lecturing and writing, surrounded by books.

I'd had two especially inspiring and generous professors at Fordham, the Jesuit university in the Bronx where I went as an undergraduate. They were—and remain—the best teachers I've ever had in my life, and I wanted to be like them. Professor Mary Fitzgerald taught Irish literature and looked like a heroine out of Celtic mythology—tall with pale skin and long, jet-black hair. In the summer of my junior year at Fordham, she invited me and a few other devoted English majors to go with her to Ireland; we studied at the Yeats Summer School and roamed around the country, meeting the poets and scholars who were her friends. We drank Guinness with Seamus Heaney (who rescued me one night at a dance from the drunken gyrations of a famous fellow poet) and talked incessantly about literature. I think about Mary these days when I'm in office hours with my own students at Georgetown. How did she put up with the company of a bunch of undergrads, no matter how enthusiastic, every day for a full month? Professor Jim Doyle was another glutton for punishment. A small, intense, brilliant, and very funny man, he taught modern poetry and nonfictional Victorian prose. My own dissertation topic—the medieval revival in art, literature, and politics in Victorian England—was Jim's specialty. To Jim, literature *mattered*—the way I imagine literature *mattered* to the New York Intellectuals or the poets of the Enlightenment or World War I. I remember him, bedraggled, coming into a seminar class on Thomas Carlyle's *Sartor Resartus* and announcing, through drags on his ever-present cigarette, that he had stayed up all night, rereading the book and trying to revise his thoughts on it. No other adult I knew stayed up all night, thinking through intellectual problems.

In the years since I graduated with a Ph.D., many of the teaching colleagues who've become my friends have shared their own horror stories about graduate school. At best, it seems a mixed experience. Nonetheless, I insist that Penn, in the years I was there, was uniquely awful because it was so nervously self-conscious about its own institutional status. In his recent memoir, *The Road to Home,* Vartan Gregorian, who served as provost of Penn during a good chunk of my time there, recalls how he was the odds-on favorite with faculty and students to be appointed president of the university in 1980. That is, until certain trustees voiced anxieties that Gregorian (who was born in Iran to Armenian parents) was "too ethnic."[1] Penn ultimately appointed Sheldon Hackney, a straight-out-of-central-casting-looking historian, to be its next president; Gregorian had the last laugh when he went on to serve, in turn, as president of the New York Public Library, Brown University, and, currently, the Carnegie Corporation.

The average citizen routinely confused Penn with Penn State. Then there were intuitively wise people like my mother, who, upon hearing where I was going to graduate school, said, "That sounds like a prison." So Penn tried to ameliorate its shortcomings by issuing sweatshirts emblazoned with the phrase NOT PENN STATE and attempting to out-Ivy the other Ivy League schools. Hence, ersatz Oxbridge customs, such as the English Department's weekly Sherry Hour. Adding to Penn's jitters was its location. Situated in West Philadelphia, across the Schuylkill River from Philadelphia proper, the campus was surrounded by a ring of crumbling row houses, bars, and twenty-four-hour robbery-friendly convenience stores that spread outward into slums and industrial waste-lands. The area looked dingy and, at night, menacing. I mostly shared apartments with friends during graduate school, but for a couple of particularly glum years I lived alone in a one-room apartment that was basically the bay window of one of these sagging West Philly row houses.

It's pretty clear to me now that my own class insecurities were exacerbated by Penn's overcompensating behavior. I remember retreating one afternoon to the solitary refuge of the university library, where, in the English Seminar Room, I stared for a long time at the JOIN THE NAVY! poster that some canny recruiter had tacked up on the wall. Maybe, I thought, I could re-create my dad's early adult life instead of the alienating one I was currently living. My first academic dinner party left me drenched in self-loathing, a feeling I waded around in for many of those years. The hors d'oeuvres tray featured artichokes—a vegetable that had never poked its fancy head into my mother's Polish American kitchen. I watched how other people scooped up some dip with their artichoke leaves. I should have watched a little longer. When I began chewing a tough scale, I realized my mistake. Worried that my faux pas would become public, I chewed some more, took a deep breath, and gulped the whole fibrous mess down. I'm probably still digesting it.

Meekly swallowing and assimilating the customs of the more powerful has always been a strategy by which the less powerful have tried to fit in. In graduate school, I learned how to swallow. The product of all my years at Penn was a mixture of education and affectation; trash and treasure. I enjoyed the luxury of time to read things like John Ruskin's *Modern Painters* and all of Jane Austen. Just as their literary stocks were sinking, I became an expert on the moldy poetic trio of Tennyson, Browning, and Arnold. A Robert Browning revival, anyone? Predictably enough, I began going to foreign films (Werner Herzog was big) and caught on that it was hip to instantaneously dismiss any work of art that had mass appeal. I got my Ph.D. just before the cultural-studies tsunami belatedly rushed toward Penn. During my first years there, I attended a lecture on Victorian literature given by some visiting Big Name and watched in horror as my own dissertation advisor, a nice man and a waning Big Name himself, stood up during the question-and-answer period and made some erudite connection between, I think, Tennyson's

"In Memoriam" and an episode of *The Incredible Hulk* he'd watched with his young son. (Back then, you always needed an excuse to go slumming.) "Did anyone else see the show?" my advisor asked. The entire audience, perhaps some three hundred people, remained motionless and silent. I *had* watched the show (sans excuse), but if I had raised my hand in an act of support, my intellectual cred would have been wiped out.

Books got me into this mess, and books got me through. When I announced to my professors at Fordham that I had gotten a fellowship for grad school at Penn, a professor within earshot, whom I didn't know too well, walked over and said, "You've *got* to read *Lucky Jim*." Always a dutiful student, I bought a copy of Kingsley Amis's classic 1954 novel about academia and social class and I read it my first year at Penn. I reread it at least once during every year of graduate school, and I still reread it frequently. So far, I think it's the funniest novel in the English language—at least the funniest I've ever read—and it contains the funniest sentence: "His mouth had been used as a latrine by some small creature of the night, and then as its mausoleum."[2] That sentence appears in the middle of a paragraph describing a gargantuan hangover suffered by the novel's hero, Jim Dixon, a hapless junior lecturer in history at an undistinguished university in England. Dixon, who's from a lower-middle-class background, got his degree at a redbrick university on the equivalent of Britain's GI Bill and fell into teaching for lack of a better idea. He's a decent fellow utterly out of his element in the snooty university world of chamber music and medieval festivals. Like Penn did during my time there, Dixon's unnamed university tries extra hard to mimic elite forms of behavior because it's not quite a first-rate place.

Forcing himself to jump through the academic hoops so that he'll keep his job, Dixon authors an article entitled "The Economic Influence of the Developments in Shipbuilding Techniques, 1470 to 1485," which gets accepted by a little-known scholarly journal. The title, Dixon thinks to himself, was:

> perfect . . . , in that it crystallized the article's niggling mindlessness, its funereal parade of yawn-enforcing facts, the pseudo-light it threw upon non-problems. Dixon had read, or begun to read,

dozens like it, but his own seemed worse than most in its air of being convinced of its own usefulness and significance. . . . His thinking all this without having defiled and set fire to the typescript only made him appear to himself as more of a hypocrite and fool.[3]

Dixon's academic success is short-lived, however, because the editor of the journal turns around and plagiarizes the article, publishing it as his own in an Italian historical review. Poor Dixon then commits professional hari-kari by getting so desperately drunk immediately before the keynote university lecture he's been invited to give on the topic of "Merrie England" that he passes out at the podium—but not before doing spot-on inebriated imitations of all the scholarly boobs he's been forced to kowtow to throughout the story.

I've read other fine academic farces written after *Lucky Jim*—David Lodge's books and Richard Russo's *Straight Man* and James Hynes's supernaturally inflected satires, *Publish and Perish* and *The Lecturer's Tale* (as well as Randall Jarrell's much revered *Pictures from an Institution,* which I didn't think was funny at all), but none come close to the Olympian comic heights of *Lucky Jim.* There are pages of that novel I can't read in public—I snort and hock up helplessly with laughter. Why do I love *Lucky Jim* so? I know I immediately identified with Jim's passive-aggressive maneuver of making faces (his Sex Life in Ancient Rome face, his Edith Sitwell face) behind his antagonists' backs. I also marveled at Amis's pitch-perfect ability to capture the bizarre quality of academic conversations, where one person has no idea what the other person is talking about because the latter's vocabulary is so archly allusive. My dissertation advisor at Penn had a fondness for using arcane Victorian slang, so that often I left conferences in his office feeling clueless, like a newly arrived immigrant who couldn't grasp her American employer's housecleaning instructions. Years after I left Penn, he sent me a note about my review of Camille Paglia's book *Sexual Personae,* which he'd heard on NPR. "You did her up brown!" he exclaimed. I was touched that he wrote and I understood that he was offering me a compliment, but once again, I had no idea what the man was saying.

What I did come to understand as I sat through classes at Penn is that reading good books doesn't necessarily make one a good person—or a smarter, funnier, or more cultivated person, either. This was a major epiphany for me—one I still struggle to come to terms with, since, as a teacher, I also have to believe that reading good books has *some* kind of influence on my students. We just can't be sure what it might be. Books are powerful. On that point, conservative culture cranks like William Bennett and Lynne Cheney and I agree. But, unlike those two purveyors of literary uplift, I think the influence of books is neither direct nor predictable. (Got a whiney kid on your hands? Give him a purgative dose of *Oliver Twist* or Robert Louis Stevenson's *Kidnapped,* advise these literature doctors, and he'll straighten out just fine.)

Books themselves are too unruly, and so are readers. As critic Greil Marcus said in *Mystery Train,* his marvelous book on the development of rock and roll: "Good art is always dangerous, always open-ended. Once you put it out in the world you lose control of it; people will fit it into their lives in all sorts of different ways."[4] Over the years I've met people—pretentious people, apparently humorless people—who, I've somehow discovered, call *Lucky Jim* one of their favorite books, too. How can the kind of people who are pilloried in *Lucky Jim* enjoy it? More puzzling still is the mystery of what happened to Kingsley Amis himself after writing his masterpiece. Amis transformed from an Angry Young Man to a club-going, Merrie Olde England Tory bag of wind. How can such things be? Similar invasion-of-the-body-snatchers-type conversions besmirch literary history: the defection of New York Intellectual Norman Podhoretz to the right; the mutation of progressive reporter Joe Klein, who had written a moving biography of Woody Guthrie, no less, into a centrist pundit and author of the anonymous Clinton parodic novel *Primary Colors.* Why? Why? Why? If reading good books doesn't necessarily make you a better person, apparently neither does writing them.

At the end of *Lucky Jim,* Jim Dixon makes his escape from academe—hence the title. Many of the abominable professional mistakes he's committed have been closely observed by a wealthy benefactor of the college, a Mr. Gore-Urquhart. When Dixon is sacked after his sodden lecture performance, he receives a phone call from Gore-Urquhart inviting him to come up to London to take a position as the rich man's private secretary, in reality his "bullshit detector." The final, exhilarating scene of the novel finds Dixon holding hands with Gore-Urquhart's lissome niece as they prepare to board a train to London together, leaving the academic world in the dust.

Lucky Jim is a male fairy tale—Dixon gets the job and the girl. In order to identify so fully with the hero of such a phallocentric (and sexist) story, I had to rely on my "learned androgyny." No problem. I don't believe in identity politics in literature—or in life much, either. Indeed the current scholarly enchantment with identity politics strikes me as a more intellectual version of the warning oft heard round Sunnyside when I was growing up: "Stick with your own kind." Family and cultural origins are crucial to self-definition, but they're not the end of the story. I certainly don't think that we readers only or even chiefly enjoy or understand books whose main characters mirror us. In fact, the opportunity to become who we are decidedly not—whether it's Amis's Dixon or Philip Roth's Portnoy or Ellison's Invisible Man or Kafka's beetle—is one of the greatest gifts reading offers. Women readers get to serve on that floating boy's club, the *Pequod;* male readers get to step into Elizabeth Bennet's shoes and teach Mr. Darcy the dance of humility; readers of either gender who are not African American get to crawl toward freedom alongside Toni Morrison's Sethe. One of the most magical and liberating things about literature is that it can transport us readers into worlds totally unlike our own.

Besides, back to the case of *Lucky Jim* and its lesser inheritors, what choice did I have? All the academic farces I've ever read have been by and about men. Pontificating for a living, historically, has been a man's job, but now that female professors have been occupying the podium for a couple of decades, you'd think that a send-up of academe from a female perspective would be a natural. Since my graduate-student days when I held on to *Lucky Jim* like a life preserver, there have been a few female memoirs about academe (Marianna De Marco Torgovnick's *Crossing Ocean Parkway,* Alice Kaplan's *French Lessons,* Lorna Sage's superb *Bad Blood*) and lots of female murder mysteries set in academe (Dorothy Sayers's classic *Gaudy Night,* Valerie Miner's amusing *Murder in the English Department,* Carolyn Heilbrun's effete Amanda Cross series), but no out-and-out farces that I know of. Odd, because the smart, sane female academics that I know have a library's worth of funny/awful roman à clef tales to tell out of school.

Nor are there many fictional sagas—period—that feature working-class women at the center. (Autobiographies have been more class-inclusive because, for so long, they were seen as the literary recourse of the unsophisticated.) *Moll Flanders* is the originating exception, but most up-from-the-working-class tales feature male protagonists. In those rare literary instances when a blue-collar gal does serve as a heroine, she almost always has to be gorgeous and preternaturally poised, a clear genetic aberration who deserves to be airlifted out of her squalid sur-roundings. Elizabeth Gaskell's Victorian melodrama *Mary Barton* pro-vides the template for this kind of fantasy. Mary is beautiful, kind, and naturally refined; she's a working-class "exception" who wouldn't offend the sensibilities of Gaskell's cultivated middle- and upper-class lady readers. The lesson I was constantly learning from literature and popular culture was that if you were a working-class young woman, you could be mouthy and shrewd like Moll Flanders (and her later real-life inheritors Roseanne Arnold and Tonya Harding) or demure and pretty (like Mary Barton's contemporary human doppelgänger Nancy Kerrigan), but the one thing you couldn't be was even vaguely intellectual.

Working-class men such as Hardy's Jude the Obscure could think their way up from the fields and shop floor, but literary fiction was devoid of women who'd made the same thoughtful journey. Working-class women could be street-smart but not intelligent or bookish. Not until I began reading women's detective novels late in my graduate-student days did I encounter women characters in the mysteries of Dorothy Sayers and Sara Paretsky—and, still later, Lisa Scottoline—who came from "distressed" or blue-collar backgrounds and who, through brains and hard work, had propelled themselves into the professional classes. These characters enlarge the menu and stretch the possibilities for how women can *be* in fiction; they also make women readers like me who've made the same kind of journey feel less lonely, less freakish. I wish I'd met them in the books I was reading at the beginning of gradu-ate school, but, except for Sayers's Harriet Vane, they didn't exist yet. It

took the Second Women's Movement and the amazing transformations
that it helped bring about in detective fiction to create a space for these
kinds of street-smart and book-smart female characters.

But in my eagerness to leave the unpleasantness of graduate school
behind, I'm getting ahead of my story. I said that Jim Dixon makes his
escape from academe at the end of the novel, but that's not quite what
happens. Dixon doesn't escape; he's delivered by a stroke of good fortune. So many characters in literature are "delivered" by fate, in the form
of love or money. For impressionable readers like myself, that's another
bad side effect of reading a lot. We bookworms think that something or
someone just has to come along to save us, because, after all, that's the
traditional trajectory of fictional plots and we tend to read our lives
through literature. In my own particular case, literary passivity went
hand in hand with Catholic mysticism (Somebody is always watching
and He knows that I'm stuck, so, surely, something or somebody will
appear to rescue me from this swamp of graduate school). Unlike Jim
Dixon, I waited a long time to be liberated, but the cavalry—in circum-
stantial and human form—did finally arrive. I slowly finished my dissertation and got that academic monkey off my back. A friend of mine
landed a job at *The Village Voice* and assigned me some book reviews to
write, so I discovered the pleasure of finding my voice in print while
being published in a venue that an educated audience of nonspecialists
actually read. I also met my future husband when both of us were called
upon by this same friend to "help" with the take-home editing test that
the *Voice* gave her. Deliverance also came in the form of a hitherto
unknown (to me) genre of literature.

It was a dark and rainy Saturday night, and I was sitting at the
kitchen table of my one-room apartment in West Philly scratching out
my dissertation on a yellow legal pad. I was bored and lonely. I had been
reading and thinking about William Cobbett, Thomas Carlyle, John
Ruskin, William Morris, and other Victorian gloom-and-doom social
critics for so long that I felt (incorrectly, I know) I had nothing left to
learn by writing about them. The best thing I could say about my dissertation was that it was ambitious: "Medievalism and the Myth of Revival
in Nineteenth- and Twentieth-Century Thought." None of those prissy
little readings of Shelley's cave (or was it cloud?) imagery in scene 2 of

Prometheus Unbound for me. My dissertation might have been dull, but it was historically sweeping in its dullness. I remember standing up from my kitchen table and abandoning whatever argument about *Sartor Resartus* or *The Stones of Venice* I was belaboring and doing a swan dive onto my daybed, where I lost myself in a paperback of Dashiell Hammett's *Red Harvest* that I'd picked up earlier that day. Someone had recommended Hammett to me, and since the plot synopsis on the back cover had mentioned something about labor unions, I bought it. (My dad was a lifelong union member and had served for years as the shop steward of his Steamfitters local.) What a relief it was to turn from the stirring but sepulchral tones of the Victorian Sages to this, the voice of Hammett's detective hero, the Continental Op:

> I first heard Personville called Poisonville by a red-haired mucker named Hickey Dewey in the Big Ship in Butte. He also called his shirt a shoit. I didn't think anything of what he had done to the city's name. Later I heard men who could manage their r's give it the same pronunciation. I still didn't see anything in it but the meaningless sort of humor that used to make richardsnary the thieves' word for dictionary. A few years later I went to Personville and learned better.[5]

That's the opening paragraph of *Red Harvest,* where the Continental Op, Hammett's otherwise unnamed, fat, middle-aged detective hero, makes his worldview known. To me, the Op's was the voice in the wilderness: smart, tough, direct, and sassy. I missed the sound of that voice in the literature I read in graduate school as well as in the people I met there. And, of course, I fell in love with Dashiell Hammett himself. Self-educated, self-destructive, faithless, brilliant, and handsome—what dame could resist him? I followed up Hammett's books with Raymond Chandler's sublime Philip Marlowe novels and, eventually, I'll admit it, Mickey Spillane's fascist fictions. (Years later I came across this Ogden Nash jingle: "The Marquis de Sade / Wasn't always mad / What addled his brain / Was Mickey Spillane.") By day, I shambled listlessly around Penn; by night, I walked down the mean streets of hard-boiled heaven.

It's probably the sturdy influence of the Catholic belief in a Big Plan that accounts for my own enduring faith that you find the books you need when you need them—even if they're not the books you start out thinking you need. Along with my burgeoning career as a book reviewer, my discovery of and subsequent addiction to hard-boiled detective fiction delayed the completion of my dissertation. But it was the kind of literature I needed to read during those rough grad-school years. The "gals, guts, and guns" school of American mystery fiction supplied me with wonderful revenge fantasies at a time when I was feeling beaten down by the academic system. Imagine Spillane's Mike Hammer on a panel at the Modern Language Association Convention. One snide question from some wise guy in the audience and—*bam!*—Mike would be feeding him a knuckle sandwich. I also really needed to hear some working-class voices in literature. I'm not reneging on my earlier dismissal of identity politics here, but I was so very conscious of my blue-collar background amidst a crowd of fellow graduate students and professors who all seemed to be deft artichoke eaters that I think I was looking for some small measure of class confirmation from the books I was immersed in.

These days, it's cool to be a working-class hero in the academy. Race, class, and gender are the Manny, Moe, and Jack of current professorial pep talk—even if most academics, like most Americans, have only the haziest understanding of the all-pervasive effects of class on American society. As Richard Rodriguez points out in his beautiful and incisive memoir *Hunger of Memory,* when academics now talk on about race, class, and gender, what they're usually talking about is race and gender. If I were so inclined, maybe I could become an Angry Young Woman and exaggerate my Queens accent, trick myself out as a tough girl with a bad attitude, and make a working-class approach to literature my "field." It's weird to make oneself one's "field," but lots of academics these days are doing it—industriously promoting their own race, gender, sexual orientation, ethnicity, and/or religion as their intellectual specialty. One of the many drawbacks of this "I teach what I am" approach is that it stifles classroom discussion. Any disagreement with the professor's expertise comes off as an ad hominem attack. When I was in graduate school, the attitude of working-class academics to their own backgrounds was equally suspect: rather than advertising their "up from the shop floor" roots, they transcended them (and, of course, many people, academics and civilians alike, still do) with an overlay of cultivated mid-Atlantic speech and careful attention to WASP rituals of dress and behavior.

Then, in 1983, Frank Lentricchia's groundbreaking book, *Criticism and Social Change,* was published. Among other things, Lentricchia helped introduce blue-collar voices—chief among them, his own—into academic discourse. I reviewed *Criticism and Social Change* for *The Village Voice* and dubbed Lentricchia "the Dirty Harry of literary criticism," a title he's been known by ever since. His book, or more precisely his book-jacket photo—which showed Lentricchia in a T-shirt, leaning against a graffiti-stained brick wall with his hairy arms crossed, looking like one of the fathers of the Italian kids I grew up with—meant a lot to me, even if, by then, Lentricchia was the holder of an endowed chair at Duke and the book itself didn't have anything to do with his roots. I came upon Lentricchia roughly around the same time I discovered hard-boiled detective fiction: both were psychological, emotional, and intellectual boons.

And a funny thing happened as I fled into the novels of Hammett, Chandler, and the other great American tough-guy (and, later, gal) writers: to me, their detectives began to sound a lot like the great Victorian Sages. Sure, their dialect and diction were neighborhoods apart, but their criticisms of society frequently were eerily similar. Like Cobbett, Carlyle, Ruskin, and Morris, detectives Sam Spade and Philip Marlowe denounced the soul-deadening effects of wage labor, the tackiness of the contemporary city landscape, and the evils that result from the unequal distribution of wealth.

This is what I mean about finding the books you need when you need them: I turned to classic hard-boiled detective fiction as an escape, only to discover that it was a popular twentieth-century American expression of some of the same "high art" nineteenth-century British social criticism that I'd grown weary of reading and rereading for my dissertation. These days I teach courses on hard-boiled detective fiction, review mysteries, and write critical essays about them. With the late scholar and renaissance man Professor Robin Winks of Yale University, I edited a two-volume collection of critical essays on mystery and suspense fiction that won the 1999 Edgar Award in Criticism given by the

Mystery Writers of America. It's been almost two decades since I've written any scholarly criticism about Ruskin and company, and I've never taught one course exclusively on their work. Like Mike Hammer, I loved 'em and left 'em. But I never would have transferred my affections to hard-boiled mysteries, which are still widely regarded as the junkyard dogs of literature, had not their purebred literary relations, the Victorian Sages, alerted me to their worth.

After twenty years of reading and studying detective fiction, I feel like I've only begun to probe the mysteries of the genre itself and how it has investigated American life over the past century. More and more, I've come to believe that detective fiction's visions of work and family, racial and class tension, and sexual identity are analogous to the "purloined letter" in Poe's famous story: American society—its problems and possibilities—has always been at the center of the hard-boiled novel, but we readers have been distracted by all that murder and mayhem lurking on the margins. Of course, murder must be given its due (if these books weren't fun, no one, including me, would read them), but the narrative pleasures of detective fiction don't stop when the shooting does.

I think it was not only the working-class voice of these novels but the very unusual fact that these books focused on work itself as a subject that first made them so compelling to me. At a time when I was floundering around trying to figure out what to do with my life, I loved reading hard-boiled detective fiction because, among other things, it presented a utopian image of the kind of work everyone would like to have. Forget specific images of a private eye's daily tasks (pistol-whipping bad guys, playing footsie with psychotic femmes fatales); I'm speaking in general terms. The work a detective does reunites head with hand, mental with physical labor. I think a lot of us fans find detective novels so riveting not because we care who-dun-it (in fact, with many of these novels, like Robert B. Parker's Spenser series, the crime is barely an issue) but because we care about *how* the detectives do it—how they work. Dashiell Hammett's 1930 masterpiece, *The Maltese Falcon,* is a classic example of the relatively bloodless crime novel: we readers tread over a few corpses but witness no "onstage" deaths. The central focus of Hammett's novel, as with most hard-boiled fiction, is the detective at work—thinking, making phone calls, casing the crime scene, walking the beat, questioning witnesses, and, sometimes, punching out or shooting down evildoers. Hard-boiled detectives are the noble craftsmen of crime—unalienated laborers who are what they do.

(Further evidence that crime is more of an occasioning excuse for the hard-boiled novel's covert investigation of American society is the famous anecdote about the making of the movie version of *The Big Sleep*. As he neared the completion of filming, director Howard Hawks sent a telegram to Raymond Chandler asking who murdered Owen Taylor, the chauffeur who's found drowned in the Sternwood-family limousine off a Los Angeles pier. Chandler studied his own novel, thought about the question, and wired back the answer, "I don't know.")

Like Hammett and Chandler and others in the hard-boiled genre, the Victorian Sages worried a lot about what constituted good work, reeling as they were from the Industrial Revolution and its corrosive effects on ordinary people. So righteously entranced were these upper-class intellectuals with the idea of the dignity of physical labor that, in one famous episode, some of them even shouldered picks and spades and backed up their convictions with sweat. In 1874, anticipating the spirit of Mao's Cultural Revolution by nearly a century, John Ruskin, who was then the Slade Professor of Fine Art at Oxford, "taught" an outdoor class in road mending. Clad in straw hats, his undergraduate chain gang composed of, among others, Arnold Toynbee and Oscar Wilde, hacked away ineffectually at a rutted lane on the outskirts of Oxford. The diggers, with good reason, were lampooned in the London press, but the impetus behind all this mucking about was one I admired. As Professor of Fine Art, Ruskin believed his privileged students needed to learn that, in the words of one of his most respected biographers, John D. Rosenberg, "labor without art is brutality and art without labor is guilt."[6]

Ruskin's most avid pupil was the socialist, artist, writer, and craftsman William Morris, now known to most people, if at all, for his wallpaper designs. Morris's utopian romance, *News from Nowhere,* is my favorite Victorian Sage rant on the subject of work. In it, a Morris-like hero identified only as "Guest" falls asleep and wakes up in the brave new world of England in 2102, which looks a lot like a prettified version of England in the Middle Ages and prefigures some aspects of England during the Swinging Sixties. Free love reigns among the inhabitants of Nowhere who wander about in arty Pre-Raphaelite getups, eating organic food in communal dining halls, sitting on handcrafted furniture, and, in general, just smelling the roses. Money is unheard of in Nowhere: when Guest enters a tobacco store, he learns that all he has to do is ask for the items he wants and he shall receive. And since money—as well as private property—has been abolished, so has crime.

What makes the nirvana of Nowhere possible is the fact that everyone does the work that he or she feels most drawn to and can change jobs at will. If you've been working as a boatman in Nowhere and want to learn the trash-removal trade, no problem. Of course, all of the female residents of Nowhere are conveniently drawn to cooking, serving food, and cleaning up after the men and children. Morris was a prophet of the possible, but he couldn't quite envision any more adventurous roles for women. There are several other aspects of his socialist utopia that Morris didn't quite think through. What do you do with antisocial loners? The chronically inept? Or people who just want to read all day long? But whenever I reread *News from Nowhere,* I'm always buoyed by this idea of a society founded on meaningful, creative work for all. As Guest says in the final sentence of the romance, after he's been whisked back to the gray nineteenth-century present, "Yes, surely! And if others can see it as I have seen it, then it may be called a vision rather than a dream."[7]

I reread *News from Nowhere* frequently because I stubbornly teach it to my freshman and sophomore students at Georgetown. Most of them don't like it, but it makes for lively classroom discussions. They find the characters thin (true), the writing too preachy (mostly true), and Morris himself naïve for believing in the essential decency of his fellow human beings and the possibility of a society grounded upon meaningful work for all. ("No, not true," I argue back, trying not to sound like that other dreamer John Lennon, singing "Imagine.") I find it hard to stomach the fact that most of my not-yet-twenty-something students are already reconciled to doing boring jobs that do nothing to make the world a better place in return for earning obscenely high salaries. They, in turn, look at me and probably think, "That sweater is from the Gap, the handbag is a sidewalk Prada knockoff; I'd never be an English professor, making nothing." Determined to back up Morris, I scrawl on the blackboard a quote from Sitting Bull: "The love of possession is a disease with them," also quoting the title of an old book by Tom Hayden. My students dutifully copy down the quote in preparation for the midterm exam and probably think to themselves, "Sitting Bull didn't make any money either."

Nevertheless, I keep on assigning *News from Nowhere* because students are at that life stage where they're faced with having to answer the daunting question "What shall I be when I grow up?" Throughout much of human history—and for billions of people in the world today—this question was and is an unimaginable luxury. Even my grandmother's flight from the Old Country, and from the farm labor that my Polish peasant ancestors no doubt had done for centuries, ended in the New World in a succession of cleaning jobs that "chose her," not the other way around. But I was lucky enough to have some freedom in determining what kind of work I would do, and so are my students. For me, it was a long process full of self-doubt, and I can tell that for all but a few of my students the decision of what to be is also scary. I hear the fear in their awkward laughter during class discussions of *Nowhere* and also sense it by the fact that when they volunteer a career choice, they almost always do so in the form of a question. ("I'm going to go to law school?" "Grad school in foreign service?") My students should be afraid: choosing what kind of work you'll do to a great extent means choosing who you'll be. This rite of passage may be a mundane, rather than an extreme, adventure, but it is, nevertheless, one of the great adventures of privileged young adulthood. And it's an adventure whose "conclusion"—the daily performance of work—has gone relatively unchronicled in literature.

That's why I have my students read *News from Nowhere:* because it discusses work that's a satisfying end in itself. The fact that *Nowhere* talks about, rather than dramatizes, such work is a literary flaw I can forgive. My students, harsher critics of all that is not perfect in life and art, pay me back for this long march through a book they find dull when, at the end of the term, they scrawl minireviews like "*Nowhere* SUCKS!" on their course-evaluation forms.

I should probably ditch *Nowhere* and instead assign Dashiell Hammett's classic 1925 short story, "The Gutting of Couffignal." Here his detective, the Continental Op, delivers a terse, two-fisted manifesto on work that encapsulates most of Morris's utopian ideas about the centrality of meaningful work to a meaningful life.

The plot is unapologetically wild and wooly. The Op has been called out to the island of Couffignal, an isolated, wedge-shaped spit of land off the coast of California, to act as a guard at a society wedding. After the reception ends and the newlyweds and guests depart into the rain-swept darkness, the Op settles down for an overnight watch next to a table where the expensive wedding presents have been piled high. Suddenly, the lights go out and the Op hears explosions and gunshots from the nearby town on the island. He rushes out to investigate and finds bodies littering the streets and the bank plundered. To cut to the chase of this shoot-'em-up tale, the crooks turn out to be a bunch of White Russians looking for some easy way of making enough money to keep them in the comfort they grew accustomed to before the Revolution came along and stripped them of their ermines and caviar. The contempt the Op has for such titled parasites knows no bounds. He's further enraged when a Russian femme fatale named Princess Zhukovski tries to seduce him away from his assignment. It's not that the Op is a saint; rather, he's a man whose sense of identity and purpose derives from his work. Here's the crucial speech he delivers to the seductress— before he shoots her:

> Let me straighten this out for you. . . . We'll disregard whatever honesty I happen to have, sense of loyalty to employers, and so on. You might doubt them, so we'll throw them out. Now, I'm a detective because I happen to like the work. It pays me a fair salary, but I could find other jobs that would pay more. Even a hundred dollars more a month would be twelve hundred a year. Say twenty-five or thirty thousand in the years between now and my sixtieth birthday.
>
> Now I pass up about twenty-five or thirty thousand of honest gain because I like being a detective, like the work. And liking work makes you want to do it as well as you can. Otherwise there'd be no sense to it. That's the fix I am in. I don't know anything else, don't enjoy anything else. You can't weigh that against any sum of money. Money is good stuff. I haven't anything against it. But in the past

eighteen years I've been getting my fun out of chasing crooks and tackling puzzles, my satisfaction out of catching crooks and solving riddles. It's the only kind of sport I know anything about, and I can't imagine a pleasanter future than twenty-some years more of it. I'm not going to blow that up![8]

My old dissertation director was fond of referring to "the Moment" when a new idea or type of art emerged in the culture. I'm borrowing his phrase and claiming that the Op's 1925 speech is the Moment when the infant genre of hard-boiled detective fiction explicitly declares that it's interested in investigating bigger questions than who killed Colonel Mustard in the library with a knife. To put it bluntly, as the Op does in his speech to Princess Zhukovski, hard-boiled detective fiction set out in the early decades of the twentieth century to investigate America—and topping the list of subjects to be investigated was work. For its founding inspiration, hard-boiled detective fiction is probably just as much indebted to the two-century-old, mostly British tradition of novels about the condition of the working class as it is to the British "Golden Age" mystery tradition.

Like other novels by and about the working class, the hard-boiled detective novel offers an unadorned picture of class tensions—the antagonism between those people who sweat to make a living and those who can afford to hire them. The class-conscious sentiments of your average gumshoe toward his or her wealthy clients would do a radical like William Morris proud. With "contemptuous tolerance"[9] in his heart and a snappy put-down ever ready on his lips, Ross Macdonald's Lew Archer is always venturing into some moneyed enclave in the California suburbs where he's hired to tidy up some dysfunctional family's dirty laundry. The message of the grand tradition of American hard-boiled detective fiction—from Hammett to Chandler to Macdonald to Chester Himes to Robert B. Parker to their many contemporary inheritors—is clear: too much money corrupts the soul. It makes men soft, even emasculates them, and the leisure lifestyle it buys is un-American.

Here's another clue that points to the fact that hard-boiled detective novels are modern utopian fantasies about work wrapped in a trenchcoat. Detecting is a fantastically autonomous line of work: gumshoes get to name their price, determine the conditions of their labor, and decide if a case is really closed or not. Even more striking is the fact that that autonomy is deeply embedded in the very plots of most hard-boiled novels. One of the baldest examples occurs in Chandler's masterpiece, *The Big Sleep*. By Chapter 21, pretty much the dead center of the novel, Philip Marlowe's work is officially done. He's been hired by the dying General Sternwood to find out who's blackmailing the old man's younger daughter, a sexy sociopath named Carmen. Marlowe efficiently sweeps up the blackmailing mess and is paid off on page 78 by the general's butler. On page 79, he decides to keep on investigating a few mysteries connected with the Sternwoods that still bug him, personally. His fateful decision to dictate how long his job assignment will last occurs in the gap between two wisecracking sentences:

> I had concealed a murder and suppressed evidence for twenty-four hours, but I was still at large and had a five-hundred-dollar check coming. The smart thing for me to do was to take another drink and forget the whole mess.
>
> That being the obviously smart thing to do, I called Eddie Mars and told him I was coming down to Las Olindas that evening to talk to him. That was how smart I was.[10]

The second half of *The Big Sleep*, what many scholars consider the greatest hard-boiled detective novel of all time (I vote for *The Maltese Falcon*), takes place only because Marlowe alone decides the work must go on. This and a hundred other examples from a hundred other hard-boiled novels lead me to insist that, as a group, tough-guy detectives are the ultimate independent contractors. If a detective takes on an assignment, he takes charge. As in the idealistic world of Morris's *News from Nowhere,* money is not the motivating force behind a detective's work. Professional pride, a quest for the truth, integrity—those are the forces that propel a detective up from his desk chair, away from that whiskey bottle, and out into the cold fog.

Where, these days, they'd probably run into their female counterparts skulking in the shadows and puzzling over the age-old problem of how to pee while conducting surveillance. In the wake of the Second

Women's Movement, a new type of female detective—liberated from the sleuthing spinster niceties of Agatha Christie's Jane Marple and the sex-kitten decorativeness of a Honey West—has gotten to talk tough, dirty her hands, mouth off to her employers, and use her brains. American Marcia Muller and Brit legend P. D. James share the laurel crown for creating this new species of female detective: Muller introduced her investigator, Sharon McCone, in the 1977 novel *Edwin of the Iron Shoes;* P. D. James's private eye, Cordelia Grey, debuted in the 1972 masterpiece *An Unsuitable Job for a Woman.* Since then hundreds upon hundreds of female detectives, professional and amateur, have crowded into the canon, and most have brought a consciously feminist edge to the issues of work and autonomy.

Whenever a spare half hour or so opens up in my day, I dive into the mystery novels written by modern masters of the form, writers such as Robert B. Parker, Sara Paretsky, Sue Grafton, George Pelecanos, Laurie King, Richard Stevenson, Peter Lovesey, Liza Cody, Lisa Scottoline, Henning Mankell, Ian Rankin, and Val McDermid. Among other things, they give shape to an empowering fantasy for overextended readers like myself: the fantasy of being in control of your work life, of calling the shots, of using your brains as well as whatever brawn you possess to get your own way. Take Scottoline, whose legal suspense novels, featuring the all-woman Philadelphia law firm Rosato & Associates, confront with hip humor the on-the-job aggravation that "lady lawyers" face—from patronizing old-boy judges to short-waisted pantyhose. One of her recurring characters, attorney Judy Carrier, has taped the empowering motto "Don't ask permission, apologize later" above her desk. Scottoline's "mouthpieces," like most other post-sixties female detectives and suspense heroines, really do get to mouth off to obnoxious clients, as well as to cops and other authority figures. That's a tantalizing carrot, I think, that female detective fiction deliberately dangles in front of its women readers: the vision of women who say what they think and damn the consequences. Unlike those tight-lipped men who've long dominated detective fiction (Sam Spade was the almost silent center of *The Maltese Falcon,* and Robert B. Parker's Spenser is distinguished by his one-sentence witticisms), feminist female sleuths use their words as one of their chief weapons.

Sara Paretsky has talked in interviews about how she consciously fashioned her lippy detective, V. I. Warshawski, to be the antithesis of the quiet good girl. Sue Grafton's enormously popular Rosie the Riveter–type tough gal, Kinsey Milhone, can't keep her big trap shut even in situations when speaking up means getting fired. In a recent alphabet outing, *P is for Peril,* Kinsey struggles to rein in her sass in the presence of her employer, a bejeweled widow named Fiona Purcell. After Fiona gives her a dressing-down for some minor infraction of their contract, Kinsey grimly reflects that she can't afford to refund Fiona her retainer and, thus, wash her hands of this troublesome boss. A nice, realistic aspect of the detective novel, male and female, as a utopian fantasy about work is that the detective's freedom is usually abridged by the need to make a living. Kinsey gives herself a sensible mini-lecture on the necessity of being a humble worker bee, but autonomy and professional honor triumph: "My temper emerged hard on the heels of injury and I had to bite my tongue bloody to keep from telling her where to stick it. This resolution lasted until I opened my mouth. 'You know what? Fun as this is, I'm already tired of taking crap from you. I've worked my butt off this weekend and if my methods don't suit you, I'm out of here.' "[11]

Who wouldn't vicariously thrill to scenes like that one in feminist mystery fiction where the heroines let 'er rip? Like many women, in tense conversations I tend to get quiet or stammer, or ten minutes later, after the other person has walked off, I think of the devastating remark I should have made. One of the great pleasures of writing book reviews is that I get to say what I think when I also have the time and space to say it right. Nobody interrupts or intimidates—it's just me and my computer. But I'm much more comfortable voicing my opinions, especially the controversial ones, in print than in person. So when I read novels by Paretsky and the rest of her sisters in crime, I'm raring to become one of their cheeky heroines and get a taste of a way I'll never be. I also get a taste of what it's like to confront physical danger, psychological distress, overwhelming exhaustion, and the eventual elation of surviving near-fatal situations. Sound familiar? Well, yes, we're back in the literary territory of the female extreme-adventure tale. I said earlier that female

extreme-adventure tales written in the wake of feminism feature heroines who don't "simply" endure but who also act. I think that contemporary women's detective fiction is a fantasy version of this "second wave"
female extreme-adventure tale. The detectives in these tales don't simply
endure, nor do they simply act; instead, they retaliate, kick butt, and set
a world gone wrong to rights. Feminist detective-fiction heroines take a
lickin', but they always come up tickin', ultimately (if only temporarily)
clearing their patch of the evil infestation of the patriarchy.

At considerable risk to life and legal practices, for instance, Scottoline's lawyers get to live out the dream of taking the law into their own
hands and do well for themselves and for society. Feminist detectives
like V. I. Warshawski and Kinsey Milhone dodge bullets and disarm
thugs to aim their own suggestively phallic pistols at male-dominated
institutions like the Catholic Church and the banking and insurance
industries that have given women grief for so long. Living on the fringe
of society in a broken-down trailer powered by illegal electricity, Liza
Cody's amateur detective and wrestling champion, Eva Wylie, uses her
muscles and her thick head to batter male parasites who've screwed up
the lives of the women and children she cares about. Sure, it's all make-
believe, but what great and empowering fantasies these contemporary
female mysteries/fantasy female extreme-adventure tales conjure up.

I had begun some detecting work of my own on and off during the
final years of graduate school. It was a missing-subgenre case. Years
before that momentous night when I ran into the Continental Op, I
had started to be puzzled by the mystery of what had happened to the
novel about work, which had appeared sporadically during the past
three centuries and then vanished with barely a trace after the 1960s.
Given my own class background and the importance that physical work
played in the lives of the adults I knew growing up, it was more and
more disturbing to me that almost none of the literature I was reading in
graduate school contained representations of the realm of work as it
would have been understood by the people I knew back in Sunnyside.
The kind of work done by the privileged classes—artists, writers, politicians, the landed gentry—was the focus of most of the fiction and nonfiction I was reading. Few pages, if any, were devoted to the kind of
skilled and semiskilled labor that, for centuries, has put calluses on the

hands of the working class. So I was determined to find out if the novel about work was really sleeping the Big Sleep or if it was living in disguise, maybe holed up in a forgotten section of the local bookstore.

My first clue was a strange passage in Ian Watt's important book, *The Rise of the Novel,* which, even these days I think, most graduate students in English at least glance at before they hurry on to the works of the more au courant theory heads. Watt, who long reigned as the dean of eighteenth-century scholars, claimed that the reason the novel was novel was because of its interest in work. He nominated Daniel Defoe's *Robinson Crusoe* as the first novel, bizarrely constructing a definition of the novel that *only* fit *Robinson Crusoe* and the handful of other novels in English that place representations of work at the center of their stories. Here's the odd pronouncement that Watt made in *The Rise of the Novel:*

> *Robinson Crusoe* is certainly the first novel in the sense that it is the first fictional narrative in which an ordinary person's daily activities are the center of continuous literary attention. . . . The Puritan conception of the dignity of labour helped to bring into being the novel's general premise that the individual's daily life is of sufficient importance and interest to be the proper subject of literature.[12]

The funny thing is that Watt's *Crusoe*-inspired definition doesn't make much sense even when applied to Defoe's next novel, about that resilient lady of pleasure, Moll Flanders. The record of "an ordinary person's daily activities" is also conspicuously absent from Samuel Richardson's epistolary bodice rippers, *Pamela* and *Clarissa;* Henry Fielding's on-the-road epics, *Joseph Andrews* and *Tom Jones;* and Laurence Sterne's psychedelic farce, *Tristram Shandy.* If we stick with Watt's choice of *Robinson Crusoe* as the first novel in English (and almost everybody does, except for a few cranky medievalists who lobby for *The Canterbury Tales*), then we're left with a puzzling history of the genre, for at the very moment of its inception, the novel picked up and almost immediately discarded the everyday work of ordinary people as a fit subject for delineation.

I was young and restless and intrigued by this literary mystery, so I would mull it over during endless afternoons otherwise spent picking at the splinters on my library carrel. The answer to the whodunit of why work was dumped as the novel's main subject had to do with centuries of theorizing about the function of art intersecting with the dawning of modern capitalism. From Plato onward, philosophers and poets insisted that art should enlighten and elevate. Art has always belonged to the realm of freedom, while work, particularly at the close of the eighteenth century, moved further and further into the realm of necessity. Industrial capitalism made work an even less appealing focus for art because it changed the very nature of work by divorcing the head from the hand. The development of the novel paralleled this split by delving deeper into the head and caring less about what the hand was doing. The public and private spheres also became more rigidly separated under industrial capitalism: the mill was where people had to go for a certain number of hours every day in order to make a living; but that by-product of work—a living—was consumed at home. Storytellers, always on the lookout for a good time, found the private sphere much more diverting than they did the cramped and coerced public sphere of work.

Other culprits also had a hand in shanghaiing work out of the novel. The people who determined aesthetic values and the people who wrote novels were not, in most instances, the kind of people who worked in the fields or, later, the factories. The novel didn't have to ignore physical labor, but most middle- and upper-class novelists were strictly brain-workers who failed to see the imaginative possibilities in other forms of work. It's not surprising that the early novelists, heirs to some two thousand years of elitist aesthetic theory, should dismiss common toil as an unworthy subject of contemplation. What is surprising is that the very first novel explicitly focused on the barbarism of its own artistic origins. *Robinson Crusoe* entertains, elevates, and educates us as it imagines what one man does with his mind and hands every day. Defoe managed the near impossible because he set his novel about work on a remote island where he could elaborate on his utopian vision of work as both essential and satisfying, giving his well-bred hero an "excuse" to engage in manual as well as mental labor.

Readers misled by the *Fantasy Island* locale think of *Robinson Crusoe* primarily as a travel tale or extreme-adventure narrative. They should think again. It takes Crusoe only five chapters to "commute" to work on his island. For the next twenty-five chapters—and thirty-five years— he's a regular Mr. Fix-It: in addition to building a fortress, he catches and cooks turtles, dolphins, and goats; he makes furniture, clothes, and a canoe; he sows corn and bakes bread; he surveys the island and keeps a journal. Generations of readers, bored with their own alienating, repetitious jobs, have been mesmerized by Crusoe's essential, civilization-building chores.

But Crusoe's fictional defenses don't hold. Moll Flanders, Pamela, Tom Jones—the whole crew go over the top, oust Crusoe and Friday, and settle themselves and their exceptional tales of mistaken identity, romance, and adventure into the charmed circle of the mundane that Crusoe staked out. The great Marxist literary critic Raymond Williams claimed that the inheritance plot and the marital-property settlement furnished roughly 90 percent of the basic plot structures of the nineteenth-century novel. This pattern holds true even for most nineteenth- and twentieth-century working-class fiction, which tended to reproduce dominant bourgeois forms. (The masons, yeomen, gardeners, and miners of Hardy, Lawrence, and Richard Llewellyn tell us less about how they work than about how they escape work through love and university scholarships.) Even that pantheon of English industrial-reform novels—books like *Mary Barton, Shirley, Hard Times,* and *Felix Holt, the Radical*—concentrates on class relations, which often translate as interclass romances, rather than on the hard day's work the characters do.

Ditto for our side of the Atlantic. *Moby-Dick* gets points for those chapters that describe the actual work of whaling, such as "Stowing Down and Clearing Up" and the famously homoerotic meditation on working with whale blubber, "A Squeeze of the Hand." But its representations of work are chiefly relegated to steerage, below the political and cosmic allegories stowed aboard the *Pequod.* Louisa May Alcott's auto-biographical novel, *Work,* which she began writing in 1863, is a more promising contender. It chronicles the trials of heroine Christie Devon as she builds up an impressive résumé: servant girl, actress, seamstress,

and, finally, stump speaker for the First Women's Movement. *Work* owes
its realistic glimpses of life in the sweatshop and scullery to Alcott's own
experience. Bronson Alcott, Louisa May's philosopher papa, was too
busy transcendentalizing to stoop to conventional employment. So,
from the age of sixteen onward, Alcott contributed to her family's survival by seeking waged work. Like *Moby-Dick,* however, *Work* winds up
subordinating its depictions of Christie's toil to grander plot concerns:
an updating of *The Pilgrim's Progress* with a dash of romance for the
ladies.

By the time I'd read all these alleged work novels, I'd become as
single-minded about tracking down traces of work in literature as Sam
Spade is with finding that falcon. I skimmed the mustiest books, for
instance, those "below-stairs" reminiscences written by butlers and parlor maids from the mid-nineteenth century into the twentieth with stirring titles such as *Life of a Licensed Victualer's Daughter* or *The Diary of
William Tyler, Footman, 1837.* Then someone told me about Robert Tressell's bizarre 1914 novel, *The Ragged Trousered Philanthropists.* Just as
James Joyce and the rest of the modernist gang were about to nudge the
novel even further away from realistic representations of work, Tressell's
book appeared—a six-hundred-page chronicle of the daily laboring lives
of a group of English housepainters and renovators. It's an epic of spack-
ling, stripping, and socialism.

I was so bowled over by *The Ragged Trousered Philanthropists* when I
first read it that I even insisted that my first-year English class at Bryn
Mawr, where I was then teaching, read the whole book. Belated apologies, ladies. Then again, maybe they got something out of the book that
they couldn't have found in the much more familiar and polished novels
of Dickens or Austen. I now concede that, storywise, Tressell's tour de
force is boring. No romances, no inheritance plots. Just this same work
plot, over and over and over:

> As a rule [the workers] worked till half-past five in the evening, and
> by the time they reached home it was six o'clock. When they had
> taken their evening meal and had a wash it was nearly eight; about
> nine most of them went to bed so as to be able to get up about half-

past four the next morning to make a cup of tea before leaving home at half-past five to go to work again.[13]

The narrator, knowing full well that novel readers expect more exotic goings-on, often sardonically apologizes for the book's obsession with the ordinary. "This is an even more unusually dull and uninteresting chapter"; "At the risk of wearying the long-suffering reader, mention must be made of an affair that happened at this particular 'job.'" And away we go into a long description of fitting venetian blinds. We're also told about how the workers clean drains, burn old paint off ceilings with paraffin torches, whitewash, apply stencils, and mix paint. Often the novel tells us about these processes more than once, because the workers perform these jobs over and over, day after day.

I dutifully read and reread Tressell, but I still wanted to see where writing about work had last been sighted, so I kept nosing around. Predictably, I ran into Britain's Angry Young Men of the 1950s, who carried forward Tressell's politics in their novels but couldn't sustain his aesthetic focus. And that's about where I came to the end of the line in my investigations. I dipped into the novels of Harvey Swados, Marge Piercy, John Sayles, Don DeLillo, and Nelson Algren and decided that, whatever their virtues, their writing explores the culture of work but marginalizes work itself. Somewhere in the midst of this quest came the moment when I discovered the novels of Dashiell Hammett and his inheritors and eventually realized that the literary subject of work was staring me right in the face. Like Crusoe, the Op and his fellow detective heroes throw themselves into a diverse round of tasks designed to rebuild civilization or at least fortify it against the wildness lurking in the shadows. Hard-boiled detective fiction, more than almost every other kind of novel that's followed *Robinson Crusoe* in the Anglo-American tradition, attempts to return us to Defoe's enclosed circle of normalcy where our greatest pleasure, as readers, arises out of watching a pro at work.

I discovered these books at a confusing time when I was trying to put together an adult life of my own—and a major part of that life would be work. I wanted work that would be creative and challenging and different each day. My father always said that part of the reason he decided, after World War II, to go to trade school and become a refrigeration-and-heating mechanic was that he didn't want to be stuck inside an office. Like him, I wanted to roam around during the workday—even if only from classroom to library—and to be, to a certain extent, my own boss. Now, given the consumer-pleasing politics of today's universities, I have, in effect, seventy new bosses each semester; they're sitting at the desks in front of me. If a teacher is not entertaining or lenient enough and her teaching evaluations plummet, she could lose the job. (Should that last statement strike you as paranoid, I refer you to the work of scholar and cultural critic Mark Edmundson, who writes for *Harper's* and who recently published *Teacher,* a very wonderful and unsentimental memoir of the high school philosophy professor who changed him from a self-professed "football thug" into an intellectually curious student. Edmundson has incisively discussed the ways college campuses have grown akin to upscale retirement homes for the very young, where the promise of intellectually demanding courses ranks far below the lure of new gymnastic facilities.)

I was immediately sold on hard-boiled detective fiction because of its focus on smart characters who spent the bulk of their days plugging away at work that gave them identity and purpose. I didn't feel I had much control over, say, my romantic life, but my life as a wage earner was something I could, in part, shape, and I was exhilarated by these dark American romances about the thrills, the deep satisfactions, even the dangers of work. A lot of these thoughts about the lost fictional subject of work and its resurgence in the hard-boiled detective novel eventually got published in an essay I wrote in 1991 for *The Village Voice Literary Supplement* called "Tales of Toil: A Work Novel Is Hard to Find."[14] I consider that essay my real dissertation—a genuine piece of original scholarship and interpretation that contributed to the understanding of a certain type of literature. And, most important, it was intellectual work itself that engaged and satisfied me. My "real" dissertation had limped to a close a few years earlier.

Just as my graduate-student career opened with a ghoulish scene—that English Department cocktail party featuring an encomium to Ira Einhorn—so it officially concluded with a Poe-like dash of the macabre. At Penn, as I think at most graduate programs, three professorial readers were required to sign off on a dissertation. The first two readers were supposed to be scholars in the designated field, in my case scholars of Victorian and Romantic literature, whom I'd invited to be on my dissertation committee. The department randomly appointed the third reader, who scrutinized the dissertation for any stray errors in grammar and format. As reader number three, I drew an old fellow, now deceased, whom I'll refer to simply as Professor Y. Graduate students in the department at that time called him Tithonus, after the Tennyson poem about a mortal man, beloved of Eros, who is granted the gift of eternal life but not eternal youth.

Professor Y suffered, as I did all throughout graduate school, from eczema. But Professor Y's eczema was acute. From his scabrous scalp to his swollen red fingers, every inch of the visible skin on his body was inflamed and flaking. The poor man couldn't stop scratching himself on his face and his hands. I would have felt sorry for Professor Y, especially given our kinship of dermatitis, but he was a martinet in matters of punctuation—a veritable Patton of the parenthesis, a de Sade of the semicolon. At the appointed time, I presented myself at his office and sat next to him for hours, going through the typescript of my dissertation, line by line, page by page, for some 266 pages. Every time he spotted an extra space after a semicolon (my trademark peccadillo) he would point a gnarled finger at the space and shake his head. And he would scratch. Gradually, every page of my dissertation became coated with flakes of dead skin.

"Congratulations on completing the requirements for your Ph.D.," Professor Y formally said at the conclusion of that long afternoon. He slowly stood up and shook my hand. More dead-skin flakes. I was one of them now.

CHAPTER THREE

"They're Writing Songs of Love, but Not for Me":
Gaudy Night and Other Alternatives to
the Traditional "Mating, Dating,
and Procreating" Plot

*W*eddings are inherently comical events—mine certainly was—that's why Shakespeare's comedies routinely end in a marriage. The vast effort expended trying to "put on the dog" for the Big Day frequently backfires and produces moments of absurdity. By the time I was in my mid-twenties, most of my old gang of girlfriends from Sunnyside were getting married. Because they were, like me, Irish Catholic, their nuptials were distinguished by mediocre food, free-flowing liquor, pre-*Riverdance*-style step dancing, and their own peculiar strains of Gaelic piety. When my best friend, Mary Ellen, announced her engagement (a Catholic doctor! Bingo!), she was fêted at a bridal shower where one of her aunts, a nun, presented her with a macramé crucifix, complete with droplets of blood sewn in red yarn. When another close friend from St. Raphael's, Cathy Sullivan, married Jim O'Brien, who was then a fireman at Kennedy airport, the wedding was held at Our Lady of the Skies Chapel at the airport (since demolished), where over the altar an aluminum statue of the

Blessed Virgin stood on a propeller whose blades were positioned to form the shape of the cross. The wedding party was then raucously escorted to the reception in nearby Astoria, Queens, by a cortège of fire trucks, their sirens blaring. And on it went. Most of my college friends were married within a few years of graduation by the Jesuits who had taught us at Fordham University. I envied the apparent seamlessness of my friends' lives—especially those of Cathy Sullivan and her sister, Pat, whose large Irish Catholic family I'd always half yearned to be a part of growing up. Everyone in their extended family was Catholic, and with the exception of a few abashed Italians, everyone was also Irish. They were like Sunnyside's version of the Kennedys—insular, good-looking, and proud of their ethnic and religious identity. Indeed, pictures of President Kennedy and Pope John XXIII hung side by side over the couch in the Sullivans' living room, as they did in Catholic living rooms across the country in the 1960s.

It's a gift of tranquillity when your adult desires mesh with your childhood background. I don't quite know why mine didn't, although I think books, again, are partly to blame. I thought my mom and dad were tops, and I liked being Irish-Polish Catholic, but I do think my avid reading left me vulnerable to the temptations of what memoirist Kate Simon dubbed "the wider world." Getting a fellowship to grad school at Penn placed me, nervously, into that wider world where, when I turned twenty-eight, I found my life's partner and he found me. But, precisely because of where we found each other—in an Ivy League grad school rather than at my Catholic college or the neighborhood bar or political club—there were problems. He was Jewish and an atheist. In addition, we were both loner types prone to overintellectualizing. There was no war on to make us pledge our troth to each other quickly, as my parents had done. (After a romantic courtship of a few months, my father proposed to my mother, on bended knee, in a moonlit park in the vicinity of what is now Tudor City in Manhattan. The next week he sailed off to the war in the Pacific.) Rich and I mulled over our relationship for years and kept our separate apartments.

I think reading at the very least intensified my hesitation to plunge headfirst into the heterosexual-female plot that culminates in marriage and children. Shy types like me tend to be drawn to solitary activities like reading, but reading also bolstered my predilection for solitude. I hated dating. Given the choice, I'd always opt for staying home and reading a book rather than going out to a bar or sitting winsomely on the *Rocky* steps of the Philadelphia Museum of Art, a favorite Sunday-afternoon pickup spot during the years I lived in Philadelphia. "Mr. Wonderful isn't just going to knock on the door," a girlfriend once said, chiding me. "Why not?" I thought. That's the way people often meet in books—effortlessly, without guile or strategizing. The literary heroines I adored—Elizabeth Bennet, Jane Eyre, Catherine Earnshaw, Harriet Vane, and yes, even die-hard childhood series favorites like Nancy Drew—were simply "discovered" by their male soul mates, who usually lived in the house or estate next-door—or, in Heathcliff's case, the barn. These young women didn't have to do anything to attract their suitors; they simply had to be. Most of these heroines are described by their creators as attractive but not outstandingly beautiful. (Catherine Earnshaw and Nancy Drew are the shimmering exceptions.) Elizabeth Bennet places second in the looks department, after her knockout older sister, Jane; plain Harriet Vane and downright mousy Jane Eyre are usually described as "neat" in appearance but nothing more. Rather, it's their wit, their intelligence, their "pilgrim souls," as W. B. Yeats said of (beautiful) Maud Gonne, that mesmerize the men in their lives.

What a welcome fantasy that was for someone like me who always felt phony flirting and rated herself as sort of good-looking but nothing spectacular. Like my literary role models, however, I knew I was smart and funny. Not smart enough, though, to figure out that, apart from Nancy Drew—who was the brainchild of Edward Stratemeyer, also the originator of the Hardy Boys, the Bobbsey Twins, and a host of other series-fiction favorites—all of these heroines were created by mediocre-looking but brilliant single women who were, undoubtedly, spinning out for their own comfort a fairy-tale fantasy of being chosen by Prince Charming. Because that's the politically incorrect angle of these progressive literary courtships in which the woman is valued for the radiance of her mind, not the radius of her bosom: the men in these novels still possess all or most of the traditional attributes of "a good catch." Mr. Darcy is moody, but his dark good looks and fat wallet more than make up for his cranky disposition. "And of this place, . . . I might have been mistress,"[1] muses Elizabeth when she catches her first glimpse of Darcy's splendid estate, Pemberley, and begins to regret her rebuff of his first proposal. Mr. Rochester is no beauty, but he, too, is conventionally wealthy and virile. The first time Jane encounters her future husband, he towers over her on a tall steed that behaves in an overtly phallic manner, rearing up and bucking. Lord Peter Wimsey boasts an aristocratic title, a bonny countenance, and an irresistible air of arrogance. He literally saves Harriet Vane from the gallows in *Strong Poison,* rendering his courtship of her perilously close to a conventional female rescue fantasy. Heathcliff starts out life without a nickel, but he eventually becomes wealthy; he's also a hunk as well as an unreconstructed "bad boy."

Leaving juvenile fiction aside for the moment, I do think Austen and her sisters envisioned something much more ambitious in their novels than a bit of literary beefcake served up with a side of clever repartee. These romances continue to captivate readers because they throw together adult men and women with complicated pasts who have to painstakingly work out the terms of their relationships before they achieve wedded harmony. That's the realistic, strikingly contemporary angle to these romances; the fairy-tale aspect enters in when these mostly plain-to-pleasant-looking poor girls win the alpha males by dazzling them with their smarts. The faithful and hot romantic partners that grinds like Jane Austen and Dorothy Sayers couldn't find in real life, they created. After all, to paraphrase another sharp Dorothy: "Men don't make passes / at [poor] girls who wear glasses."

Of course, once safely tucked away in their marriages, our heroines, like fireflies trapped in a bottle, flicker and fade into gray domesticity. Austen and company devote, at most, a couple of pages to imagining the postnuptial lives of their lucky brides—and with good reason. Jane Eyre and Elizabeth Bennet spawn children, tend to their peevish husbands (Mr. Rochester probably made even more so by his temporary blindness), and carry on the debilitating round of social visits expected of upper-crust ladies. Nancy Drew fortunately remains frozen at age eighteen; although, as Bobbie Ann Mason observes in her terrific book *The Girl Sleuth,* even in her chaste late adolescence, Nancy displays incipient tendencies toward becoming another proper Mrs. Bobbsey. Harriet Vane makes a wan postnuptial impression in *Busman's Honey-*

moon, where she defers to Lord Peter in the detecting department. In her last published literary appearance, a short story entitled "The Haunted Policeman," Harriet is not seen at all. She's secreted away in a back bedroom in the Wimsey mansion giving birth to a male heir as the sleepless Lord Peter directs his urbane attention to solving a neighborhood crime. Only Catherine Earnshaw's mystical marriage with Heathcliff, which takes place in the netherworld after her premature death, can be described as truly "blissful."

It would be too pat to say that witnessing this grim literary wedding march made me skittish about serious relationships myself. More accurately, it was probably the fact that I was someone who spent so much of her time reading, standing apart, and observing that made me hold myself aloof. If I was, indeed, influenced by the literary heroines I loved, it was in the low-level way of wanting to remain in a heady state of becoming, rather than "settling down" or "for." Maybe reading Laurie Colwin's magical short stories, which usually feature happily mated, yet complicated and vital female characters, would have helped nudge me out of my singleness, but I didn't know that wonderful writer back then.

If a young woman doesn't marry and start a family at some point in her twenties, she detours around the age-old normative markers of female adulthood. It's harder to discern, then, exactly when one becomes a grown-up—especially if, as in my case, the young woman in question is still in school throughout her twenties. Even when I finally was awarded my Ph.D. at thirty-two, I hadn't yet held down what my parents considered a "real" job. For years before and after I officially became Dr. Corrigan, I was what they call in the profession a "gypsy scholar"— one of a multitude of excess eggheads who roam from campus to campus, teaching introductory courses like "Composition." I became practiced at moving into temporary teaching positions and other people's offices. Once, at Haverford College outside Philadelphia, I was assigned the office of a recently deceased faculty member; the office hadn't been cleaned out yet, and a few days before the fall term began, I unlocked the door to find a dirty room whose bookshelves were crammed with empty bourbon bottles and crucifixes—mute testimony to the limits of literature as a sustaining comfort in life.

"It didn't get you anywhere, did it?" my mom worried aloud when I'd announced to her that I'd gotten my Ph.D. The question stung at the time, but she was right. Adventures are supposed to achieve something in the end, and it wasn't clear, even by the time I'd accepted Professor Y's scaly congratulations, what I'd gained by the great solo adventure of my young womanhood. It took me several years more—years of consistently bombing out on interviews for tenure-track jobs—to realize the great lesson that my unhappy graduate-school years had taught me about my own inclinations and limits: that is, that in an age of specialists, I was most happy being a generalist. Much as I admired those scholars who lived and breathed their subjects, who immersed themselves, as, say, my old dissertation director did, in the work of John Henry Newman or Walter Pater, I gradually came to terms with the awareness that that kind of holy intellectual devotion was just not for me. Instead, I happily spent more and more time reviewing a hodgepodge of books for *The Village Voice,* roaming from the popular to the canonical and making connections between the two. I also loved being able to talk about those books in educated but accessible language. Without being conscious of moving in any particular direction, I began to put together a career that allowed me to be part of the academy but also to stand outside it—a career in which I could make a living talking about all kinds of books to a wide range of people. By becoming a book reviewer, I finally discovered that community of readers I had originally hungered for when I entered graduate school—even if that "community" was linked by the printed page and, later, in the case of *Fresh Air,* by satellite transmission and the Internet.

Since writing those early reviews for the *Voice* didn't cover the grocery bills, I also worked during and after graduate school at a succession of odd jobs. I mean "odd" in the primary sense. I picked up part-time work at a few only-in-Philadelphia places that were guaranteed to rattle my nerves, already plenty shaken up by the *Touch of Evil* atmosphere of graduate school. I worked for a couple of years as a proofreader at Lippincott Publishers, scrutinizing the proofs of medical textbooks packed with illustrations of skin cancer and venereal disease. Also in the medical line, I worked as a temporary curator's assistant at the Mütter Museum, a medical museum founded in the eighteenth century and tucked away on a quiet street in downtown Philadelphia. The Mütter Museum since my tenure there has been "discovered"—its current curator has even made several guest appearances on *Letterman*. But back in the early 1980s, it was a little-known local curiosity. Housed in a marble-halled mansion, it often rented out its upper floors for weddings; its basement, though, contained a semisecret chamber of medical horrors. Visitors could see centuries-old tumors afloat in glass bottles and pickled in gin; a chair used by the famous nineteenth-century Siamese twins, Chang and Eng; skeletons of nineteenth-century ladies whose rib cages had been deformed by too-tight corset stays; and John Wilkes Booth's shattered tibia bone. One of my chores was to regularly dust these and other gruesome exhibits, and in the course of my cleaning, I must have come into contact with some hardy eighteenth-century spore because my legs broke out in a vicious pox that none of the dermatologists I consulted could cure.

Besides creepy images that haunt me to this day, the legacy of my time at the Mütter Museum was the draft of a Nancy Drew novel I wrote. I took inspiration for my plot from the museum's collection of ancient baby-feeding instruments: pap boats, iron nipple shields, bubby cups, and the like. In my tale, Nancy and her sidekicks, Bess and George, are visiting Philadelphia on one of those educational vacations that Nancy's stately father, Carson Drew, regularly arranges for them. They're called upon to discover the whereabouts of a pap boat (an object, shaped like a gravy boat and designed to hold gruel) rumored to have been used by the infant Thomas Jefferson, that has vanished from the Mütter Museum. I was proud of my Nancy Drew draft. I thought the plot contained local color, suspense, historical background, and restrained patrician humor in just the requisite proportions. The present-day editors of the series, however, thought the plot also contained allusions to something that has always been forbidden in Nancy's life: sex. The fact that Nancy is rummaging around in a collection of pap boats and nipple shields, I was told in a rejection letter, brings up the unwholesome suggestion that Nancy herself has breasts. As squeamish Bess Marvin would say, "Eeek!"

Around that time, I also began teaching composition and literature as an adjunct professor at two elite colleges, Bryn Mawr and the aforementioned Haverford, in the WASPy Main Line suburbs of Philadelphia.

Like a lot of other bashful introverts, I discovered that I liked teaching a lot because it's like acting. When I stepped into the classroom, I stepped into a role, one that allowed me to forget myself. Talking about a favorite novel or poem, I felt erudite, funny, enthusiastic, and seductive. Because I've always settled for being a second-class (nontenured) academic citizen at first-class institutions, I was usually blessed with smart, engaged students.

My students ushered in new ways of responding to and interpreting familiar works—some provocative, some wacky. Occasionally they've even made me laugh as much as I do when reading *Lucky Jim*. Every teacher has one—the sentence in a student paper that is so earnestly wrong that it lodges permanently in your brain. My most cherished student howler popped up in a paper on E. L. Doctorow's novel *The Book of Daniel*. Doctorow's book is a brilliantly inventive reworking of the Rosenberg case, and after many rereadings, it remains on my short list of the best English-language novels of the twentieth century. I once had a student who, in his paper on *Daniel,* decided to focus on the Rosenbergs' (called the Isaacsons in the book) electrocution scene. The day before the paper was due, he showed up at my office with a draft. The latest revisions included this declaration: "The Isaacsons were put to death by electrolysis." I bit my cheek and asked him if he knew what "electrolysis" meant. Unperturbed, he said it was a synonym for "electrocution"—a word, he'd wisely recognized, that he'd used too lavishly throughout the essay. As a British friend of mine dryly observed when he heard this story, "Well, Ethel maybe."

During the mid- to late 1980s, I not only taught English at Bryn Mawr but also served as the assistant to the president—a detour into college administration I made in despair over the shrinking job market. My job was to help draft speeches and letters, meet and greet visitors, shuffle paper, take minutes at meetings, and order sandwiches. I think of those as my "Into the Belly of the Beast" years—the "Beast" being the WASP upper class and myself being the intrepid accidental tourist. Bryn Mawr was an institution where newly arrived freshmen were treated to an indoctrination screening of *The Philadelphia Story,* starring the college's most famous alumna, Katharine Hepburn. This was also the college that Ira Einhorn's smart and pretty Texas girlfriend/victim, Holly

Maddux, attended and intermittently dropped out of for six years. As Steven Levy details in *The Unicorn's Secret*, Maddux was plagued by profound feelings of not "fitting in." I can imagine to a certain extent how she felt. Not just the clothes you wore (for the faculty: Pendleton or Talbots) or the makeup and jewelry you didn't, but every vowel out of your mouth—and certainly, most of all, your name—marked you as "us" or "them." My own name marked me as one of the help, and in fact, at Bryn Mawr I learned that I had the makings of a good Irish parlor maid. The president I was "assistant to" was Mary Patterson McPherson, and she was a rangy, white-haired Juno of a woman who was a walking advertisement for Bryn Mawr's much touted aim to educate women to be "leaders." In other historical circumstances, I would have followed her blindly over the trenches or onto the beaches of Normandy—such was her personal magnetism, kindness, and good humor.

Aside from expanding my anthropological knowledge of WASP rituals and dress, my two years as assistant to the president at Bryn Mawr also gave me limited entrée into the most fascinating alternative-family life I've ever been a part of, however tangentially. Still trying to assert my adult female identity to myself and to my family and old friends without the traditional imprimaturs of marriage and motherhood, I found at Bryn Mawr a community of women who'd done just that—most of them in the "dark ages" before the Second Women's Movement. Most of the female administrators at the college and many of the faculty were single, and I observed them with a fluctuating mixture of admiration and dread. Maybe it was my early mostly positive exposure to nuns and/or my happy childhood-through-late-adolescence memories of being part of a tight-knit pack of girlfriends, but I've always felt drawn to communities of women, both in literature and in life. I love the picture that Barbara Pym paints in her sunny first novel, *Some Tame Gazelle,* of the two well-off spinster sisters, Belinda and Harriet, living together in their rambling house in the English countryside, tending flowers, sitting down to their Sunday joint of beef, and, well into advanced middle age, still gracefully rebuffing suitors. Describing an evening tea of potato cakes and Belgian buns the sisters share with a woman friend, also single, Pym writes: "At tea they were all very gay, in the way that happy, unmarried ladies of middle age often are."[2] Like every other female reader I've ever discussed *Little Women* with, I experience Father March's return from the Civil War and Meg's marriage to the donnish John as rude intrusions into a sororial circle that managed just fine without men, thank you. I'm always delighted by the map of St. Mary Mead that's included in some editions of Agatha Christie's Miss Marple mysteries. There's Miss Marple's house, nestled among other spacious houses, many of them owned by "old cats" like herself.

I was predisposed to be charmed by the female community at Bryn Mawr that functioned like a big alternative family. Some of the single women there were discreetly gay; others were hetero; still others were sexual ciphers. Some lived in their own houses and apartments around the campus, while many others shared homes and lives. These women exercised together in the mornings; worked together till late in the day; sipped cocktails and dined together, often at college functions, in the evening; and vacationed together on rugged "walking tours" of the British Isles in the summer months. They were strong, splendid, no-nonsense types who lived for the college and for their intellectual pursuits. Men seemed superfluous. That's where my feelings of dread entered in. While I could sometimes see myself settling into this single-sex life, it also felt too hermetically sealed—in terms not only of gender but of class as well. The single-sex world of Bryn Mawr was one I ended up visiting as an extended guest, rather than living in. But I've always liked returning—through literature—to that fantasy vision of a community of women who are mostly sufficient to one another. Beyond what Barbara Pym called her "excellent women," or Miss Marple, or the March sisters, the female community of Bryn Mawr found its literary double in a novel I serendipitously read for the first time while I was teaching there, Dorothy L. Sayers's remarkable 1936 mystery, *Gaudy Night*.

I once taught an adult course on female mystery fiction at the Smithsonian Institution called "Sleuthing Spinsters and Dangerous Dames," and in that crowd of some two hundred overwhelmingly female readers was a woman who had read *Gaudy Night* fourteen times. I may be up to my seventh or eighth reading by now, and with each reading, I better understand that woman's passion for the book. It's an extraordinarily compelling fantasy about a woman who's been badly hurt in a romantic relationship with a man returning to the refuge of an all-female community that offers intimate friendship and mental stimulation. What makes the story mythic in its allure is the sense the reader has that our heroine, Harriet Vane, is not simply indulging in a time-out sojourn at her old Oxford alma mater, Shrewsbury College, but that she's unconsciously seeking to escape into an earlier stage of heterosexual female development, when the bonds with her girlfriends seemed all-satisfying, before men came lumbering along to muck things up or, as Dylan Thomas put it, "before I knocked and flesh let enter." I think that, for Harriet, the single-sex community of the fictional Shrewsbury College represents a return to a youthful oasis of possibility where the limits and problems of adulthood—including romantic relationships with men as well as copyright wranglings with publishers—have not yet materialized.

Gaudy Night anticipates today's feminist-inflected detective fiction, which, as I've said, constitutes an updated version of the female extreme-adventure tale. (Sayers's feminist visions of education and work arose out of the frantic, shift-for-yourself circumstances of her own life. She was part of that extraordinary first generation of women, along with Winifred Holtby and Vera Brittain, who desegregated Oxford. Sayers received her degree from Somerville College in 1915. While writing the first three Wimsey mysteries, she worked at an advertising agency. Later on she supported her son, who was born out of wedlock and subsequently cared for by a cousin; nursed her sickly husband; and tended to her elderly parents before their deaths.) Like contemporary hard-boiled heroines, Harriet is intellectually, economically, and even physically self-sufficient. In *Gaudy Night,* she fights her way out of near-fatal disaster and wins the husband of her dreams, with whom she expects to fashion a progressive marriage. Like all such marital fantasies, however, *Gaudy Night* stumbles when it comes to working out the gritty specifics of its vision.

The tale begins with a journey. Harriet is behind the wheel of her little roadster, motoring from London to Oxford and steeling herself for her reception at the Shrewsbury College reunion or "gaudy." The occasion is fraught with tension for her because of her notoriety: some years earlier, Harriet had been charged with the murder of her live-in lover, Philip Boyes. In the public spectacle of the trial, Harriet's bohemian sex-

ual behavior had been crudely discussed. Only the intervention of another man, Lord Peter Wimsey, saved Harriet from the hangman's noose.
Wimsey fell in love with Harriet in the course of investigating the case,
but ever since, she's kept him at arm's length, not wanting to confuse
gratitude with love. Her autonomy is at stake. Harriet was a scholarship
girl at Oxford, and though she's subsequently carved out a successful
career as a mystery writer, marriage to the moneyed and titled Lord
Peter would effectively diminish her hard-won sense of self.

For five years "the stark shadow of the gallows had fallen between her
and that sun-drenched quadrangle of grey and green."[3] Harriet has
allowed herself to be coaxed back to Shrewsbury only because of the
entreaties of a seriously ill classmate. Eager to banish her still-persistent
class anxieties, Harriet takes pains to convince herself that she has, in
fact, become Somebody. The dresses she's packed for the college festivi-
ties are high-quality and severe. The dresses the other alumnae wear turn
out to be much splashier. (Like overzealous religious converts, climbers
originally from the lower rungs of society tend to go overboard when
they ape the upper class.) Stopping to lunch on the road, Harriet orders
wine and tips the waitress generously: "She was eager to distinguish herself as sharply as possible from that former undergraduate who would
have had to be content with a packet of sandwiches and a flask of coffee
beneath the bough in a by-lane."[4]

The dreamlike atmosphere of the journey lingers well into Harriet's
arrival. She's settled in the neighborhood of her old undergraduate
rooms, and when she does finally take a deep breath and make her en-
trance into the welcoming reception, she basks in what every reunion-
goer longs for: the golden acknowledgment, by glance and by word, that
she is the star of her class. The college dean, sensing that Harriet is
uneasy about her notoriety, looks her in the eye and sternly pronounces:
"Nobody bothers about it at all. We're not nearly such dried-up mum-
mies as you think. After all, it's the work you are doing that really
counts, isn't it?"[5]

Work, work, work. Just as with the American hard-boiled mysteries,
work is one of the great themes of *Gaudy Night*. The novel affirms a
feminist ideal of work in which women are recognized as full-fledged
adults and sustained—mentally, emotionally, and financially—by their

labors. Harriet, with good reason, worries about what would become of her work life should she marry Lord Peter. Staving off that momentous decision, she decides to accept an invitation from the dean to come up to Shrewsbury some months after the gaudy and investigate some vicious pranks that have been played on the college. A manuscript has been defaced, academic gowns have been stolen and burned in a bonfire, and students have received anonymous hate mail. Her residence at the college allows Harriet the space to pursue not only her amateur detective work but a more "literary" form of writing as well: she begins research on a scholarly biography of the eighteenth-century thriller writer Sheridan Le Fanu. (Foolishly, Dorothy Sayers second-guessed the value of her chosen genre. Harriet's move from suspense to scholarship parallels Sayers's own migration from the Wimsey books to her now largely unread but high-toned essays on the Bible and her translations of Dante.) It's the cloistered environment of Shrewsbury that inspires Harriet to return to her undergraduate intellectual passions. Here's a key passage from *Gaudy Night* that captures the nurturing spell of the college:

> If only one could come back to this quiet place, where only intellectual achievement counted; if one could work here steadily and obscurely at some close-knit piece of reasoning, undistracted and uncorrupted by agents, contracts, publishers . . . —then, one might be able to forget the wreck and chaos of the past, or see it, at any rate, in a truer proportion. Because, in a sense, it was not important. The fact that one had loved and sinned and suffered and escaped death was of far less ultimate moment than a single footnote in a dim academic journal establishing the priority of a manuscript or restoring a lost iota subscript.[6]

Harriet goes overboard here in extolling the nobility of academic work—many academics I know would speedily trade in tenure in exchange for authorship of a bestselling mystery. But the call to turn inward and remove oneself from the world, to transform from a queen bee into a drone, is one Harriet heeds. For a brief space, she's happily one of the hive. Shrewsbury, like Bryn Mawr, is a single-sex community whose stated purpose is to support women, emotionally and intellectually. Harriet dines in the Senior Commons Room, sips whiskey at night with the warden, and discusses prosody with her old English tutor. Many of the administrators and faculty at Shrewsbury belong (fictitiously, of course) to Sayers's own pioneering generation of Oxford "undergraduettes." Theirs is a cordoned-off and robust sanctuary, like that of Bryn Mawr, in which most men are relegated by the female gaze to being distant objects of study.

In addition to its many other attractions, *Gaudy Night* enthralls so many of us women readers because it engages the two top female "guilty pleasure" fantasies of retreat and rescue. Let's start with the latter. Harriet plugs away at her detecting, but it's not until her paramour, Lord Peter, elegantly strolls into the Senior Commons Room that progress is made on the case. Thanks to his superior efforts, Harriet is saved from death by strangulation and the identity of the college's poltergeist is revealed. The culprit turns out to be a "scout" or cleaning lady named Annie, whose husband had been a tutor at another institution before a female scholar destroyed his career—a misfortune that prompted his suicide. Annie has borne a psychopathic grudge against academic women ever since. (Despite her seeming sympathy for Harriet's class insecurities, Sayers was something of a snob. Note that the villain of her story turns out to be a working-class woman who's too ignorant and normative to realize the worth of the intellectual work done by the refined ladies of Shrewsbury.)

Feminist critics of *Gaudy Night* make much of the novel's ending, in which Lord Peter (yet again) proposes to Harriet using her Latinate academic title, "*magistra*," and she finally accepts. The form of the proposal indicates Lord Peter's respect for Harriet's intellectual accomplishments and foretells an emancipated union. But romantic fantasies—even those penned by the likes of pathbreaking Oxford graduates like Dorothy Sayers—are never quite that politically correct. The fact that Harriet escapes death by strangulation because she's wearing a heavy leather dog collar that Lord Peter gave her for protection should give one pause. *A dog collar?* Reinforcing the suspicion that what we female readers might also be naughtily relishing in *Gaudy Night* is the spectacle of a strong woman being saved and o'ermastered by her male counterpart is the fact that when Harriet and Peter consummate their union in the novel that follows, *Busman's Honeymoon,* Sayers tells us that Harriet gasps out a rapturous "My Lord!" at the decisive moment. Harriet pays for that episode of giddy sexual submission by spending the rest of her married life in Lord Peter's suave shadow. Utopian moments—in art or life—are, by nature, fleeting.

Refuge is the other forbidden female fantasy that *Gaudy Night* serves up. Rest! Regenerate! Meditate in silence! . . . while a crew of unobtrusive workers washes your soiled linen and cooks up your meals. Put in these terms, Harriet's retreat into Shrewsbury sounds like an ad for the Golden Door. To escape from the needs of others and to tend to one's own well-being and ambitions is a luxury most women throughout history could only dream about in their most secret moments. What a lark Harriet's withdrawal must have been for Sayers to write. Vicariously, Sayers and many of us female readers bask with Harriet in the solicitous solitude of Shrewsbury. Her creative energies undepleted by the usual tedious weekly routine of meetings with agents, publishers, friends, and the fawning Lord Peter, Harriet sits down at her writing desk and produces . . . what? A monograph on Sheridan Le Fanu and a fragment of a sonnet.

That's the irony of the fantasy of refuge that *Gaudy Night* offers: like the dream of rescue, its pleasures are momentary and don't bear up under scrutiny. Sayers seems to be dramatizing Virginia Woolf's immortal pronouncement that, to write, a woman needs "a room of her own."[7] (A pronouncement Woolf made, by the way, in the course of two lectures she delivered in 1928 at Oxford. Woolf was thinking of the "room" she had been denied at university.) Fair enough. But most women writers aren't used to rooms of their own, and Harriet, for one, doesn't do her best work when she's uncharacteristically undistracted. No matter how hard Sayers tries in *Gaudy Night,* she can't make that monograph sound compelling. Harriet herself is pleased with her piddling literary output because it's highbrow, but the mysteries she's managed to write in her London flat with the hubbub of her real-life responsibilities swirling about her are more inventive than her tortuous efforts at Oxford. Perhaps, because the room of her own she inhabits at Oxford is relatively airless, so is the writing she produces there.

The vast majority of women writers throughout the ages have had to "make do," sneak in a few scribbling hours here and there, fit in writing after the "necessary" work of the day was done. For almost all of their adult lives, the Brontë sisters were cooped up together in that parsonage tending to the needs of Papa Patrick and drunkard brother Branwell or sent out to earn their keep as governesses. While entertaining her brother Frank, his family, and several visitors over the course of weeks, the forty-year-old Jane Austen wrote her sister, Cassandra, that she yearned for "a few days quiet, & exception from the Thought & contrivances which any sort of company gives—I often wonder how *you* can find time for what you do, in addition to the care of the House. . . . Composition seems to me Impossible, with a head full of Joints of Mutton & doses of rhubarb."[8]

Like the Brontës, Louisa May Alcott sang for her supper by writing those breast-heaving thrillers that are still coming to light in order to make up for the economic deficiencies of her philosopher father, Bronson. Sure, there have always been exceptions. Lots of men—John Keats, Edgar Allan Poe, Wallace Stevens—have scrambled to write while making a living doing something else. Then there are those cagey female invalids, like Emily Dickinson, who have made productive use of sickness (Alice James and Virginia Woolf are also in this passionately frail company). Some lucky female writers, such as Mrs. Gaskell and Edith Wharton, were emancipated from the distracting demands of work inside and/or outside the home by their personal fortunes. But historically, male writers have an easier time taking themselves seriously, while society still doesn't encourage women to give themselves over to Art. I'm reminded of that crucial moment when Dashiell Hammett quit his job as an advertising copywriter, moved out on his wife and baby daughter to take an apartment by himself in San Francisco, and threw himself into writing. Granted, Hammett had been told by his doctors that he was a "lunger"—a tuberculosis victim—so he decided (erroneously) that he had only a few years left to prove himself as a writer. In the detective-fiction classes I teach, I've always talked about that episode in Hammett's life with admiration. Yet when Agatha Christie skipped out on her personal responsibilities—*for eleven days*—she would never be allowed to forget it. After the death of her mother and the infidelity of her first husband became too much to bear, Christie left her baby daughter in the care of the nanny and "went missing" for those infamous eleven days in 1926. The widely publicized episode dogged her for the rest of her life.

Judging from the lives of many twentieth-century literary women, "the second shift" isn't about to be phased out anytime soon. Stevie Smith did office work and cared for her aged "Lion Aunt" at home; Toni Morrison worked for years as an editor while she was writing; Eudora Welty tended to her ailing mother and brothers for more than a decade in the middle of her by then flourishing writing career; Anne Lamott teaches and is a single mother to Sam, the son she made famous in her wonderful memoir, *Operating Instructions.* Mary Higgins Clark, America's reigning "Queen of Suspense," was a young widow raising five young children on her own *and* holding down a full-time job writing radio scripts when she began rising before dawn to write her first mystery, *Where Are the Children?,* published in 1975. The writer many critics, including me, regard as Sayers's latter-day inheritor, P. D. James, began her detective-fiction career while her husband, whose schizophrenia surfaced after his service in World War II, languished at home and in mental institutions. I had the thrill of interviewing James face-to-face for *Fresh Air* when her 1997 novel, *A Certain Justice,* came out. She was gracious and erudite, and she wore tweeds. I fell at her feet. In that interview—and in the hundreds of others that she's given—James recounted how she started writing her first novel, *Cover Her Face* (completed in 1960 and published two years later), at the kitchen table in the early morning, before she went off to her day job as a bureaucrat in the National Health Service. Because of the hectic circumstances of her early life (she also pretty much raised her two daughters single-handedly), James didn't begin writing until she was thirty-nine. But as so many of her deliriously enthusiastic critics have observed, her inside knowledge of government departments and hospitals and human suffering graces her mysteries with a hard-won authenticity.

James especially came to mind one December a few years ago, when I skipped off to a junket for mystery writers and critics sponsored by, of all things, Club Med. Two male mystery writers, the bestselling Dennis Lehane and the lesser-known but very entertaining Lev Raphael, talked about taking the risky step of committing themselves full-time to their writing. Listening to them made me depressed. Maybe if I had gone to a women's college like Shrewsbury or Bryn Mawr, I would have felt empowered to take myself and my work seriously, too. Maybe I would have risked a full-time writing career. I brought my husband and then two-year-old daughter along on that junket. On the first day, we were given a list of all the conference participants, their hotel-room numbers, and their affiliations. Next to my name, before the initials "NPR," was one word: "Crib." "Maureen Corrigan, Crib, NPR." To me, that entry spoke reams about my own version of the contemporary female juggling act. Reading the biographies of Sayers and other multitasking women writers reminds us, as Yeats immortally said, that great art also arises out of "the foul rag and bone shop of the heart"—as well as the typing pool and the Xerox room; the kitchen, the sickroom, and the nursery.

As any self-respecting feminist would, Harriet dithers about being "rescued" by marriage to Wimsey; in the end she succumbs, no doubt hoping that Wimsey will make good on the promise of equality implicit in his form of proposal. Sayers couldn't manage to conjure up such a marriage in her later writings about Harriet and Lord Peter—perhaps because human history up to Sayers's own time gave her so few models to draw upon. As a female reader who was then, too, dithering about the threat of being overwhelmed by marriage, I appreciated seeing Harriet's thoughtful deliberations dramatized on the pages of *Gaudy Night*—as well as in the Harriet/Lord Peter novels that preceded it. One of the great, largely unacknowledged advantages of series fiction is that a story line can be strung out over several novels, allowing a character to think, falter, and reverse direction, as Harriet does. Sometimes novels just companionably mirror your own confusion, and I think that's what *Gaudy Night* did for me when I first read it in my late twenties.

Retreating into the all-female haven of Bryn Mawr was never a real option for me, since, for one thing, I was never issued a permanent invitation, and unlike Harriet at Shrewsbury, I was plugging away at three jobs during my time there. The college's isolated and serene atmosphere was something I experienced as a day worker rather than as a full-time resident. While teaching and functioning as a low-level administrator, I forced myself to finish my dissertation and wrote a lot of essay reviews for *The Village Voice.* My mother once excitedly reported to me that she saw a man on the New York subway reading my long review of Helen Vendler's book on Keats's sonnets. What a kick! I could never agree with Harriet that penning a scholarly footnote was more rewarding than writing an essay thousands of people might read, even if they would throw it away a day later. An even greater thrill was the on-air reviews for *Fresh Air* I'd started doing. Adding to the thrill was the fact that, at the time I began contributing pieces to *Fresh Air,* the show's regular book reviewer was John Leonard—then and now the greatest all-round popular critic of literature and culture in America.

Although while working at Bryn Mawr I remained fitfully enthralled by what the late-Victorian novelist George Gissing would have called its "odd women" and the alternative family life they had constructed, that fascination, I noticed, was not shared by the contemporary novels I was reviewing at the time. In fact, new fiction made *Gaudy Night* look all the more radical in its feminist hesitation about romance and marriage. The books I was reading and reviewing were almost always concerned with one or two heterosexual people, their search for love, how the relationship went wrong, and how it was finally fixed or not. Sometimes, in a really ambitious novel, a dysfunctional nuclear family would be featured. Community, society, history, politics, work, and utopian alternatives to convention—all of these subjects seemed to have dropped out of the novel's view. Or, I should say, the literary novel's view. For here's a development that I first became aware of in the mid-1980s or so: as literary fiction struggled to maintain its anorectic figure, a more expansive and daring vision of romantic and familial relationships was being developed in, of all places, the lowbrow form of popular American detective fiction.

Yes, after my woozy seduction by Hammett and Chandler, I was still stuck on the tough guys—except that now, in the contemporary hard-boiled fiction I had worked my way up to, the tough guys were sometimes girls. Or gay. Or dark-skinned. The straight, white tough guy of yore hadn't disappeared, he'd just moved over to accommodate a variety of colleagues in his bare-bones office. While the contemporary literary novel had grown more pinched, these ambitious hard-boiled mysteries injected sweeping social criticism into their suspense. That in itself was nothing new: as I've said earlier, the classic hard-boiled detective story has, from its earliest days, offered a utopian vision of work along with its shoot-'em-up scenes. The surprise about many of these post-1960s mysteries, however, was that so many of them were also suggesting alternatives to the nuclear family that the classic hard-boileds had demonized.

The home base of the traditional tough guy had been a one-room dive outfitted with a rumpled Murphy bed, overflowing ashtrays, and a kitchenette stocked with liquor. As the social revolution of the 1960s began to infiltrate the very formula of detective fiction, however, a funny thing happened to the detective's bachelor pad: it began to look less like a low-rent version of Superman's Fortress of Solitude and more like a hippie commune where gumshoes, their friends, and adopted family members dwelt in hard-boiled harmony. These days, post-1960s hard-boiled detectives have accumulated such large alternative families that it takes pages and pages at the beginning of each mystery just to catch up on everybody's doings. Sara Paretsky's V. I. Warshawski, for instance, has dogs; a father-figure neighbor in Mr. Contreras; a mother-figure close friend in Lotty Herschel; and, occasionally, a steady boyfriend. Ditto for most of her contemporaries in the detecting business.

The fellow chiefly to blame for the "family affair" atmosphere of post-1960s hard-boiled detective fiction is Robert B. Parker. When Parker introduced his sensitive male detective, Spenser, in *The Godwulf Manuscript* in 1973, he inaugurated a series that helped transform the macho politics of the private eye and also the profession's preordained monkish lifestyle. For most of his series life, Spenser has maintained a committed (mostly) monogamous relationship with Susan Silverman, a Jewish feminist therapist. Almost as close to Spenser's heart is his best friend, Hawk, a laconic African American gun-for-hire. In *Early Autumn* (1981), the seventh novel of the series, Spenser became an adoptive father to the teenaged Paul Giacomin, who grew up to be a professional dancer and choreographer. Other Spenser intimates include Rachel Wallace, a radical lesbian feminist writer; Henry Cimoli, a gym owner who talks like Huntz Hall; straight-arrow white cops Frank Belson and Marty Quirk; a gay cop named Lee Farrell; a Chicano mob enforcer called Chollo; and Pearl, a hunting dog the resolutely childless Spenser and Susan coyly refer to as their "baby." Strictly speaking, Spenser does not live with any of these folks (he and Susan alternate sleepovers, and Paul visits Spenser periodically), but then again, how could he? The only space large enough to accommodate the Spenser clan would be one of those sprawling manor houses straight out of the pages of Golden Age mystery fiction.

When I began reading them, the Spenser novels were pretty much out there in terms of their depiction of utopian alternatives to the traditional nuclear family. It was a subject that intrigued me, particularly at the time, because I found myself in an alternative-family environment at Bryn Mawr and because I was semiconsciously struggling with my own feelings about marriage and children. The Spenser books were investigating the crucial mystery of how to be emotionally committed to another human being without allowing oneself to be swallowed up. (As is well known to fans of the series, Parker himself lives in semi-autonomous harmony with his longtime wife, Joan, in a Victorian mansion in Cambridge, Massachusetts, that has been divided into "his" and "hers" apartments.) Whenever a new Spenser novel appears, usually every spring, I still read it in one or two sittings. By now, the plot is almost beside the point. Instead, I read the latest greatly diminished Spenser novels to check in with his extended alternative family: I'm curious about what Hawk is up to these days and about Paul's ongoing search for love and Susan's latest home purchase. Reading the Spenser novels now is a little like reading one of those chatty holiday letters that come tucked in Christmas cards. The story lines are predictable, but still, it's nice to keep up with who's lost weight, gotten married, or had a set of brass knuckles smashed into his face.

The question of the literary value of mysteries and whether or not reading them—as much as I do—is mere escapism or just as worthwhile as reading highbrow fiction really comes to the fore with the Spenser series. Lots of critics sneer at Parker, claiming his novels are, at best, interesting for their sociological content. Similarly, lots of critics and readers look down their noses at the entire genre of detective fiction, disparaging it as "beach reading." A standard cliché in positive reviews of mystery fiction is to claim that a particular book "transcends the genre." As someone who teaches college-level courses in detective fiction, who's co-edited a two-volume scholarly book on them, and who reads and reviews them constantly, I'd say, in ruminating on this charge that mysteries are junk, that sometimes they are and sometimes they aren't. Just like autobiographies, literary fiction, ghost stories, biographies, and books of every other literary genre, mysteries can be stunning or simply awful. Both Charlotte Brontë's *Villette* and many of those candy-colored bodice rippers displayed on supermarket shelves are, strictly speaking, Gothic novels. No genre is inherently beneath contempt.

When mysteries are great, they're some of the most magical, psychologically insightful, metaphysically complex, and narratively sophisticated novels ever written. Take one of my most beloved classic mystery tales, Arthur Conan Doyle's *The Hound of the Baskervilles*. Its subject, aside from the entertaining MacGuffin of that supernatural hound, is epistemology, the study of knowledge itself. Throughout that tale, Holmes—the great defender of reason as the pathway to truth— struggles against the forces of chaos and primitive irrationality as represented by the Great Grimpen Mire, a formless bog that sits in the center of the action. The Mire, and the novel's obsessive focus on it, owes something to Freud's theories about the id, which were becoming popularized in 1902 when *The Hound* was published. Toward the end of the tale, Holmes just barely escapes being sucked down by the Mire, and ultimately the contest ends in a draw. What a subject. And what profoundly evocative language and symbolism grace this tale that the unenlightened dismiss as a traditional kind of boys' blood-and-thunder story.

My dad was an enthusiastic reader of the Holmes stories and a faithful follower of the Spenser series, too. In the fall of 1997 I interviewed Robert B. Parker onstage for the Smithsonian in Washington, D.C. My father was very weak from the combined effects of a year of dialysis and nearly six decades of cigarette smoking. He wanted very badly to take the train down from New York to see me talk to this author he admired. "I'd give my right arm to be there," he told me on the phone. It was just as well he missed the event. I played pedantic stooge to Parker's "aw, shucks," unreflective natural man of letters. (No hard feelings, Bob.) It's odd that my dad liked the Spenser mysteries as much as he did. While he was no racist, he certainly wasn't socially progressive. Similarly, his unspoken policy on "women's libbers" and the differently sexually-oriented seems to have been to express disapproval from afar and, in personal encounters, to take individuals as they came. He once drove down to the Steamfitters' union hall in Manhattan to confront the bureaucrats there who had denied his black partner, Adam, membership in the union. "If he's doing the job, he should be in the union," said my dad, who also, paradoxically, identified with Archie Bunker when *All in the Family* was a hit. Another time, when he and my mother had some problems with their old console television, they called a neighborhood repair store. An hour or so later, they buzzed a repairman into their apartment house. They heard the clatter of high heels coming up the stairs, and then there before them was a transvestite TV repairman in full drag. "But she did a really good job," my dad conceded later, still shaking his head in disbelief whenever he told the story.

Parker, with his assemblage of "others," certainly wasn't my father's political soul mate. Yet it speaks to the power of evocative writing—in Parker's case, the strong presence of Spenser and that wonderful rat-a-tat dialogue, especially in the earlier novels—that my father was transported beyond the boundaries of his own personal tastes and political inclinations to become a fan of the series. Literature doesn't work on readers in predictable ways. Sometimes we readers put up with views we don't like in a novel or any other kind of art in exchange for other compensations. That's certainly true for me whenever I read Hammett and Chandler, or Philip Roth, for that matter—and have to tolerate their disturbed depictions of women. Sometimes, works of literature forever alter the way we see ourselves, our world. And sometimes they just give us the sense that we're not alone in our confusion or yearnings.

Sayers's progressive fantasy, *Gaudy Night,* along with the Spenser series and the other contemporary detective fiction I was reading at the time, made me feel less lonely. Over the years that I was first reading those mysteries, I was trying to put together my adult identity without the transformative marker of marriage and also trying to figure out what kind of meaningful work I could do, what kind of relationships I could hope for. The Spenser books investigate that same terrain of work and family, and so they kept me company in my thoughts, maybe gave some inspiration—as, in its different way, *Gaudy Night* did. The hero and heroine of those stories were, like me at least in this regard, not so eccentric or defiant that they didn't want to somehow stake out a place for themselves on a tributary of the mainstream. I wrestled during my twenties and early thirties with feelings that there was "something wrong with me" because I wasn't married and, thus, hadn't fully become an adult. That's the way the collective eyes of the Irish Catholic world I grew up in viewed me, and I was still, and always, a daughter of that world, so I saw myself, disparagingly, as odd—an "odd woman." At the same time, I felt a dim sense of entitlement to my own life's adventure, apart from whatever husband and children might be floating in what Shelley nicely called "the clouds of futurity." The books I read helped give me the courage to keep on flying blind.

This period of my reading/real life closes, as many youngish women's stories do, with a wedding. "Reader, I married him." That, of course, is Jane Eyre's famous announcement of her marriage to Mr. Rochester. I felt a little like Jane Eyre in that my path to marriage, too, was long and hesitant. I had found a man who loved me and, most times, understood me, a man who didn't threaten to overwhelm me. Rich also valued his solitude; a much more talkative person than I, he is also an insatiable reader, so he likes to have time to himself, too. It now seems quaint, but one of the big obstacles to matrimony, apart from the personal *mishigas* each of us brought to the union, was that Rich is an atheist Jew and I am a Catholic, sort of. My parents were upset. (I can still hear my father's hollow voice on the phone saying: "He's not of our faith.") Rich's parents were also unhappy, especially because they heard my parents were unhappy. It was very hard for me, even as an adult, to go ahead and buck their disapproval; but I did. My reading gave me a shove; so many of the novels and plays about marriage that I had read featured lovers who had tensions to resolve.

After spending years in the company of characters whose ethnic, religious, racial, and class backgrounds differed from mine, I didn't regard it as such a big deal to step outside my own context and be with someone "not of our faith." My reading, and the life it helped create for me, put me more and more in contact with folks, fictive and real, who would have stuck out in Sunnyside. As evidence, consider the framed sketch of a frowning Buddha, floating above a skull with a flower dangling out of its mouth, that hangs above my desk these days. Not pretty, but precious. The haphazard inscription on the drawing reads "Allen Ginsberg,

D.C. 1/28/93; For Maureen Corrigan." A wonderful student of mine at Georgetown, named Sean Burns, went to hear Ginsberg read on that date at a revival movie house in Washington. After the reading, Sean, who was goofy and very smart and very friendly, went up to Ginsberg and told him that he had read "Howl" in the freshman poetry course I was then teaching at Georgetown. Sean also mentioned to Ginsberg that poetry was a hard sell at Georgetown, where pragmatic careerist subjects usually trump those whose payoff is not as tangible. That's why the Buddha is unhappy: because, as Ginsberg told Sean, "teaching is hard." As Sean talked Ginsberg began drawing and eventually handed him the sketch to give to me. I love a lot of Ginsberg's poetry and his courageous Whitman-esque embrace of his unique self, so that drawing on my wall is a treasure. Every so often, though, the wondrous improbability of this connection between me and the "nearsighted, psychopathic" Beat poet who resolutely "put [his] queer shoulder to the wheel"[9] hits me. All because of books.

In life, as opposed to literature, almost none of the couples I then knew well were different from each other in significant ways, so I felt like something of a pathbreaker. In my weaker moments, I would have preferred the safety of sameness: the church wedding at St. Raphael's, the reception marked by the music of the Clancy Brothers intermixed with a few token polkas, where everyone would dance and drink too much and have fun because everyone, in a cultural sense, knew everyone else. It would have been easier and I would have felt a lot less of an oddity. My wish for normality would have made my hero, Ginsberg, howl.

Our wedding was less like the final section of *Jane Eyre* and more like the last frantic hitch-up scene in *The Taming of the Shrew*. My old friend Mary Ellen came to the rescue. She had just moved with her husband and two kids to a big new house in rural Pennsylvania, and they offered us their backyard, with a view of rolling hills, for the summer ceremony, which was to be pagan. I dithered about the feminist politics of buying a white wedding dress. (Harriet Vane, I remembered, dressed for her Big Day in an eye-catching golden ensemble, no white for the soon-to-be-Lady Wimsey, a public fallen woman.) A few months before the ceremony, I felt a rush of defiance. Why shouldn't I assert my right to be a bride? So Mary Ellen and I went off to Brooklyn one weekend in search of an inexpensive but classy bridal gown. At the Mona Lisa Bridal Shoppe in Bay Ridge I found a bargain off-the-shoulder number that I thought looked a little like those evening costumes Jean Harlow and Carole Lombard slunk around in. Wedding photos suggest that the dress looked more flamenco dancer than Hollywood glamour.

My parents and Rich's parents met, for the first time, at the rehearsal dinner and made awkward but well-meaning conversation: Rich's parents mentioned having met a Catholic cardinal once, and my parents volunteered that they liked lox and bagels. The dads were both World War II veterans, which helped. The day of the ceremony I had teal blue flowers stuck into my hair at the local beauty parlor, shimmied into my dress with the help of friends, and stood with Rich in Mary Ellen's backyard, under a sweltering July sun, as the local traffic-court judge married us in a five-minute boilerplate ceremony (both of us far too self-ironic to express "personal vows"). The guests gathered around us in a circle and wisecracked when the judge asked "if anyone here has any objections . . ." Afterward, people made toasts that played on the theme of the two of us melding our mammoth book collections. It felt good to have everyone—our parents, the rest of our families, friends—there that day to see us together, to be happy for us, even despite themselves. The wedding photos don't show a Spenserian alternative family—for one thing, everyone is white—but it was an alternative-enough gathering by old Sunnyside standards: Jews, Catholics, a few lesbians, one nun, a token WASP, a "best man" who was a woman—even a few Republicans.

The reception, during which most of the guests changed into shorts and ate and danced far into the night, was a blur. Afterward, I heard of funny moments that I missed: my mother swaying to Motown with my new husband; Rich's mother trying to get the deejay to stop playing polkas and substitute the hora; the out-of-town guests (including my parents), who stayed at the local top-of-the-line hotel, being woken up by telephone calls from prostitutes soliciting customers. I do clearly remember us getting into our rental car late at night, preparing to embark on the first leg of our trip to Vermont. I remember my dad standing in the dark beside the car saying, "I hope you'll both be very happy." Not original, but words I cherished. I didn't want to be normative, but much as I might admire renegades, neither was I, say, a defiant heroine out of a Marge Piercy novel. I wanted to follow my heart *and* to have my father's man-of-few-words blessing. Packed in my suitcase was a copy of Dashiell Hammett's *The Thin Man,* to read as a kind of literary talisman for my new life as part of a twosome. It was the only novel I could think of at the time that featured a married couple of equals who were both witty and as fascinated by each other as they were by the world outside. I chose to overlook the fact that Hammett, no troubadour of wedding ballads he, kept Nick and Nora drunk throughout most of the book. Like the lovers at the end of Chekhov's great short story "Lady with a Lapdog," I knew that nothing had been, could ever be, entirely resolved—the hardest part was yet to come. So, I put my "queer" shoulder to the wheel, and we drove off.

Looking for a Ship/Looking for My Dad

About a decade ago, John McPhee wrote a wonderful book called *Looking for a Ship* about the history of the United States Merchant Marine and its current debilitated state. I passed it on to my dad to read because he had served in the Merchant Marine before joining the Navy right after Pearl Harbor. I always gave him any books I read or received as review copies that had anything to do with the sea; I also sent him any promising thrillers and detective novels and, of course, any book, even the dryest-looking histories, that had anything to do with World War II. Sometimes there were surprises. When I gave him a review copy of the first volume of Clay Blair's history of U-boat warfare—a book filled with pages and pages of eye-straining statistics—he was delighted. Magnifying glass in hand, he would sit at the kitchen table and read for hours, finding the names of merchant ships he had served on. One of those ships had been torpedoed, all the men lost. My dad was supposed to have boarded it at the Philadelphia Navy Yard, but when he reported for duty he found that he had left his seaman's papers behind at his sister's house, where there had been a boozy send-off the night before. By the time he raced back, got the papers, and returned to the Navy yard, the ship had left. My dad always said he felt like the rest of his life was bonus time after that brush with death.

My dad, like me, thought I had stumbled into one of the best jobs imaginable—a book reviewer! Someone who got new books for free and got paid to read them and, especially, talk about them on the radio! But, he often qualified his wonderment with the warning that there was no future in radio—it was a thing of the past. Whenever I tear open boxes of review copies and spot a book with a ship or swastika on the cover, I still think to myself, for a second, "Oh, great, I'll send that to Dad." Then there's the moment of correction, experienced as a faint, internal bodily jerk. He's gone.

I was especially missing him that summer day in my office at Georgetown (and I was certainly avoiding work) when I decided to do an Internet search for his ship, a destroyer escort called the USS *Schmitt*. It was always somewhat awkward, my dad recalled, to serve on a ship with a German name during World War II, but the *Schmitt* was named after a genuine hero. Father Aloysius Schmitt was a Catholic chaplain serving on the USS *Oklahoma* when it was bombed during the surprise attack on Pearl Harbor. He helped some sailors trapped with him belowdecks to escape through a hatchway. He himself drowned.

As I quickly found out, the *Schmitt* crew had had a few reunions in the 1950s. Then there was a thirty-year break and the reunions started up again, this time yearly. Clearly, the sense of time running out had galvanized some old members of the crew. My dad had told me that he had been all set to attend a reunion when I was a small child, but that I came down with chicken pox and he decided to stay home. The other version of that story—the one my mother tells—is that my dad didn't want to go to any reunions. He didn't like that sort of thing. Chicken pox and loner tendencies aside, I think that my dad stayed away from reunions because his time on the *Schmitt* was so important, certainly the most crucial time of his life, and he wanted to remember his shipmates as they were, not as the old men they turned into.

I e-mailed Alton Blanks, the crewman now living in North Carolina who was listed as having been in charge of the most recent reunion, in Lancaster, Pennsylvania, in the summer of 1999. Later that same day, Alton's wife, Sylvia, e-mailed back. (As I eventually learned, Sylvia is the computer-savvy half of the couple.) Her note was gracious and welcoming. She said that many of the family members felt as I did, "that they had served on the *Schmitt* too." We began exchanging information. For my part, I sent her copies of my dad's list of the crewmen; Sylvia sent me information on recent reunions, including a roster of known crew members who had died. That's how I found myself, on Columbus Day weekend 2000, checking in to a Hampton Inn in Crestwood, Illinois, along with my magnanimous husband, eighty-one-year-old mother, and two-year-old daughter—a strangely assorted crew in search of any word about our missing member at that year's reunion of the USS *Schmitt*.

We got to the hotel late Thursday night, but Alton, undeterred, had been waiting up for us in the lobby. He was a lean man, still in shape, and he hurried over to the check-in desk and introduced himself: "Welcome, welcome. You must be the Corrigans." He turned to me and shook my hand. "I didn't know your father—I joined the ship in California right after he was discharged. I went to the library and checked his dates. But we'll ask the other men tomorrow at breakfast. Did you bring any pictures?"

Oh, yes, we had brought pictures. There were snapshots of my dad and his buddies in their white sailor uniforms, all smiling, all looking impossibly young and handsome. (My Aunt Peggy, my father's sister, always maintained that my dad resembled the movie star Dana Andrews. He sort of did. When young, Aunt Peggy herself looked like Myrna Loy. Their dashing black-Irish looks became diluted in my generation. People have told me I look a little like Margaret Atwood. Swell.) In some shots my dad is grinning behind bars, holding a liquor bottle—obviously a prop setting in some photographer's studio. In others, taken when the *Schmitt* was in Hawaii, steaming toward the South Pacific, he and the guys are wearing grass skirts. Some shots feature other crew members manning five-inch guns; a few are of the ship seen from a distance. It looks so small; it *was* so small, this ship that dodged U-boats and submarines in the Atlantic and Pacific; convoyed men and equipment to Europe in preparation for D Day; shot down two kamikaze planes; sailed into Tokyo Bay to check for booby traps (the second American ship to do so after the Japanese surrender); and, much of the time, braved the dangers of the sea alone, as most destroyer escorts did.

Alton's words that first night were fateful because they were repeated, with some variation, the next morning at breakfast. "No, I'm sorry, I didn't know your father," said one old salt after another as the thirteen crew members at the reunion stopped by our table to say hello and look at the pictures. They tried. They were kind men and they squinted through the fog of fifty-some-odd years trying to remember. Some claimed to recognize his face; others managed a snippet of information about one of the other guys in the photos. ("He worked in the engine room, didn't he?") One old crew member looked at a snapshot of my dad and Uncle Paul—who had also served in the Navy, but not on the *Schmitt*—and said, pointing to Uncle Paul: "No, I didn't know your dad, but *this* guy I remember."

"Okay, nobody here knew your father," said Rich later that day. "Can we go home now?" He was only semi-kidding. We were holed up in our hotel room watching a cartoon channel we had located for Molly. Hours earlier, we had taken the hotel minivan to the Crestwood train station and traveled into Chicago, where we piled into a cab and rode to Marshall Field's. It was too cold to walk around the city, and with my slow-moving mother and antsy toddler in tow, together with the stroller, diaper bag, and packages we picked up along the way, the trip was exhausting. Now we were marooned back in our room at the Hampton Inn next to a suburban strip mall. The temperature outside was dipping into the thirties, light snow was predicted, and none of us had brought warm coats. And nobody here remembered my dad.

I'm not going to say that the rest of the weekend wasn't without its awkward moments, but of course, we stayed for the whole reunion, and I'm glad we did. Those old crewmen and their wives were so good to us. They bought Molly stuffed animals and puzzles and tried to entertain her—one man played the harmonica; another showed her his trick finger that popped out of its socket. They treated us to dinner and wouldn't hear of us contributing to the reunion fund. The men were all elderly, and some were frail, some sickly—shades of what they once were. But in spirit most of them retained the cheerful, self-deprecating attitude that characterized their generation, the generation that had lived through the Depression and won the War.

I felt as though I had been made an honorary member of a rapidly dwindling alternative family. My mom and I stay in touch via phone calls and Christmas cards with some of the *Schmitt* crew. We—all four of us—might go back to another reunion or two if they're held nearby, until, inevitably, they end. Those men may not have known my dad, but they knew the *Schmitt,* and from my earliest years, that ship loomed large in my life, too. Like so many of my aging boomer cohorts, I grew up with World War II as almost a felt memory—dressing up in my dad's old sailor suit to mug for home movies; studying the enlarged picture of the *Schmitt* that always hung above my dad's dresser; singing "We Gotta Sink the *Bismarck* to the Bottom of the Sea" with my dad as he and I walked along Queens Boulevard, lugging a Christmas tree home one year. I must have been about five years old, and I still remember the smiles on the faces of passersby as they looked at us. Back then, they all would have known that song, too.

The highlight of the trip (even if he didn't remember my dad, either) was meeting my dad's old commander, Captain Melusky. Captain Melusky looked pretty good—handsome and fit. Part of the reason he's still around to attend the reunions is that he was so young when he assumed command. The captain told me he took over the *Schmitt* right out of a Navy ROTC program. I felt like my dad's earthly emissary when I told the captain what an honor it was to meet him and how my father always talked about him with such respect, even reverence. After, again, fruitlessly showing him the photographs she'd brought, my mother asked Captain Melusky whether he remembered the ship's dance held at the St. George Hotel in Brooklyn in 1944. That dance had been my parents' first or second date. They'd met when the ship was docked for a couple of months at the Brooklyn Navy Yard, where it was being outfitted for service in the Pacific. "Sure, I do," said the captain. "We even printed a group picture taken of that dance in one of our earlier reunion booklets. I'll show it to you." He went up to his room and came back with the booklet. He opened it to the photograph, and there, in the very front row of a huge ballroom crowd of sailors, officers, and their dates, were my parents, smiling. My dad is in his dark winter sailor suit; my mom is wearing a light-colored dress, and her hair is waved and long. They're both so young and slim and beautiful. They look—as they had—like they've just fallen in love. A few weeks after that picture was taken, my dad proposed, then sent my mother an engagement ring bought at some Navy PX in the South Pacific. ("That's a blue-white diamond," he would remind her whenever she expressed dissatisfaction at the size of the stone.) Another of those whirlwind World War II romances that lasted a lifetime.

On Sunday morning the captain spoke at the memorial service that traditionally concludes each reunion. Like so many of us, he turned to books to make his meaning clear. He cited Tom Brokaw's bestseller *The Greatest Generation,* which he'd generally liked. He said, however, that the problem with the book was that it talked about those who had served in World War II as "heroes." "We weren't heroes," Captain Melusky said without a trace of false humility. "We just did the job we had to do." And his modesty evoked a more generous and democratic thought from me: perhaps my students, or any of us, would, if called upon, "do the job" the way these ordinary men had so long ago. The quiet, unsentimental, no-big-fuss way the captain and other crewmen there regarded themselves reminded me of my dad. He always joked, for instance, that the motto of refrigeration mechanics like himself, who installed huge air-conditioning systems on top of buildings, was "Never stand back to admire your work." Also, the way Captain Melusky and the others talked about making the next reunion an especially good one, "because we all know it might be the last," seemed to echo the courage they had shown more than fifty years ago when they had faced death the first time, then, as young men.

Sometimes I see my dad as being out on the ocean, on the *Schmitt,* just beyond the horizon. I have a brown-tinted snapshot of a bunch of crew members—I can't tell whether my father is among them, the faces are so faded—but they're all on the ship's deck, facing the camera. I think of these guys as the shipmates who've passed over, and now my dad is in their company, in safe harbor, reunited with the family he loved second only to the one he left behind when he died.

Sometimes, though, I think of death as more horrific, capricious, meaningless. Once or twice my dad told me this story to illustrate what a good leader Captain Melusky was. One night a sailor was crossing the *Schmitt*'s deck to go to the galley to get some cherry pie and coffee. That's what he told the guys he was on duty with as he left them. A freak wave smashed into the ship and washed the sailor overboard. Captain Melusky ordered the ship's lights to be turned on to search for the man in the black waters. The captain's decision was absolutely against wartime regulations because turning the lights on made the *Schmitt* a sitting duck for any enemy ships or submarines in the area. You could argue that it was a stupid, even irresponsible, thing to do. Nonetheless, Captain Melusky gave the order: the lights were turned on and the ocean searched. That poor guy was never found. I think about him sometimes, out there in the black ocean, maybe just out of reach of the lights, terrified and screaming for help. His fate was a lot like Pip's in *Moby-Dick*. (Books, books, always books.) A guy who just felt in the mood for cherry pie, swallowed up by the Infinite.

I occasionally sit, feeling exposed and self-conscious, at Mass in the neighborhood Catholic church, waiting for a sign, trying to reach my dad. I talk to his picture. I imagine I feel his hand on my shoulder, or hear his voice. Sometimes I feel his presence almost superimposed on me, when I'm sitting in our La-Z-Boy recliner late at night, like him, reading, lost in a book.

CHAPTER FOUR

Praise the Lord and Pass the Ammunition:
What Catholic Martyr Stories Taught Me
About Getting to Heaven—
and Getting Even

*I*t first occurred to me that maybe other people found Catholics a little peculiar in the fall of 1965—October 4 to be exact—the day that Pope Paul VI came to New York to address the United Nations. I was in fifth grade, and I was lined up with my other classmates from St. Raphael's School under the shadow of the El along Queens Boulevard, the main artery from what is now Kennedy airport into Manhattan. To catch a glimpse of the pope as he rode by, we had all walked (in line) about ten city blocks from our school, newly built and situated in a factory zone of Long Island City, adjacent to sprawling Calvary Cemetery. I remember it was an unseasonably raw day and my teeth were chattering because the nuns had insisted that we all leave our coats back at school. It was very important, they told us, that the pope see our green plaid uniforms. For the girls, those uniforms consisted of thin pleated wool jumpers worn over even thinner white nylon shirts, a snap-on green bow tie, "flesh"-colored leotards, green kneesocks, and durable green oxfords. The ensemble was topped off by a green-and-gold Robin Hood–style felt hat and complemented by the requisite white cotton gloves. Thus, most of our major body parts were encased in something green or white and/or scratchy. Still, we were ridiculously underdressed for the chill October weather—even though the boys had the advantage of green woolen pants.

Hours and hours went by and still no pontiff. But at some point during that windy vigil, a man came out of one of the neighborhood Jewish delis and cornered the nuns. I couldn't hear what he was saying. I just saw his hands moving up and down and all around like he was really angry. He disappeared back into the store but came out again quickly, and this time he was carrying containers of hot chocolate. We all got some, even the nuns.

I finally did see a white papal blur whiz by that day. (Pope Paul, we were later told, was late for his UN appearance, and so the Popemobile raced down Queens Boulevard.) And, what did the pope see, I wonder, as he sped past us? A smear of green? The subway El that might have reminded him, vaguely, of a Roman viaduct? The worshipful faces of some of the nuns—many of whom, I now realize, would have been, at most, in their early thirties? Though no one knew it at the time, Pope Paul was speeding toward an even more fateful destiny than that historic address to the UN. The modernizing changes in Church liturgy and doctrine that his predecessor, Pope John XXIII, set in motion through Vatican Council II would, within a few short years, make that scene on Queens Boulevard look as quaint and otherworldly as a painting of a New England ice-skating party by Grandma Moses. Nuns in long black habits, shivering children unquestioningly obeying the commands of those nuns even as the nuns and the children's parents obeyed the commands of the local parish priests. All changed, changed utterly. But I'm getting ahead of myself here.

Beyond the pope or the cold or the hot barley soup my anxious mother made me for dinner that night (she always made barley soup and gave me a shot of blackberry brandy to combat colds), my most vivid memory of that day is the outrage of that righteous Jewish deli guy upon seeing us kids out there freezing to death in our green plaid uniforms. Years later, I realized his agitated hand gestures translated into one word: *meshugene!*

Not only did our uniforms set us Catholic schoolkids apart, but so did our mind-set—one of silently "offering up" all sufferings, great and small, to God. It was a mind-set that was drummed into us, through word and deed, by our parents and teachers. Granted, some of its sources were secular. Many of those parents, like mine, had grown up during the Great Depression, when the philosophy of grin-and-bear-it became a national coping mechanism. In addition, much of St. Raphael's parish was then composed of first- and second-generation Irish Americans, and as Pete Hamill recalled in *A Drinking Life,* his great memoir of growing up Irish Catholic in 1940s and '50s Brooklyn, the standard retort of "Who do you think you are?" was one any Irish Catholic kid who whined to his or her parents could count on hearing. There was a strong class element to this attitude, the "Bronx cheer" of the working class directed against any of its offspring who tried "to put on airs" or otherwise demand attention. (In *The Gatekeeper,* his superb memoir of growing up Irish Catholic during the late 1940s and '50s in Manchester, England, literary critic Terry Eagleton says that his family's aim was to have the words "We Were No Trouble" engraved on their gravestones.[1]) Working-class self-deprecation and Catholicism went neatly hand in hand; despite dazzling exceptions like the Kennedy family, Catholicism is not popularly associated with the ruling class. It's the religion of immigrants and first- and second-generation strivers: the whiff of steerage still mingles with all that incense and candle wax.

Above all, we Catholic-school students were taught that the state of our souls would largely be determined by our fortitude. The more God tested you, the stronger you became spiritually—that is, if you didn't falter and complain. This pedagogical tough-love message persisted into college. During my first days at Fordham, the Jesuit university in the Bronx, we entering freshmen were required to write a composition to assess our skills. The assigned topic, as I vividly remember it, was "There is no free lunch in America." By then I was an expert on that theme. Our parents and teachers transmitted this message to us, but we also were exposed to it constantly through our reading. In my case, at least, the martyr stories—spiritual and secular, overt and covert—that we read in grammar school made an indelible impression.

Of course, we heard the Gospel stories in religion class, as well as at Mass on Sundays. In school we read about the lives of the saints. I remember my attention level soaring whenever we read and talked about a martyr story: not only were the tales of saints like Agnes, Dymphna, and Sebastian less familiar than the life of Christ, but their deaths were often gorier (multiple wounds to the body, beheadings, salivating lions) and, in the case of the female martyrs, much more sexually provocative. Many of the early-Christian female martyrs died protecting their virginity. Throughout grammar school, I didn't have the murkiest idea of how, exactly, a woman "lost" her virginity, but I knew that there was something enticingly sinful and secretive about the process.

The martyr stories we learned in religion class most blatantly preached the spiritual rewards of "sucking it up"—in the sense of enduring whatever life threw at you. Even secular subjects such as English, art, and spelling provided occasions for reinforcing this most fundamental of pre–Vatican II Catholic-school life lessons. I remember working on some kind of construction-paper collage in my second-grade art class and having trouble because we weren't allowed to use scissors. I must have asked the "art nun," Sister Mary Matthew, for help and she must have told me to figure things out for myself, because when I finally hit upon the idea of folding and tearing the paper into shapes, she stood over my shoulder and tersely said, "Now you're using the brains that God gave you."

Spelling, that most ideologically neutral of disciplines, turns out to have been a veritable indoctrination course in the virtues of spiritual and secular martyrdom. Purely by chance, I still happen to have my fifth-grade spelling book, *The Brooklyn Catholic Speller*—copyright 1939(!). (The fact that in 1965 we were using such an ancient speller demonstrates just how slowly changes infiltrated my childhood corner of the world.) Read today, *The Brooklyn Catholic Speller* seems like a soft-sell version of Mao's Little Red Book in its propagandizing techniques. Each unit introduces new words by means of an introductory essay or poem and then goes on to list opposites, spelling rules, rhyming words, homonyms, prefixes, suffixes, and usage tips. It's actually a good no-nonsense primer—the kind that I sometimes wish my own spelling-challenged college students had been required to study.

About 75 percent of those essays and poems preach the rewards of having a stiff upper lip or, conversely, meditate on the dangers of enjoying one's self too much and forgetting one's duty to God or others. There are straightforwardly religious essays on the rosary, the North American martyrs, the "perfect obedience"[2] of Saint Joseph, and Christ's death on Calvary. More intriguing to me at this distance, however, are the secular essays and poems that slip in homilies on self-sacrifice. In an essay entitled "The New Club," some boys, bored in the wintertime, decide to form a club whose aim is to encourage its members "to perform a helpful deed each day."[3] Any boy who misses a meeting will be fined a few pennies, which will go toward setting up a fund "to buy cigars for the old men in the hospital." The poem "Useful Advice," which kicks off the book, is a veritable finger wag in rhyme on the dangers of succumbing to self-absorption:

Useful Advice

Gloomy children never grow
Into handsome people. So
I advise you to be gay!
Laughter, troubles sweep away.
Laugh then, and you'll loving be.
Gentle, helpful, that's the key
Winning loyal friends for you.
Yes, glowing beauty will come, too.[4]

Perhaps I'm imputing too much meaning to a pair of little essays called "Saved" and "Brother and Sister," but prolonged exposure to *The Brooklyn Catholic Speller* tends to turn one into a paranoid reader. In "Saved,"[5] an anonymous child narrator describes his or her new home by the ocean. While the writer's parents take pleasure in a round of golf, the narrator walks near the edge of a cliff to catch a glimpse of an ocean liner and, of course, falls in. The child is indeed "saved"—certainly from drowning and, maybe, too, from reveling in the dangerous worldly delights of that new house with its luxurious view of the ocean—by the heroic efforts of a stranger.

"Brother and Sister"[6] describes how Martha and Fred are spending a companionable day at home: Martha is ironing towels and Fred is reading and studying "postals" he's collected in a writing tablet. The phone rings: it's a nurse from the hospital letting them know that "a close relation" has taken a turn for the worse. Martha quickly makes a soothing custard, and she and Fred dash off to the hospital. Well, after all, what *were* the two of them doing having a cozy time at home while that relative was lingering, alone, in the hospital?

I don't mean to indulge in retrospective Catholic bashing here. I'm still on the fence about my childhood religion. One priest I talked to after my father's death labeled me a "skeptical Catholic." He's right. I think skeptical Catholicism is my denomination. Like millions of others, I have serious problems with the Church as an authoritarian institution and with its official views, to name a few, on abortion, women, gays and lesbians, and the proper way to handle the crimes committed by some of its own priests. I don't understand the existence of evil in the world, and I don't know what to think about the Bible stories or life after death. Though he didn't go to church often, my dad was more of a believer than my mother is: part of my literal-minded mother's torment since my father died derives from her difficulty in believing that there's anything beyond death. Also, there's a legacy of resentment toward the Church on my mother's side. When my grandmother Helen's first husband died, she was left a young widow with a baby. Grandma Helen went to the local parish priest for help. As the story goes, the priest looked at her and pointedly said, "You have two hands, don't you?" Thanks to that humanitarian, an unswerving, respectful awe of priests and nuns never prevailed in my family the way it did in the families of my childhood friends.

All these doubts aside, however, I still think of myself as a believer, sort of. I erratically pray—mostly "petitioning" prayers but sometimes simple prayers of thanksgiving. Occasionally I go to Mass. I cherish the mostly loving memories I have of my Catholic childhood. The nuns at St. Raphael's were the first teachers to encourage me as a reader and writer. I even made my first writing money there, cooking up a theme song for the school to the tune of "Downtown." At bottom, I have a slim but persistent faith—and for that, as well as for the progressive social gospel they preached—I'm indebted to the nuns and priests and neighborhood parents, most of them kind and intelligent, who shaped my childhood.[7]

Self-denial, generosity, acceptance in the wake of tragedy, the beauty of a life of service to others, even a sense of cosmic unworthiness: these core values that *The Brooklyn Catholic Speller* and so many of the other books I read in St. Raphael's pounded into me seem more and more attractive as this, our current Age of Entitlement, flourishes. The spiritual training, which is what my teachers at St. Raphael's would have called it, that I received in grammar school and that was diffused in the atmosphere of my neighborhood and family has unquestionably shaped my character, for better and worse. In person, at least, I'm uncomfortable promoting myself. Historically, whenever I've launched into a litany of my extraordinary qualifications for the job in question, I've heard my father's voice, rumbling one of his favorite axioms: "Self-praise is no recommendation."

The books of my Catholic girlhood have also influenced my adult reading tastes. I like books that don't call too much attention to their own cleverness, ones that aren't too pleased with themselves. I know I should give them yet another chance, but Great Books Untouchables such as Virginia Woolf and Henry James have always struck me as purring a bit too loudly over the beauty of their own sentence structure. The tone of a lot of academic literary theory repels me, given that it exudes a musky scent of superiority to the writing it purports to interpret. Many of the books I like at least assume a pose of shaky self-esteem.

But there's a flip side to all that breast-beating we Catholic kids of a certain vintage did in church and all the instruction in self-denial we underwent in school. We think we're better than other people. Down deep, maybe we still do.

As kids, we were taught to be the psychological equivalent of Navy SEALs—an elite parochial-school unit, drilled to take life's blows on the chin without wincing. Or to stand in the bitter winds of winter, coatless, without complaining. If we did feel pain, well, we were supposed to. After all, we Catholics—not the Jews and certainly not the baffling Protestants, who had broken away from the one true Church—really were God's "chosen people." Suffering was a test from God, a sign of His love. The Kennedy assassination, which took place when I was in third grade, made some kind of grim sense when seen through the lens of this theology of suffering popular among Catholics. On that terrible November day in 1963, America's first Catholic president also became the country's most visible secular martyr. Like everyone else old enough to remember, I retain sharp images of that day. Sister Mary William, my wonderful third-grade nun, was called outside our classroom and told the news. In shock, she broke into tears—which, in turn, upset the class. I remember her big white handkerchief and her rosary beads. After we were dismissed from school that day, my friends and I played listlessly on the street. My father came home from work that night and said something that shamed me. "He was a bum," my father said of Kennedy. My father might have said other, gentler things about Kennedy before or after this blasphemy, but I remember only those words, which, for years, I never repeated to anyone. In conversations we had much later, I learned that my father had never forgiven JFK's father, Joseph Kennedy, for being an enemy of Franklin Roosevelt and, to boot, against the U.S. entry into World War II.

Whatever else you might say about them, the Kennedy family, over and over again through subsequent tragedies, would conduct themselves stoically in public. I remember reading an interview years ago with Senator Ted Kennedy in which he recalled that one of the key family lessons he learned growing up was that "to whom much is given, much is asked." I'm sure that I, too, heard this phrase, or some variation of it, throughout grammar school—even though none of us at St. Raphael's were remotely in the Kennedys' league. But we were Catholics; we had been given the greatest gift of all—our faith. That made us and the Kennedys equals in the most crucial way.

Submitting to suffering silently and accepting blame without excuses, deservedly or not, made our souls stronger. Our school motto might well have been "When the going gets tough, the tough get going." It wasn't; we didn't have a motto. Instead, on top of the first page of every homework assignment we students submitted at St. Raphael's, we were required to draw a cross and, under it, the initials A.M.D.G. Translated from the Latin, those initials stood for the phrase "For the

Greater Honor and Glory of God." Imagine: every scrap of homework, no matter how inconsequential, dedicated to God. The great payoff of the Catholic popular theology of suffering in silence was the knowledge that Someone was always watching, keeping score. There was no need to complain or call attention to yourself or your trials or triumphs—God knew all about them already. To be a loudmouth was akin to being a Doubter. Squeaky wheels never got the grease at St. Raphael's Parochial School; they got admonitions from the nuns to put up and shut up, as well as, no doubt, private prayers for salvation.

I had no problem absorbing this lesson in popular theology. Indeed, it was a message preached to the public at large during the 1960s heyday of cinematic Catholicism when movies like *The Sound of Music, The Trouble with Angels,* and *Yours, Mine and Ours* affirmed a "zip your lip" program of self-abnegation. Popular films like these underscored the more potent gospel of self-denial I encountered in my parochial-school reading. I especially loved the autobiographies and novels about "Catholics under duress" and remembered their plots vividly, if not always accurately. And, though I've seen hardy traces of the unflinching "offer it up" attitude of these tales in contemporary Catholic fiction by Ron Hansen, Alice McDermott, Mary Gordon, and even America's Queen of Suspense, Mary Higgins Clark, the secular-martyr stories were a historically specific product of pre–Vatican II Catholicism. All but the most hard-line Catholic literature written after Vatican II displays a more humane attitude toward the souls being tested, a recognition that self-esteem (in small doses) can also be a virtue. For instance, in her 1978 masterpiece of updated martyrology, *Final Payments,* Mary Gordon charts the self-immolation of a beautiful young woman named Isabel Moore. Isabel has nursed her father through his long final illness. Now that he's gone, this good daughter finds herself tortured by guilt over an incident that happened decades earlier: Isabel's father, a longtime widower, showed interest in marrying his housekeeper, but the young Isabel contrived to break up that romance. In penance, Isabel now decides to care for the former housekeeper, becoming that bitter and infirm woman's domestic slave. In the course of her servitude, Isabel gains a lot of weight and cuts her gorgeous black hair, perming it into a dull frizz. But in a post–Vatican II deus ex machina, she is redeemed from her self-lacerations by the interventions of an enlightened priest, who restores her sense of self by reminding her that personal happiness and beauty are gifts from God. Had Gordon written that same story in the 1940s or '50s, Isabel probably would have gone on to run a Catholic rooming house for other friendless and unappreciative old ladies, waiting on them ceaselessly until her life of service (and all that extra weight) brought on an early death.

I've delighted in meeting up with vestiges of the popular pre–Vatican II Catholic theology of self-sacrifice in contemporary Catholic-inflected literature, but like many an avid adult reader, I wanted to make a pilgrimage back to the source—the source not only of this traditional Catholic sense of superiority through martyrdom but also the source of my own passion for reading. About ten years ago, I began to try to reread as many of the autobiographies and novels as I could from my early years at St. Raphael's. At an early point in this quest, I walked into a mega-bookstore that had just opened in downtown Washington and began to search for some of the autobiographies whose titles I remembered. No luck. I approached a clerk for help. He told me there was no separate section for autobiography. The autobiographies of literary figures, he said, were shelved in the literature section; all other autobiographies were shelved according to what their authors did. That system didn't help me much because, as I've noted, what the Catholics whose life stories I was searching for "did" was to suffer and sometimes die without complaining too much.

Remarkably, the children's section of my local public library still had a few of those decades-old out-of-print titles on its shelves. (The District of Columbia public library system is as underfunded as St. Raphael's was during my time there, when we were studying the ancient *Brooklyn Catholic Speller*. The librarians at my local D.C. branch are always too grateful when I walk in laden with shopping bags full of cast-off review copies.) In recent years, via the Internet, I've located little reprint houses that had still more of these secular saint stories on their lists. That's how I've enjoyed the great luxury of revisiting parts of the literary world of my Catholic girlhood. And what I found in those memoirs and novels was the presence of something grander than a simple spirit of submission. If, as the Gospels tell us, "the first shall be last and the last shall be first," the authors of those uplifting Catholic sagas—and, in particular, the autobiographies—must have decided that they weren't going to wait for the next life to be recognized. Their tales of forbearance provided them the excuse to elbow to the head of the line and shout out that most Luciferian of profanities: "Pay attention to *me*!"

That same semi-sacrilegious homily—one that suggested that good Catholics could not only get to heaven but also get even in this life—wafted through the plots of the novels I unearthed and reread. Over and over again, key (Catholic) characters come out on top in their stories precisely through pious renunciation, while their more grabby comrades are consumed by thwarted ambitions, envy, and a sinking realization of their own second-rate destinies. Of course, most martyr stories—sacred and profane—contain an element of superiority. The self-denying hero or heroine is "rewarded," at the very least, by capturing the admiring focus of the narrative, while everyone else recedes into the background. Think of Sydney Carton, the guillotined martyr who gets to deliver the stirring closing words of Charles Dickens's *A Tale of Two Cities:* "It is a far, far better thing that I do, than I have ever done; it is a far, far better rest that I go to, than I have ever known."[8] Unlike the Catholic martyrs of autobiography and fiction, however, most non-Catholic martyrs like Carton need to sacrifice themselves to prove that they're as good as the other characters. Catholic martyrs already know that they're better than their peers; their sacrifice is evidence of their spiritual supremacy, and their stories confirm their mystical sense of election.

As I reread these Catholic autobiographies and novels, their odd pridefulness became clearer to me. Much of the Catholic juvenilia I so dearly remembered preached a cover story of self-denial along with a covert sermon about the spiritual and worldly superiority that would result from this self-denial. Writhe and shine.

Was I aware of this devout double-talk as a child reader? I'd like to claim premature powers of critical perspicacity, but who knows? It's impossible to figure out just how literature influences young people, what messages they pick up or retain. I know that the lessons of the Catholic juvenile fiction and nonfiction I read meshed nicely with my shy personality and reinforced the "don't get a swelled head" gospel that prevailed at home and in the neighborhood. I also sense that their pious

egotism has something in common with my own. As a book critic for
Fresh Air, I enjoy a certain amount of celebrity. As a college professor, I
get to stand up in front of my classes and show off what I know. But in
both cases, I'm shining my light in service to Literature, much as those
exhibitionist secular saints served God and Family. (Plus, there's a curious and fitting self-effacement involved in being a "radio celebrity,"
since listeners don't see your face.) This early reading diet of mine fed
the desire for distinction that, I guess, is nascent in most children; it
also cautioned against making a spectacle of oneself, towering too tall
amongst one's peers, being different. Wanting to stand apart and wanting to fit in—the contradictory impulses that have pushed and pulled
my life—have their literary source in the books I read in parochial
school.

Upon rereading these stories as an adult, I wasn't at all surprised to
find that the meek and pious prevailed; maybe I half remembered that
the plots turned out that way. And, certainly, as I've acknowledged, the
message that we Catholics were better than the non-Catholics around us
was so fundamental to our culture that it barely needed to be articu-
lated. Indeed, a nonverbal memory comes to mind when I try to recall
whether I would have realized that, through these ostensibly humble
martyr stories, I was learning how to become a top dog here on earth
and, eventually, in the hereafter. The image I see is Sunday Mass at St.
Raphael's Church. We knelt longer at Mass way back when I was young,
especially at the pre–Vatican II Latin Masses, and I can still see the arro-
gant set to certain parishioners' backs as they knelt stiffly on Sundays.
That oh-so-correct posture had to have been a strain, but worth the
pain. It was a public display intended to be seen by God as well as by the
rest of the congregation—especially by those weaker worshippers who
rested their rears on the pews for support. Those straight-spined parishioners could justify their exhibitionism by telling themselves that they
were setting an example, even educating the rest of us. That's certainly
the justification that, particularly, the writers of the autobiographies I
read in parochial school offered for their own immodest literary self-
display. So, as a child, did I see the contradictions inherent in the way
these authors flaunted their martyrdom to magnanimously provide spiritual models for the rest of us? I'm guessing, but I think that kind of

behavior, both in books and in life, used to be as familiar to me as, once upon a time, Horn & Hardart fish cakes and macaroni were for Friday-night supper.

The Catholic literature of my childhood is fascinating to me *not* because it encourages obvious connections to contemporary literature or social attitudes but precisely because it doesn't. Sometimes we read books to escape the confines of the familiar, the here and now. Reread-ing these autobiographies and novels, I've felt as though I were reenter-ing a world I once lived in but whose beliefs and cultural assumptions are now radically "other." I don't think you have to be Catholic to enjoy delving into these books (any more than I've had to be Jewish to enjoy Philip Roth's novels, or Protestant to "get" John Updike). The lost world these books both create and invoke is so vivid, any curious reader can enter and be swept away.

I thought Karen Killilea had died. Somewhere toward the end of the second of the two memoirs that her mother, Marie Killilea, wrote about her, I had a memory of Karen, like Beth in *Little Women,* breathing out a final sigh, closing her eyes, and giving up the ghost. After all, Karen, like Beth, was depicted in her story as a Victorian angel in the house, a self-less spirit whose brief time on earth would be spent showing others, par-ticularly those lesser beings who blatantly *wanted* material comforts and success (think Jo and Amy), the right way to live. Angels in the house always die in the books they preside over because early ascension into heaven is their reward—and because their goodness makes them boring. Their creators have difficulty sustaining such static characters through-out the entire length of a book. But memory played a trick on me: Karen didn't die. One of the bonuses of revisiting dearly remembered childhood literature is that we learn anew how faulty our recollections really are, and, in this particular case, how fictional plots can superim-pose themselves on those memories. Karen Killilea, after all, was a real person. And like many other celebrated lives, hers refused to conform to neat societal or novelistic expectations.

Karen's exceptional life was the subject of two bestselling memoirs written in the 1950s: *Karen* and *With Love from Karen.* For decades these memoirs were required elementary and high school reading for both parochial- and public-school kids. Together they traced the life of the ever-expanding Irish Catholic Killilea family from the 1940s into the mid-'50s. The originating cause of the first book was the birth, in 1940, of Marie and Jimmy Killilea's second daughter, Karen, three months premature, weighing under two pounds, and given little chance of survival by the attending doctors. When she was close to one year old, Karen was diagnosed with cerebral palsy. The Karen books are now out of print (although a special Thirtieth Anniversary Edition of *With Love from Karen* was published in 1983, attesting to its importance). The books, however, still grace the shelves of libraries and used-book stores, and they hold up as a devastating historical record of the widespread medical and popular attitude toward severely handicapped children in mid-twentieth-century America.[9]

They also hold up as a record of the particular kind of spiritual extreme-adventure tale that we Catholic-school students were required to read. Along with swashbucklers by Robert Louis Stevenson and A.E.W. Mason (author of *The Four Feathers*), we were nourished on a steady diet of secular-martyr fiction, in which ordinary men and women, boys and girls, found their faith—and, often, their emotional and physical fortitude—tested. The intriguing and exhilarating thing about these spiritual extreme-adventure tales was that they routinely featured women in the primary role. Indeed, aside from the Nancy Drew series, the secular-martyr stories were among the few books, fiction or nonfiction, that I can remember reading from grammar school that featured women as heroines. After all, women were just as capable as men of suffering through dark nights of the soul—no muscles were required. As the Karen books illustrate, however, female martyrs often cloaked their remarkable acts of faith and courage in a mantle of ladylike humility—even as they gloried in doing ferocious battle with the sacred and profane forces of the patriarchy. Reading the Karen books as a young girl, I think I internalized some lessons about being simultaneously devout and determined, pious and self-promoting.

Karen Killilea's life, as described by her mother, is the kind of story all readers love: a true story of ordinary people who are thrown into extraordinary circumstances and who persevere and triumph against all odds. When baby Karen was diagnosed with cerebral palsy, many of the top doctors in New York City and around the country whom her panicked parents consulted predicted that she would never live beyond childhood. Other medical experts decreed that she was retarded, that she should be institutionalized and forgotten.

But the Killileas desperately push on in their search to find hope for their baby daughter. Finally, when Karen is three and a half, Marie reads in the local evening paper that "Dr. B, cerebral palsy specialist,"[10] will be visiting their local hospital the next day. She boldly places a person-to-person call to the doctor's home late that night and insists that he squeeze Karen into his already overcrowded clinic schedule. When the sleepy doctor demurs, Marie tells her readers,

> I wasn't going to let this chance slip away. I forgot all Mother's teaching and my convent training. I took a grip on the phone and boldly and frantically I said: "Doctor, doesn't your train come into Pennsylvania Station?"
>
> "Yes, it does."
>
> "Doctor, I believe you're our last hope. I feel that if you say our case is hopeless, we must accept the verdict. But, I also feel that if you saw Karen you would not say so."
>
> "But—"
>
> I interrupted him and went on. "If you'll tell me what time your train gets into Penn Station, I'll get a redcap to take Karen into the baggage room. If you'll just look at her for five minutes, that's all I ask."
>
> "But—"
>
> Again I interrupted. "Oh, Doctor, please. Just to tell me—shall we keep on looking or is it hopeless. Is it as they say?"
>
> There was a long pause. A life hung suspended in the silence, to be saved or shattered by his reply. "Dear God, make him say yes!"
>
> "Very well, Mrs. Killilea"—his voice was sweet—"bring her to the clinic tomorrow and we'll see if we can't fit her in."[11]

The next day, Dr. B, who turns out to be a decent man, gives Marie the verdict she's been dreaming of through all those long, agonizing years: he tells her that Karen will need a lot of help but that she's mentally fit and capable of learning to sit up, use her hands, and walk. For the remaining 250 pages of *Karen,* Marie provides a chronicle of the Killileas' formidable physical-therapy routine with Karen, as well as their role in helping to found the United Cerebral Palsy Association in 1948.

Adding to the appeal of *Karen* and its sequel are the ofttimes black-comic travails of the Killilea family (which, by the end of *Karen,* includes not only Karen herself, Marie and Jimmy, and older daughter Marie, but baby Rory and daughter Gloria, who was adopted as a teenager). But what really distinguishes *Karen* as a secular-saint story with a profane attitude is Marie's fed-up narrative voice. I don't want to take away from the personhood of the Killileas or their very real and inspiring struggles. So I'm not trying to diminish the Karen books or their subjects by suggesting that, in those memoirs, Marie zealously records the suffering of two martyrs, not one.

Marie Killilea, like so many other mothers of seriously ill or handicapped children, lives out a particularly tortured version of the traditional female extreme adventure. As she chronicles in the Karen books, Marie wears herself out, physically and emotionally, in the quest to give her daughter a shot at life—initially, by finding competent medical care, and later through daily physical-therapy sessions and judicious applications of tough love to make sure that the maturing Karen doesn't fall into the abyss of self-pity. Karen's father, Jimmy, is a partner in this mission, but since he works "outside the home," as we would say these days, he's just not around that much. Of course, Marie works hard, too, but her work doesn't come close to the utopian ideal concocted by socialist dreamer William Morris or feminist detective-fiction writers Sara Paretsky and Lisa Scottoline. Instead, the grueling demands of Marie's role as mother to a handicapped child fit the traditional, prefeminist, and very Catholic idea of work as service to others. Her work doesn't sustain her mentally or financially. Rather, it's the work of writing the Karen books that fulfills those seditious functions.

No wonder the nuns were so enthusiastic about the books. "Write on, sister!" some of them might well have whispered to Marie in their heart of hearts. For in their revision of the patriarchal spiritual script whereby good women simply serve and submit, Marie's memoirs are as cagey as any of those nineteenth-century protofeminist challenges to Milton's *Paradise Lost* that Sandra Gilbert and Susan Gubar excavated in *The Madwoman in the Attic*. Like Emily Dickinson's poems, Marie Killilea's Karen books appear on the outside to be ladylike literary vessels—yet they are vessels that barely contain their witches' brew of potent female ambition and rebellion. No, I don't think that, like Dickinson, Marie Killilea is consciously subversive in her writing—not all the time. I do think, though, that even at her most innocent, she was exhausted and angry, particularly infuriated with all those sanctimonious male authority figures, the doctors and priests, who made pompous pronouncements about Karen and the other members of her family. That righteous fury—always, ostensibly, on behalf of others, of course—finds its outlet in her writing.

The Karen books, functioning as they so powerfully do as testaments to the Killileas' faith, also were a sanctioned way for Marie to bask in the spotlight through being of spiritual service to her readers. It's a weird coincidence, by the way, that soon after the Killileas move to a new house in Larchmont, New York, at the beginning of *With Love from Karen*, their new next-door neighbors turn out to be Walter and Jean Kerr—he the famous *New York Times* drama critic and she the author of that family classic *Please Don't Eat the Daisies*. The Kerrs, like the Killileas, were also Catholic, and Jean's bestseller, though it's much lighter in tone and subject than Marie's memoirs, also takes advantage of the opportunity to write about a big, energy-sucking family as a way of drawing attention to a mother's labors, self-sacrifice, and know-how. What were the odds of two Catholic author-mothers, living side by side, tending their brood by day and brooding over their subversive pages by night?

What really distinguishes the Karen books from their literary neighbor, however, is their recognition of the very real existence of evil—a recognition that's one of the enduring strengths of the two memoirs. Karen's cerebral palsy is a heavy cross to bear, a tragedy that the Killileas' mid-twentieth-century Catholicism interprets as a sign of God's greater love for Karen. Marie chronicles the family's struggles not just to win independence for the handicapped Karen but also to win Karen's soul

for God by arming her against the satanic siren calls of bitterness and
self-pity. In an electrifying scene toward the end of *Karen,* Marie recalls
her first confrontation, verbal and physical, with the demons that lie in
wait for her young daughter. Karen and her friends are playing "doctor"
in the nursery, and Marie momentarily leaves the room to answer the
telephone. As she returns, she overhears Karen demanding that one of
her playmates fetch something for her:

> I didn't at all like her tone. As I walked into the room she said in a
> tone of revolting complacency, "You have to do it for me—I'm
> crippled."
> Mama struck.
> Maybe it was good. Maybe it was bad. I still don't know. But the
> action was a simple reflex. Eight years old and capitalizing on her
> handicap! I knew from harsh personal experience the abundant
> misery that stems from such a trick and I reacted as I would if I saw
> a black-widow spider crawling toward her—I'd crush it instantly.[12]

You could imagine how that scene would play itself out today. Mom
would remove her wayward child from the room for a "time-out" and
lots of talk. But as rock-'em-sock-'em Marie endearingly admits, who
knows what the best approach is? *Slap!* When a Catholic bishop administers the sacrament of confirmation to adolescent boys and girls, he
slaps them on the cheek, signifying that they have become soldiers for
Christ. *Slap!* When Marie delivered that blow to Karen, she was knock-
ing into her small daughter not only some sense but also a sense of
spiritual duty. The hands-on approach apparently succeeds: at the very
beginning of *With Love from Karen,* Marie writes, with relief, that despite the then-twelve-year-old Karen's many physical and emotional torments, "she never complained. A large statement—of a large truth."[13]

Not complaining is a redeeming virtue in the world of the Karen
books, as it was in the Catholic world of my childhood. "Ask not what
your country can do for you," declaimed our nation's first Catholic president, "but what you can do for your country." JFK's famous words were
of a piece with the gospel of self-abnegation I would hear throughout
my Catholic schooldays. The burdens that Marie and her family endure

throughout the time span of the two memoirs range from the calamitous to the traumatic. So, what's a good but overburdened Catholic mother to do if she can't complain to her family and friends? One answer is to start writing memoirs.

Marie always stresses the altruistic motives behind her autobiographical self-advertisement. In the foreword to *With Love from Karen,* she notes that the Killileas had received nearly thirty thousand letters thus far in response to *Karen.* Thus, she was called upon to write this sequel out of a sense of duty. Marie's two-volume marathon litany of the Killilea family's trials would be burdensome reading were it not, as I've said, for her unusual narrative voice. As a martyr, Marie is wry rather than whiney, fuming rather than always forbearing. Here is a very partial list of the Job-like afflictions the Killileas weather through the course of the books: fourteen bouts of pneumonia endured by daughters Gloria and Marie; daughter Marie's episodes of rheumatic fever and TB; Jimmy's severe hearing loss; a persistent money shortage; Marie's near-fatal allergic reaction to some sleep medication; and Marie's chronic miscarriages and "secondary" infertility. (She and husband Jimmy have been trying for seven years to have a fourth child. Altogether, Marie tells us in *With Love from Karen,* she's been pregnant eleven times.) Karen's sufferings, which are the raison d'être of the books, include a series of tonsillitis attacks and ear infections, pressure sores from ill-fitting braces, excruciating muscle spasms, sleeplessness, two dislocated hips, hours of repetitive physical therapy every day, and unremitting thirst (her water intake eventually needs to be restricted to alleviate her spasticity).

When the subject is the Killilea family's troubles, Marie is unapologetic about demanding not only her readers' attention but also God's. After all, God, in the language and theology of pre–Vatican II Catholicism, is figured as male, and men, throughout the Karen books, tend to be a lot less focused than their female compatriots.

Again, there's a proper Catholic cover story that cloaks Marie's paeans to female drive and competence, as well as her own frequent exasperation with male ineptitude. The flip side of the Catholic Church's misogyny is its Mariolatry: the veneration of the Virgin Mary and, by extension, the idealization of all good Catholic women (particularly mothers) whose job it is to civilize and spiritualize their wayward men-

folk. Marie is no ur–Betty Friedan: she doesn't voice any explicit challenges to the patriarchy, spiritual or secular. The vision of women her
books offer is somewhat empowering; but it's also essentialist and, therefore, inadequate. There's a subtext of grudging female strength that
underlies the Karen books—a subtext whose theme could be summed
up in the slogan "If you want the job done right, especially if it's a dirty
job, call in a woman." Like Joan of Arc, Marie upholds the status quo,
but armored and angry, she also clearly relishes doing battle with those
male authorities who get in her way.

That nervy phone call to Dr. B is fun to read, not only because it
marks the happy turning point in Karen's young life but also because
Marie is acting like a tough broad and is obviously proud of herself
for doing so. What makes the scene even more peculiar in terms of
proper gender-role stereotyping is that Marie is wrestling with Dr. B all
by herself. Husband Jimmy is flat on the mat, supine. A week earlier,
he'd been rushed to the hospital with a ruptured appendix. His recovery,
Marie tells her readers, was "unusually slow."[14] You get the sense that
Marie thinks she herself would have been up and vacuuming again an
hour after being stitched up. Her exasperation with Jimmy's sluggish-
ness becomes even more smilingly acid a page later when she recalls: "It
was only a week before Christmas and we were involved in the welter of
preparation peculiar to families with children. We were hoping that
Jimmy would be home before Christmas, but the only thing we could
count on him for was expert direction in the concoction of egg-nogs,
from a horizontal position on the couch."[15]

As the crucial moment of Karen's examination and Dr. B's pronouncement approaches, Jimmy's absence—along with Marie's super-
woman self-reliance—is (always regretfully) underscored. To get to the
appointment, Marie drives Karen through a dangerous sleet storm in a
borrowed car with malfunctioning windshield wipers. "All nature," she
harrumphs, "appeared involved in a gigantic conspiracy to make my trip
as unpleasant and hazardous as possible."[16] As she gamely steers the car
through the ice, Marie prays and ruminates on the missing Jimmy, presumably safe and snug in his hospital bed. In the Karen books, Jimmy
emerges as a good husband and father who, like the rest of the family,
exhausts himself in the colossal effort to help Karen become as indepen-

dent as possible. But he's a male, so he's weaker in spirit and even in flesh than the women of the family.

Blessings have to be earned the hard way. That's a belief affirmed again and again by the Karen books. Of course, their historical context has a lot to do with their worldview: Marie Killilea would have been a young adult during the Depression, and *Karen* opens just before World War II. But, the books' message that blessings have to be worked for—as well as the complementary belief that any gratuitous good fortune will have to be paid for—is familiar folk Catholicism. "This is too easy; something bad has to happen," sighed my friend Mary Ellen during a phone conversation a few years ago in which she was telling me about a great job offer that had just appeared out of nowhere. "Yeesh, you sound so Catholic," I replied, and we laughed, knowing we both had a fear of falling into premature (i.e., preheavenly) contentment that parochial school had implanted deep in our young psyches. Certainly other cultures, religious and ethnic, have their superstitions about luck and happiness. For Catholics, however, there's an atavistic worry that the good life will diabolically soften one's soul. The theological term for the Catholic Church on earth, after all, is "the Church Militant." Catholics are always supposed to keep themselves in fighting trim, and there's no better way to tone the abs and biceps of muscular Christianity than through suffering. I said that we schoolkids at St. Raphael's were trained to be the psychological equivalent of Navy SEALs. If that claim is anywhere close to the truth, then Catholics like the Killileas were our drill instructors.

None of the Killileas can let their guard down even for a second: when they do succumb to the temptation to relax, disaster strikes! This narrative/theological pattern is so endemic to the memoirs that it almost functions as comic relief: after a while, we readers just know that if anyone is having a good time, there'll soon be hell to pay. Early in *Karen,* Jimmy and Marie run away from the kids for a few hours to go to a baseball game and then on to a cocktail party. They return to find steam pouring from their house and the children, babysitter, and assorted pets out on the street, crying. It turns out that Marie forgot to turn off the ancient gas water heater and the pipes exploded, stripping linoleum from the floors and veneer from the furniture. A few days later, as Marie is still contemplating the soggy wreck of her home, a package arrives from Laurette Taylor, the star of *The Glass Menagerie,* then on Broadway. Inside is a glass unicorn for Karen. Marie comments: "Whenever we had a crisis, and they seemed to occur with satanic regularity, it was inevitably followed by some such nice pick-me-up."[17]

Which is then inevitably followed by an even bigger knock-me-down. Toward the end of *Karen,* Marie takes the children to the doctor for their regular checkups. Everyone, for once, is fine, so Marie decides that she and Jimmy should go to a movie and dinner to celebrate. Uh-oh. They drive off from the house "feeling young and carefree" and "splurged and ordered cocktails and then spaghetti with red wine." We "came home," she concludes, "feeling . . . quite buoyed up as one is apt to be by unwarranted extravagance."[18] By now, the hardened reader can hardly breathe in anticipation of the Big Cosmic Bill that surely must come due soon. Sure enough, it arrives two days later, when daughter Marie shows her mother the lump on her arm where the family doctor had administered a tuberculosis test.

Shortly after *With Love from Karen* opens, the Killileas move into their new home, a shambling turn-of-the-century handyman's special by the Long Island Sound. It's Christmastime, and adult daughter Gloria gives her parents the lavish gift of theater tickets and weekend reservations at a hotel in New York. Off Marie and Jimmy go to enjoy their rare escape, only to find, upon returning, that the family's beloved Irish setter, Shanty, has been dognapped. (Shanty eventually turns up at the house days later, wounded and starved, having escaped his captors.)

Then there's that ill-fated Labor Day weekend trip. The entire family piles into the station wagon for a gay time at a distant country fair; at the fair, a hurricane whips up out of nowhere, and on the perilous ride home, they narrowly avoid a head-on collision with a drunk driver. Or, consider the consequences of a working-weekend getaway Marie and Jimmy enjoy in Providence, Rhode Island. Marie delivers a lecture on cerebral palsy on Saturday night; Sunday morning, while attending Mass, she experiences a "familiar and most distressing sensation—at once physical and mental; . . . a heavy weightiness in my chest that had no confines, simultaneously with a sense that was a *knowing* of coming disaster."[19] A freak blizzard turns the usual five-hour drive home into a sixteen-hour ordeal. When the couple stumble into the house and open the closed door of Karen's room, they find Karen comatose from the leaking fumes of her bedroom's separate coal-gas heating unit.

Enough already. The sermon that man (and woman) was made by God not to loll about in Edenic comfort but rather to soldier on with head held high is woven into the basic plots of the Karen books—just as it was a staple of my own childhood training, secular and religious.

> *Good better best*
> *Never let it rest*
> *Until your good is better*
> *And your better best.*

The nuns at St. Raphael's often incanted that jingle as they surveyed sloppy penmanship, slouchy postures, poor pronunciation. The concept of "self-esteem" would become big in primary schools and in children's television programming during the following decade; but at St. Raphael's Parochial School in the sixties, self-esteem (a word no one there would have ever been tempted to use, since it sounded too synonymous with the Luciferian sin of "pride") came from being of service to God, without complaint.

But the internal pressure generated by this command to always maintain a stiff upper lip had to be vented somehow. Maybe that's why, in *With Love from Karen,* Marie begins firing off a gun.

In that memoir, Marie proudly announces to her readers that for Mother's Day one year, "the family gave me a Smith and Wesson 22."[20] Huh? Marie became interested in target shooting when her son-in-law tried to teach the sport to Karen, whose ears turned out to be too sensitive to stand the sound of the shots. Target shooting becomes a prime activity when Marie is confined to bed rest during her much-longed-for pregnancy with daughter Kristen, toward the end of the book. During those weeks in bed, Marie says, she meditated and read detective stories, as well as lots of books by now moldy Catholic authors like Cardinal Newman, Ronald Knox, and Wilfred Sheed. She also shoots at some suggestive targets. Jimmy buys his wife an air pistol and sets up a target right "under the altar on my mantel. . . . On good days I would fire for several hours."[21] Some pages later, Marie recalls how she and Jimmy, restless for activity one night, "dry fire" her pistol at her bookcase.

Under the altar? And the bookcase? The very one that contains those volumes of canonical Catholic literature? If the Karen books were works of fiction rather than memoirs (and I know that current literary theory tells us there's little real difference between the genres), I'd feel freer to say that Marie was taking aim at the Church—particularly its repressive, restrictive attitudes toward women—attitudes that have turned the bedridden Marie into a mother/martyr who's now become more immobile than her handicapped daughter. Given the avowed depth and sincerity of her faith, however, I think it's enough to marvel at Marie's aggressive choice of a hobby and how it helps her "pop off" in an acceptable way. I don't think Marie's choice of targets is her covert way of saying "*Non serviam*"; the Karen books themselves trumpet that message, loud and clear.

"*Non serviam*" not to God, or to Marie's particular vocation as a wife and mother, but to the overarching Catholic mind-set of "just accept." The Karen books are defiant because, even while they traditionally affirm that Karen's disability is a mark of her divine election, they also chronicle the Killileas' monumental effort to amend this heavenly gift. Like those of us Catholic schoolkids who blasphemously prayed that the finger of God would skip over us and tap our neighbor's shoulder to summon him or her to be a priest or a nun, the Killileas—and Marie, above all—resist what conventional Catholic wisdom told them was God's plan for their daughter. Just before setting out alone on that life-altering visit to Dr. B in *Karen,* Marie confides to her readers: "I didn't want anyone to know about this trip since, with the exception of our mothers, there was a pretty general opinion that we had carried this searching business a bit too far. Certainly beyond the realm of good sense. 'You must learn to accept and stop fighting this thing,' was the usual advice."[22]

Of course it would have been. Meekness, humility, and above all, acceptance are still cardinal Catholic virtues. But the cry of rebellion shrieks through the Karen books as the fighting Killileas ceaselessly prevail, together and individually, against what seems to be foreordained. Marie delights in her clan's give-'em-hell spirit and especially revels in her own grit and shanty-Irish gift for back talk. So, how did two such sassy, seditious, even protofeminist memoirs wind up on the required-reading list for generations of Catholic schoolkids? Once again, that memory of upright parishioners ostentatiously kneeling at Sunday Mass comes to mind. Marie kneels so ramrod straight all throughout her memoirs, it's easy to miss the glint in her eye.

I loved the Karen books when I was a kid, and I still love them today. I hope, while talking about them, I haven't sounded condescending. That's a danger in reviewing and teaching literature for a living: you can develop a kind of knee-jerk superiority to the material you're "decoding." If that literary material is Catholic, there's an even greater temptation to patronize it. In the academy these days, any "exotic" religion (that includes Judaism) is talked about in respectful-of-difference tones, but the gibes fly fast and loose whenever Catholicism is mentioned. Catholicism is different enough to be vaguely irritating but not so different as to evoke serious anthropological respect.

When I've laughed at aspects of the Karen books here, I've felt as though I'm sharing an inside joke. The assumptions and codes of behavior of the Killileas' pre–Vatican II Catholic world are utterly familiar to me. I may not live in that world anymore, but then, I couldn't; it no longer exists. Almost everyone who rates a mention in the Karen books is Catholic. In *With Love from Karen,* even her doctors at Temple University Hospital in Philadelphia kindly advise the visiting Killileas on the local Mass schedule. That self-confident, cohesive Catholic community is the one I lovingly remember from childhood. It was broken up, undoubtedly for the better, by the changes wrought by Pope John XXIII, as well as by feminism, the civil rights movement, and the other social revolutions of the 1960s, and also by an increasingly profane and powerful mass culture, by urban migration, and by dozens of other factors that I'm not taking into account.

Nevertheless, I miss that world from the safe distance of memory. I wonder about the Killileas' lives beyond the Karen books. How did they ride out the upheavals of the coming decades? Did Gloria and her divorced beau, Russ, like Newland Archer pining for Madame Olenska in Edith Wharton's *The Age of Innocence,* later regret all those years of their youth spent petitioning Rome for an annulment of Russ's first marriage when, these days, hardly anyone would care and they could probably find some progressive priest willing to marry them out on a beach somewhere without the papal seal of approval? What of that devout young man named Joe who was always hanging around the house in *With Love from Karen*? He liked fashion and was always available to escort daughter Marie to dances but never seemed romantically interested in her or any other girl. Surely he must have been in the closet, maybe even to himself. Did he come out? Leave the Church? Join the priesthood and/or sleep with men (or, God forbid, altar boys)? Or repress, repress, repress? And what about Karen? In the 1983 preface to the Thirtieth Anniversary Edition of *With Love from Karen,* Marie tells readers that Karen had become a secretary to "one of the busiest priests in the world"[23] and sat on the board of the Cardinal Hayes Home for Children in the Bronx. Is she still there?

I could satisfy some of my curiosity via the Internet, but I won't. Just as I often wonder, but don't really want to know, about the adult lives of my classmates from St. Raphael's who gradually disappeared from the old neighborhood after eighth-grade graduation. The Karen books, as they stand, mean too much to me as literary traces of the lost culture of my own childhood. I don't want their stories updated. Better to reread and enjoy them in their 1950s "uncolorized" version. Just as I suspect it's better for me to remember my classmates as it felt to be standing with them on that long-ago autumn day, all of us in our prelapsarian states, excitedly waiting for the pope.

*T*raditional female secular martyrs were shrouded in a double bind of ladylike meekness and Catholic humility—a double bind that Houdini-esqe narrators like Marie Killilea managed to elude as she proudly, yet piously, recounted the spiritual extreme adventures that constitute the Karen books. For male secular martyrs, there was more leeway allowed in terms of boasting of their trials in prose. After all, men in the Church were supposed to show off more. While the nuns of my childhood were always swathed in black from head to toe, the parish priests slipped out of their black suits on Sunday and donned beautiful vestments whose bright colors, keyed to the liturgical calendar, would have pleased a peacock. A glance at the work of one of the most widely read secular male martyrs of the 1950s and '60s illustrates how masochism and machismo went hand in hand in God's service.

"Through my fault, through my fault, through my most grievous fault." Before the changes of Vatican II, that's what we Catholics used to chant midway through the Mass as we beat our fists against our hearts. Like those ostentatious kneeling displays at Sunday Mass, energetic breast-beatings were once an even more explicit way for parishioners to signal simultaneously their piety and their preeminence. "Through my fault—*thump,* through my fault—*thump*—through my most griev-ous fault—*thump.*" That's the sound I hear when I think of Dr. Tom Dooley and his three enormously popular memoirs, *Deliver Us from Evil* (1956), *The Edge of Tomorrow* (1958), and *The Night They Burned the Mountain* (1960).

Dooley was an Irish American Catholic Navy doctor who set up field hospitals in Vietnam and Laos during the 1950s. He was also a central figure in the formation of MEDICO, a humanitarian aid organization that was later folded into CARE. After a few brief and intensely frenetic years spent establishing clinics and tending to the sick and the victims of war in Southeast Asia, Dooley died young, at age thirty-four, from malignant melanoma. In my grammar-school mind, Dooley was con-flated with the youngest of our three parish priests, Father O'Hagan, who was also Irish, handsome, and energetic—what we Catholic girls would learn to call in high school "a real Father What-a-Waste." The good-looking Dooley wasn't a priest, but he seemed to be fiercely celi-bate, devoting all of his time to tending the sick, accompanied only by the young American, Laotian, and Vietnamese men he trained as aides. A jaded contemporary reader will suspect that something more than bandage rolling might have been going on between Dooley and "his boys." Sure enough, according to a well-received 1997 biography of Dooley by James T. Fisher called *Dr. America: The Lives of Thomas A. Dooley, 1927–1961,*[24] Dooley was "out" to homosexual circles in the United States and Southeast Asia. Shortly after his bestseller *Deliver Us from Evil* was published, the Navy, acting on information gleaned from months of investigation of Dooley's private life, quietly booted him out with a dis-honorable discharge. Undaunted, Dooley fabricated a cover story that he resigned from the Navy in order to carry out his maverick humanitarian work without the interference of military bureaucracy.

Nor are those the most dramatic of the revelations concerning Dooley. According to Fisher, the CIA was onto Dooley's potential as a propaganda machine very early. The required "situation reports" Dooley filed as a medical officer in Vietnam were, in contrast to the cut-and-dried language of his colleagues, both melodramatic and fervently patriotic. The top brass suggested that Dooley shape his reports into a book that would help garner public support for Operation Passage to Freedom— the moving of hundreds of thousands of North Vietnamese refugees to the South, ostensibly to protect them from the Communists and, coincidentally, to create a constituency for the newly reinstalled South Vietnamese president Ngo Dinh Diem. Ngo was a Catholic, and so were many of the refugees fleeing North Vietnam. Later, in Laos, Dooley would perform an even more hands-on mission for the CIA, smuggling weapons into the country along with his pharmaceutical supplies and surgical gear.

But that's not all Dooley was. Even in Fisher's revisionist biography, Dooley registers as a very religious young man and a hardworking doctor who really did heal people and save lives. If only human identity weren't so messy, we could crack the riddle of moral enigmas like Dooley as easily and as glibly as I sometimes "solve" Gatsby or Madame Bovary in class for my students.

In light of Fisher's later revelations, this is going to sound self-congratulatory, but it's nonetheless true that, while I admired the Dooley I met in the memoirs we students were required to read, I didn't feel comfortable with him—certainly not the way I felt with Marie Killilea and her family. Had I known about Jonathan Edwards when I was at St. Raphael's, I think I would have compared Dooley to the great Puritan sermon writer. In print, both men have an icy, disdainful quality about them that alternates with a wrathful temper. In a 1961 memorial volume entitled *Before I Sleep . . . The Last Days of Dr. Tom Dooley,* many of Dooley's friends reluctantly acknowledge his overbearing arrogance that rubbed lots of people the wrong way. As holy men go, Dooley is more in the Saint Paul or Archangel Michael mode, rather than that of the kindly Saint Francis. He demonstrates a charming, self-deprecating sense of humor throughout the memoirs, but he never lets his readers forget that these lighter moments are but short respites from his Important Work.

Throughout the late 1950s into the 1960s, every self-respecting Catholic read Dooley's books or their excerpts in *Reader's Digest;* like the Killileas, Dooley was a secular saint, a practicing Catholic who suffered in silence an extreme adventure of the body and spirit. The fact that Dooley's torment took place in the public and traditionally masculine extreme-adventure arena of war, rather than in the private and feminine domain of the home, like the Killileas' saga did, makes Dooley sound tougher, more swaggering. But the crucial difference between Dooley and the Killileas was that he *chose* to climb up on his cross; the Killileas had martyrdom thrust upon them. His martyrly volunteerism accounts, I think, for the condescending tone he often adopts toward us, his readers. The very fact that we're reading his books, rather than living his life, confirms that that's what we are—passive readers, not "doers" like Dooley.

If Dooley could forsake all the luxuries of his American life and go off to Southeast Asia where torments of biblical proportion (war, fire, disease, starvation) awaited him, how could we, the chairbound, dare complain about anything—least of all Dooley's disdain for us? For me, reading Dooley the second time around was like making a dimly remembered act of penance. As the pages turned, I felt worse and worse about my own timid sense of faith, my ever-present longing to curl up with a good book. Bless me, Father, for I have sinned. But Dooley was a doctor, not a priest; maybe that's why he never administers absolution to his readers.

Dooley's final memoir, *The Night They Burned the Mountain,* is the one I remembered best from childhood. That's not surprising, because it's the most flagrant in its Catholic commingling of self-renunciation and self-display. In that book, Dooley describes his discovery of the malignant melanoma that would speedily claim his life. The memoir opens in August 1959 just as Dooley has been mysteriously summoned back to the United States from Laos because, as we later learn, his medical superiors have just done a biopsy of a tumor and diagnosed his cancer. Dooley knows something's up, but he doesn't know what. On his trip home, he has dinner with an informed medical friend who takes pity on Dooley in his anxious state and breaks the bad news to him. Here's Dooley's response: "I had no reaction. . . . I felt nothing. . . . It seemed for a moment that all was quiet."[25]

This lack of affect is understandable: shock renders lots of people numb. What's weird, however, is that this scene occurs toward the end of Chapter 1 and is followed by more than a hundred pages where Dooley ostentatiously changes the subject to discuss the hospital work he's left behind in Laos. The narrative structure of *The Night They Burned the Mountain* dramatizes Dooley's superhuman act of self-silencing. We readers plow through the central chapters of his memoir, waiting for Dooley to break down and unburden himself, but he keeps his chin up and his lips sealed—suffering in silence. Interestingly, he's not so silent about other topics that, spiritually speaking, are kind of dodgy. Dooley often sounds like he's been reading too much Nietzsche (or, at least, Emily Dickinson) as he exults in overheated language about his solitary sense of election. For instance, back in Laos, Dooley observes that he and his two young male medics "had that strange kind of loneliness that men have who find themselves swinging out beyond the boundaries of normal existence. . . . We felt as though we were standing on the mountain peak and had, just for a quick moment, a tremendous view of the world."[26] Lest those two medics share too easily in Dooley's mystical apartness, he quickly adds: "The loneliness I knew was different from the loneliness of my boys."

Dooley's outsized sense of self-importance was grounded in the reality that, for months at a time, he was the only Western doctor in the surrounding area, literally charged with the care and salvation of thousands. Given that the only fellow westerners he could turn to for company were his subordinates and that many of his day-to-day interactions were with Cambodian and Laotian refugees, it's understandable that Dooley would fall prey to the *Heart of Darkness* syndrome. His Irish temper also kept the locals at bay and the folks back home cowering. In a letter to his mother included in *The Night They Burned the Mountain*, he rages about the deluge of irritating fan mail he receives from the States: "Don't people in America know I've got my own problems from day to day? . . . I must battle . . . and work out the problems of war, death and chaos. People write and ask me to write another book and tell me how I must find words. Don't they realize I have other things to do now."[27]

Marie Killilea also complained about the torrents of mail she received from her readers, but her tone was good-naturedly guilty; she might have been complaining about piles of dishes left undone. (And she was probably flattered by all that fan mail.) Like other Great Men throughout the ages, however, Dooley, down deep, takes himself ultra-seriously, which is another reason he's not easy to read. He exudes an Olympian disdain for his badgering readers: it's they who must please him, not the other way around.

The final framing chapter of *The Night They Burned the Mountain* returns Dooley to the United States, where he's about to undergo surgery. In an extraordinary scene—one that quintessentially illustrates how resourceful saints can be when it comes to showcasing their suffering—Dooley permits his operation to be filmed for a television documentary on cancer, *The Biography of a Cancer,* the brainchild of Fred Friendly. When it aired on April 21, 1960, on CBS, the program was watched by millions. While Dooley was anesthetized, motionless, and mum, draped in surgical gowns "in the middle of [a] huge [operating] amphitheatre,"[28] the God's-eye-view TV cameras watched every detail of his ordeal. I can think of no other scene in the entire canon of Catholic secular-saint stories that so brazenly demonstrates that genre's characteristic conflict between the desire for self-display and self-abnegation.

I still admire Dooley in a qualified way and feel sad when I think of him in his splendid solitude—isolated by culture, by sexuality, by his inherent arrogance, and, finally, by his illness. The official ascension of a human being to sainthood entails a slow, sometimes centuries-long bureaucratic process within the Catholic Church, during which witnesses must come forward to attest to miracles the prospective saint, even after death, has managed to perform. Were it not for all the revelations that have come out about him, Dooley would have been a shoo-in. He practically said as much in his own memoirs. If Dooley, somehow, were to ever be canonized, I'd like to see him made the Patron Saint of the Perpetually Incensed—intercessor to those who must work surrounded by their mental and physical inferiors, those who write books destined to be read by readers too unenlightened to understand.

*A*s is frequently remarked, we're currently enjoying an autobiography craze in American literature. But there are secular memoirs and then there are secular-saints' memoirs. I'm uncomfortable even imagining the books written by Dooley and Killilea rubbing covers on the same shelf with, say, a memoir like Kathryn Harrison's *The Kiss,* which chronicles the details of her sexual affair with her father. I cite Harrison's book as an extreme example of this latest generation of memoirs in which the reader is treated as a confidant, someone who will understand even the most aberrant of behaviors. Notice I said "understand" rather than "forgive" because I don't think Harrison and her contemporaries are looking for forgiveness from their readers. "Coming through" and "surviving" are the sought-after states; if there's any forgiveness desired, the autobiographers (not their readers, or God) dispense it to themselves. The chasm between pre–Vatican II secular-saint memoirs like Dooley's and Killilea's—which were ostensibly written to serve as instructional guides in faith and sacrifice—and the current crop of first-person narratives is as deep as the chasm separating the pious Middle Ages and the humanist Renaissance.

It's not just that being an Irish Catholic American is the norm in these Catholic secular-saint stories I've recalled so far, it's that being Irish Catholic is synonymous with being a true-blue American. The election of the country's first Catholic president looms on the horizon as a casual inevitability in these memoirs, whose multivolume narratives concentrate on the 1950s but whose life-changing brushes with destiny (Karen Killilea's premature birth; Dr. Tom Dooley's first Navy tour of duty) occur during World War II. The war finally made Irish Catholic Americans "white," concluding a process of immigrant assimilation that had begun decades earlier—as historian Linda Gordon says in her brilliant work of narrative history *The Great Arizona Orphan Abduction.* And, as I've suggested, the wartime spirit of patriotic self-denial found a congenial ethnic counterpart in the Irish Catholic martyrly temperament. The

Sullivans—that doomed family of *five* sailor brothers who all drowned on the same ship early in World War II—might well serve as the spiritual emblems of this specifically Irish Catholic strain of patriotic martyrdom. In fact, at the very end of the rousing wartime film made of their story, *The Five Fighting Sullivans,* the grinning faces of the five sailors float, ghostlike, on the screen, letting the audience know that even death can't dampen their boyish Irish American spirits.

Irish Catholic patriotic martyrdom is the prime ingredient of a popular fictional series of secular-saint stories, the Beany Malone books, which were published from 1943 to 1969. The Beany books are a kind of Catholic version of the Nancy Drew mysteries—with spiritual and moral dilemmas, rather than missing jewels or haunted houses—at the core of the plots. Girls—in particular, Catholic girls—were the intended audience for the Beany books, and consequently, they functioned as primers in how to behave as a good Catholic adolescent and young woman. But the Beany books also leavened their lessons with action and adventure. Over the course of their long serialized run, these novels presented—over and over again—age-appropriate versions of the female spiritual extreme-adventure tale to impressionable young readers like myself.

The Beany books were written by Lenora Mattingly Weber, a veritable one-woman female-juvenile-fiction factory. For more than forty years she wrote books and short stories, but she's best known for the Beany Malone series. Weber's life (apart from her writing) sounds like *Little House on the Prairie* crossed with *Annie Get Your Gun.* Raised by her homesteading family on the plains of Colorado, the teenaged Weber tamed broncos, chopped railroad ties into firewood, and rode in rodeos and Wild West shows. As an adult, Weber was not only a successful author but also the mother of six and an avid cook, swimmer, and horseback rider. What a gal! While lesser girls'-series authors have faded into obscurity, Weber's legend lives on. There's now a Lenora Mattingly Weber Society and a Lenora Mattingly Weber website, and the Beany Malone books have all been reprinted.

The Beany novels served up many of the charms of the Karen memoirs in fictional form, and for me, certainly, paramount among those charms was the lure of a big family. Marie Killilea evoked a picture of a house bursting at the seams with children, relatives, friends, neighbors, animals, music, and laughter, as well as commingled tears. Indeed, the life of the Killilea house exerts such a powerful pull that, in that second memoir, both now-adult daughters, Gloria and Marie, drop out of the public spheres of office work and college, respectively, to return home and busy themselves there. As an only child, I envied the Killileas their pandemonium. I wanted brothers and sisters so that my own place in the sun wouldn't be so hot. Rereading the Karen books, I can remember as a child even fantasizing that, should anything happen to my parents, I, too, like daughter Gloria, would be adopted by a big family just like the Killileas.

Lots of interesting siblings, a big old house, animals, recurring calamities, and the subtle curb of Catholicism to keep everything and everyone in check—there you have the entertaining lures of both the Killilea memoirs and the Beany books. Consider the surefire lure of the opening sentence of the very first book, *Meet the Malones*. "Mary Fred Malone had just bought a horse."[29] Ahhh. As the scene unfolds, we learn that sixteen-year-old Mary Fred Malone (more about that masculine moniker in a minute) has bought the horse, called Mr. Chips, from his stable owner with the fifteen dollars that she had in her pocket to buy a prom dress. Sweet Mr. Chips, beloved by all the girls who, like Mary Fred, have learned to ride on him through the years, has strained a tendon. Because World War II has just begun (the attack on Pearl Harbor takes place a month before this story opens), there's no room in the stable for him to recuperate: all stalls have to be filled with able horses in order to meet the demand for military riding lessons. Mary Fred to the rescue! Through a snowstorm, she leads the limping Mr. Chips home to the Malone house on the then-bucolic outskirts of Denver and settles him in to the stone garage that originally had been a stable. Fortunately, the Malones' mother has been dead three years, so she can't object, and their father, crusading newspaperman Martie Malone, is a benign and distant patriarch whose work often takes him far from home. The Malone kids—four in all—are largely on their own.

Absent parents! Autonomy! A house with an empty stable to spare for a horse! What girl reader could resist the opening of the Beany Malone books—especially a girl reader like me who would have had to lead that horse up two flights of apartment stairs and park it in the living room, where my always present parents would worry about what the landlord would say?

When Mary Fred enters her comfortably shabby and sprawling house, we alert readers will recognize, in fictional form, many of the same elements that made the Karen books so appealing. First, there's the large whirling dervish of a family. Apart from the erratically present paterfamilias, Martie, there's oldest daughter Elizabeth, who throughout the series is given the saintly tag description: "her hair was an aureole about her face."[30] Indebted to Jane Bennet of *Pride and Prejudice* and Meg March of *Little Women* for her characterization, Elizabeth is sweet, pretty, and, like those lovely old sisters of classic girls' fiction, rather dull. She's recently married to Lieutenant Donald McCallin and off living with him in a succession of Army camps. Next in line is Mary Fred herself, whose distinct physical features are her "unruly dark hair" and her gray eyes framed by dark lashes, "put in [by God] with a dirty finger"[31] as the Irish say. Mary Fred's younger brother, fifteen-year-old Johnny, is the literary genius of the family. Kind and endearingly absentminded, Johnny often has to be reminded to push his swoop of black hair out of his eyes and to tear himself away from his typewriter for meals. (Johnny is the same lanky, black-Irish physical type as Dr. Tom Dooley and, until late in the series, he shares Dooley's distracted disregard of the fairer sex.) Thirteen-year-old Beany (real name: Catherine Cecilia) is the most practical family member; in the parlance of Harkness High, which all the young Malones pass through, Beany, like Mary Fred, is a "mop squeezer" rather than a "stude" or a "queen."[32] When we first meet Beany, she's planning to sew curtains and buy paint to redecorate her bedroom by herself. To complete the character-as-defined-by-hair lineup of the Malones, Beany sports stubby "roan" braids, as well as a sprinkling of freckles across her face and the same sooty eyes as Mary Fred.

The other literary feature that the Beany Malone series shares with the Karen books is its basic plot trajectory: temptations, minor calamities, and major crises arise, and all are met, eventually, by the Malones' Catholic ethos of self-abnegation. The Beany Malone stories are much lighter in tone than the autobiographical sufferings of Karen and her family, but the presence of sin and tragedy also pervades the series: beloved characters die, young children are neglected and abused, the old are forgotten and lonely. The Malones, like the Killileas, offer up their own silent sufferings as a spiritual bulwark against, not a solution to, the evils of this world.

In *Meet the Malones,* the paramount crisis is war. World War II figures here as much more than a backdrop or a plot device; in this first novel of the series, wartime self-denial explicitly joins forces with the Catholic propensity toward martyrdom to make the Malones and, perhaps, by implication, a nation of gallant American families like them, unbeatable. The story has barely begun when father Martie volunteers to replace his newspaper's injured war correspondent and flies off to Hawaii, where he remains for most of the story, but not before delivering a rousing, blink-back-your-tears speech to his children: "I'd rather stay home and argue with you kids, and have old Red [the Malones' Irish setter] sleeping on my foot in the evenings. But it's like going into service, you can't think of what you'd like, or what you wouldn't."[33]

No sooner has one Martie temporarily disappeared (as he does in all the novels) than another Martie materializes. Two-week-old Martin Donald MacCallin arrives in the company of his exhausted (but still lovely) mother, Elizabeth. When her officer husband was called to battle, the pregnant Elizabeth began a railway journey back to the Malone-family homestead, planning to have her baby there. But her train was sidetracked in order to let troop trains go by, and Elizabeth had her baby alone, in a hospital in a small Wyoming town. When her money ran out, Elizabeth left the hospital early and forged her way, by train and car, to the Malone doorstep. In her first conversation with Mary Fred, Elizabeth immediately proves that she's a self-denying chip off the old block:

> "You should have telegraphed us," [says Mary Fred].
>
> "No," [Elizabeth] said slowly, "it wouldn't have been right to worry you. . . . In times like these, . . . everyone has his own burden, and no one else should add his. Don has his; Father has his; and this was mine."[34]

After her strength begins to return, Elizabeth really shows herself to be an apostle of the timely creed of patriotic martyrdom when, still bedridden, she delivers these orders to Mary Fred and her friends as they prepare to attend a square dance at the local airfield: "'Now listen, gals, be sure you go out there to this soldiers' dance with only one idea—not to have a good time yourselves but to give them one. Because you've got other good times ahead of you. But these kids—we don't know what's ahead for them. . . . Just forget about yourselves. Though I suppose it's hard for youth not to be selfish,' she added."[35]

The epic battle that takes place within the souls of young girls between the innate selfishness of youth and the selflessness called for by God and country is the overarching motif of all the Beany Malone books.

The typical plot of the thirteen novels that follow *Meet the Malones* finds Beany being temporarily seduced by the pleasures of this world proffered by school chums or other family outsiders. At the eleventh hour, Beany always realizes that the saintly virtues of self-denial, modesty, generosity, and love of one's fellow humans are the only worthy values for a Malone to embrace. After all, the Malones, being upright Irish American Catholics, are spiritually and morally superior precisely because they know how to tough things out. "The Malones," pronounces their housekeeper, "are the beatenest. . . . The Malones can stand up to things that'd just flatten anybody else right out."[36]

Beany assumes the mantle of series heroine in the second novel, *Beany Malone* (1948). But why? Wasn't spunky Mary Fred suitable in just about every way to carry on as the everygirl heroine of Weber's series—not the oldest, not the youngest; not the prettiest, not the plainest? The answer, I think, resides in the first book's description of Mary Fred as a "fresh air fiend" with "unruly hair." Note, also, that she's vigorously athletic and the kind of girl who forks over prom-dress money to buy a horse. From the get-go, in fact, Mary Fred's dethronement was foreordained by her dubious first name. With the towering exceptions of Jo March in *Little Women* and Laura Ingalls in the *Little House* books—and maybe, just maybe, one or two more characters I'm not thinking of—no unreconstructed tomboy over the age of twelve serves as the primary heroine in girls' juvenile fiction—and most certainly not Catholic girls' juvenile fiction. The figure of the tomboy, while entertaining, is too disturbing, too potentially subversive, to flourish. More often she's a foil, confirming, by contrast, the heroine's femininity. The archetypal example is George Fayne in the Nancy Drew novels. Sporty, close-cropped George despises daintiness and squeamishness—as embodied in the character of her plump, pretty blond cousin, Bess Marvin. Consequently, for nearly eighty years, Nancy Drew has maintained her position as the ideal feminine compromise candidate, smack in the center between George's butch bravado and Bess's girly-girl fragility.

Similarly, Beany figures in Weber's series as the happy attainable medium between Elizabeth's Madonna-like presence and Mary Fred's slapdash self-presentation. The series's estimation of Mary Fred as being an untraditional (and, therefore, problematic) female character extends even into the last novel, *Come Back, Wherever You Are.* While in that book Beany is a merrily frazzled mother of two, Mary Fred and her husband struggle with what we would now term "infertility problems." In keeping with the suffering-in-silence ethos of the series, Mary Fred ultimately decides to mother the troubled children her psychiatrist husband treats and to give up the selfish quest to have children, biological or adoptive, of her own.

Beany is sixteen years old when she displaces Mary Fred. In *Beany Malone,* she also takes over the care and feeding of her family. The family patriarch, pneumonia-weakened Martie, on doctor's orders, has departed for Arizona to recuperate from a plane crash he survived in a Wyoming blizzard. (Like any self-respecting martyr would, Martie contracted pneumonia when he insisted that another passenger take his place on the rescue truck and then had to wait hours in the freezing cold for the truck to return.) Beany chafes at her many domestic duties, especially when she compares her life to that of her new friend, Kay Maffley, a shy beauty with taffy-colored hair and perfect clothes. Kay lives in a playhouse of an apartment with her mother, Faye, who credits her youthful looks to her philosophy of "never put[ting] myself in a position that might turn out unpleasantly."[37] Beany envies Kay her soft cocoon and temporarily tries to emulate Faye's "don't stick your neck out" attitude, until she sees—with a jolt—what collateral damage such selfishness can cause. In the final novel of the series, *Come Back, Wherever You Are* (1969), Kay dies young, leaving a husband and a little boy to Beany's care. Her nurse ascribes Kay's death to Faye's maternal narcissism: "You might say she was doomed . . . maybe from the time she was a child, and had no one to see that she built up health and strength."[38] (While the Beany books condemn Faye's parental neglect, Martie Malone's absences are approved because he's always called away to be of service to others, and of course, he is the dad, not the mom.)

Weber ingeniously rings changes on this formulaic struggle between the forces of self-interest and self-denial throughout her series—an advantage that series fiction has over one-shot novels and nonfiction. Some of the novels stand out for their ingenuity, others because they mark watershed changes in the Malones'—or the nation's—life. In *Beany Has a Secret Life* (1955), for example, Beany briefly joins a "secret club" at Harkness High that, in this McCarthy-era novel, serves as a miniaturized representation of the Communist Party. In the penultimate book of the series, *Something Borrowed, Something Blue* (1963), Beany gets married. Like many another smart, courageous, and independent heroine in fiction, Beany settles for a schlemiel. Throughout the course of the series, Beany sequentially kept company with two young men: Norbett Rhodes, a junior Heathcliff with attitude problems, and Andy Kern, a handsome and cheerful Marine who, significantly, always wants to "play it light."[39] Toward the end of the series, Beany begins to take inexplicable notice of Carlton Buell, the judge's son who lives next door and who has served, throughout most of the books, as Johnny's silent sidekick. Weber works hard to make over Carlton into a hunk, but even her mighty efforts fall short. To highlight Carlton's caretaking, altruistic side, Weber has him running a recreation center for underprivileged kids when he and Beany fall in love. The kids at the center charmingly mispronounce his name as "Mr. Bull,"[40] but stolid Carlton always seems more like an ox. His romantic appeal isn't enhanced by his chaste habit of mumbling "Brakes!"[41] and pulling away whenever his smooching sessions with Beany grow dangerously rapturous.

Beany and Carlton get the kind of modest, homemade, Catholic wedding that befits their unpretentious station in life, complete with the underprivileged kids from the recreation center crowding the church and Beany's kindly old priest friend, Father Hugh, and his seminarian assistant, Andy Kern, presiding at the altar.

Say it ain't so—Andy Kern! Beany's dishy Marine turned into a Father What-a-Waste! All too true, I'm afraid. I can't take leave of the Beany Malone books until I give a nod to the weirdest depiction of martyrly self-denial in the entire series. Here's how extraordinary that scene is: five summers ago, I showed my fellow St. Raphael's alumna, Mary Ellen, my newly assembled collection of Beany Malone books. I began to describe the climactic Andy Kern scene in *Pick a New Dream* (1961), the eleventh book in the series, when Mary Ellen grabbed the book out of my hand, opened to the relevant pages, murmured, "I remember this," in a hollow voice, and lost herself in a reading reverie. Some three and a half decades after she had last read it, Mary Ellen had never forgotten that scene, and neither had I. No wonder. It dramatized a barely conscious fear that haunted us Catholic girls. It was the complement to the dread of being zapped with a religious vocation; it was the fear that one day we might be called upon to sacrifice our potential husbands to a hungry God.

In *Pick a New Dream,* eighteen-year-old Beany and her Marine beau, Andy, seem to be getting serious. Andy keeps talking to Beany about being at "the crossroads of life."[42] So, one evening when Andy telephones Beany from Father Hugh's rectory in the nearby mountain town of Twin Pines and urges her to drive up there *now* because he has something to show her, the eavesdropping Mary Fred is certain she hears wedding bells for her sister.

Beany drives up to Twin Pines in an emotional tumult, partly due to the fact that Weber has contrived to have her develop a belated crush on boy next door Carlton. As Beany pulls into the sloping driveway of the rectory, she spots a stranger in clerical black coming down the rectory steps. The horror, the horror of this scene—and the oddity of Andy's silent self-display (shades of Dr. Tom Dooley!) must be quoted in full:

> [Beany] climbed out, lifting her eyes above the oncoming figure, expecting to see Andy come leaping down the steps and toward her. And then her eyes dropped and met the twinkling ones beneath the black biretta. She stumbled back a step, leaning against the car and breathed out an amazed, "Andy!" And that's all she could say.

"Don't just stand there with your mouth gaping open like a capital *O*. How do I look in a Roman collar?"

She couldn't answer.

He took her arm and gave her a little shake. "Why, Knucklehead, I didn't mean to bowl you over. I'm ashamed of being such a ham. But I thought you must have guessed what I was beating around the bush about a time or two."

"I never guessed." She was ashamed of how *wrong* she and Mary Fred had been.

He guided her toward the gate. "This is just a preview. I won't be wearing them for real until September when I enter the seminary."

And still Beany could only repeat after him, "Until you enter the seminary."

"The coat's new, and so is the biretta, but the rest of the outfit some priest outgrew and left with Father Hugh. He brought me up to try them on, and I wanted you to be the first to see me in them. Look. Black shoes, black socks."

Father Hugh was holding the door open for them. "Now, don't be blaming me, Beany, for proselytizing. He was the one that came to me and said he wanted to be a priest. And I was the one who told him, 'It's nothing you can go rushing into. Wait, lad—wait, till you get to the point where the wanting is bigger than you are.'"

A dazed Beany sat with them on Father Hugh's screened porch. She drank the lemonade his housekeeper brought, and tried to absorb all they were telling her.[43]

Is it my cynical imagination, or is there something unkind about this scene? The two men playing dress-up out there in the woods, the coy phone call to Beany, the way she's ambushed by the sight of Andy, and his and Father Hugh's relentless cheerfulness as the poor girl sits there, stunned and dumb. What else can she do but be a good loser?

After Andy leaves the room to change, Beany assures Father Hugh in an intimate tête-à-tête that there was no "heart involvement"[44] with Andy, but we loyal readers know better—and, dammit, so does Andy!

When Beany gives him a lift home that night, Andy teases her at his door by "tilt[ing] her head and press[ing] a feathery kiss on her forehead. He added with his roguish grin, 'After September it'll be only a fatherly—not a brotherly—pat on the back.'"[45] There is a nasty compound word for women who behave in this smugly flirtatious way toward men; there's probably a nasty word for their male counterparts, and if I knew it, that would be the word I'd apply to Andy Kern here.

Acting like a priestly peacock, Andy ostentatiously displays his sacrifice of himself in this scene, while Beany must suffer in silence. In this particular round of the ongoing, centuries-long contest Catholic women have waged with God for available straight men, Beany has lost; and, since she's no Meggie from *The Thorn Birds,* Beany relinquishes Andy to his Maker without a struggle. Indeed, even the U.S. government colludes with God in sending Andy into the seminary early. We're told that his Marine CO decided that Andy could get out of his tour of duty ahead of time, or, as Father Hugh firmly puts it: "In this case the U.S. service could give way to God's service."[46] Thus, Andy's induction into the priesthood extends the particular connection the Beany Malone books make between being a good, martyrly Catholic and being a patriotic American. Against the combined forces of God and country, poor Beany doesn't stand a chance. She meekly accepts her second-best fate: marriage to sturdy old Carlton and bearing Carlton's kids. Playful Andy Kern gains gravitas as he transmogrifies into Father Kern, while the lively girl with an Irish temper we first met as a thirteen-year-old in pigtails dissolves into Mrs. Carlton Buell.

"That's so sick!" my Jewish husband said when I recounted for him one evening the martyrly plot pattern of the Catholic juvenilia I read in grammar school. Caught up short by his response, I nimbly rushed to these books' collective defense. "No! You're stupid!" Granted, the Karen books and Tom Dooley's memoirs are too neurotically guilty about partaking of the pleasures of this world, but they're not sick. In many ways, the suck-it-up sermon of these books is infinitely preferable to me than the victimhood that's displayed in so many autobiographies today, or the widespread sense of entitlement our culture fosters. As I've said, I'm drawn to books and people that don't put on airs. Of course, one probable reason is that they remind me of the fast-vanishing atmosphere of my childhood. I inhabited that atmosphere again, a few years ago, when I picked up Alice McDermott's *Charming Billy*—her dead-on, poignant novel about Irish Catholics in Queens and on Long Island. In the opening scene, a scruffy bunch of Irish Catholics, family and friends, are sitting around a restaurant in Queens. Every time the waitress comes by to fill their water glasses or put down a plate, people at the table quickly say "Thank you." I find myself doing that, too—scrupulously thanking anyone in a restaurant or store who's serving me. It's a holdover from the world of my childhood where we were taught to feel gratitude for any service done for us—and where almost all the parents we knew held down blue- or pink-collar jobs, so there was no sense of superiority to someone working as, say, a waitress.

These days, I sit at too many restaurant tables with people oozing privilege who barely acknowledge the waitperson. I'm more comfortable, for whatever "sick" reasons, being seated with McDermott's table of penitents, eating humble pie. And, sure, by the Jesuitical logic of Catholic martyrdom, this embracing of my own unworthiness does indeed signify that I'm a morally and spiritually superior person. Praise the Lord and pass the potatoes—and the haloes. More "semicolon" qualifications: it's also true that a wobbly sense of entitlement can be a bad thing. I've seen my parents, old friends, and myself be super-deferential to people in authority (teachers, doctors, bosses) who don't deserve such consideration. My mother tells a story about how my grandmother Helen took time off from her two cleaning jobs to visit my mother's grammar school and bring a present to an ill-tempered teacher who was humiliating my mother in class. I wince when I imagine that scene of my grandmother bowing and scraping to "buy" decent treatment for her daughter. And, if I could, I wouldn't think twice about telling that teacher where she could stick her haughty attitude. But I've had the empowering advantage of a higher education; as I've said, my grandmother Helen couldn't read.

In an era when having an "attitude" was akin to committing a mortal sin, we kids at St. Raphael's, along with our doppelgängers in thousands of parochial schools across the land, were given these secular-martyr stories to read as a crucial part of our religious training. But maybe our nuns assigned these books to us for another reason. Maybe they sensed that reading itself is essentially an antisocial and even voluptuous indulgence. So, to combat the dangerous siren call of literature, they needed to toughen us up with books that preached a message of hard work and self-sacrifice, deference to others, and service to society.

If the secondary aim of this early curriculum of secular-saint stories was to turn us away from the pleasures of the word out into the work of the world, it failed. Reading those books as a child, rereading them as an adult, I could hardly tear myself away.

My New York:
September 8, 2001

I've never identified with those up-from-the-working-class stories where the hero (almost always it's a hero) packs his bag and leaves his humble place of origin never to return. Even in Pete Hamill's New York memoir, *A Drinking Life,* which I love and always assign in the course I teach on the literature of twentieth-century New York City, Brooklyn all but disappears when the young Hamill leaves it—first, for a stint in the Army and trips to Mexico, then, most irrevocably, for Manhattan. Sunnyside, my old neighborhood in Queens, has never disappeared from the routine geography of my adult life. After I "left" for college in the faraway Bronx, and then for graduate school in Philadelphia, I always made frequent trips back there to visit my parents. During the year and a half when my dad was seriously ill, I'd spend at least one weekend a month in Sunnyside with my parents, shopping for groceries at the corner markets, sometimes renting a car and taking them for a ride to Bayville or Teddy Roosevelt's house, Sagamore Hill, on the North Shore of Long

Island, the places we used to go to almost every summer weekend when I was a kid. That was in the days when people said, "Let's go for a drive!" Reading took me away from Sunnyside, but it didn't sever the connection.

Now I go back to visit my mother, to help her in the slow chore of packing up thirty years of her life in that apartment—old home movies (keep), the long rayon slip from my prom dress (ditch), a bureau drawerful of my dad's brown and black dress socks (Who would want them? But it's so hard for her to just throw them out). She's planning to move to Washington, to be close to us. She's been planning it for six years now. Maybe it will actually happen, maybe not. As she tells me, "Everyone in Washington is a teacher," meaning they're educated. My mother doesn't really fit in in Sunnyside anymore, either. She's part of a dwindling band of elderly longtime residents in the neighborhood, which has become home to newer waves of immigrants—from India, Romania, China, and Ireland. Yet Sunnyside is still, in a loose sense, "home"— hers and mine. Another strike against Thomas Wolfe, whose florid novels a short-term boyfriend convinced me I *had* to read; his famous pronouncement, "You can't go home again," has achieved the status of woeful fact. Maybe it is, for a lot of other people—most of whom I suspect, based on a completely subjective survey, are male. I know a lot of women in my situation who are always going home again, and again, and again.

This was not a "help-out Mom" trip back to Sunnyside. The reason Rich and I and Molly were driving up the interminable Jersey Turnpike that Saturday morning was a fiftieth-anniversary party in honor of Joe and Ellen Sullivan, the parents of two of my closest friends from childhood. I've mentioned Cathy and Pat Sullivan before, the "Irish twins" (born eighteen months apart), who, together with Mary Ellen Maher, were my constant companions during some of the happiest years of my life. My friendship with the Sullivans was sealed one afternoon when we were all playing in the alley behind their apartment building. Cathy Sullivan asked me which baseball team I rooted for, the Yankees or the Mets. I took a lucky guess and said, "The Mets." For well over a decade afterward, the four of us constituted a quartet as solid as the Beatles. Indeed, we even played the Beatles in the living room "concerts" we staged in the mid-1960s. Years later, I felt a shock when I read Barbara

Ehrenreich's smart discussion in her 1986 book, *Re-Making Love,* of what she identified as a widespread phenomenon of preadolescent girls acting out fantasies of androgyny by assuming the identity of their favorite Beatle in playtime concerts. We thought we came up with the idea ourselves. I believed my love for George Harrison—naturally I would be George, "the Quiet Beatle"—was a mark of my superior discernment.

"Be prepared for starchy food and an open bar; this is going to be an old-fashioned Irish party," I told Rich, whose Russian Polish Jewish roots dictate exactly the opposite approach to party throwing. (His family thinks that a cranberry-juice cocktail really *is* a cocktail.) I knew from whereof I spoke. All the years of my Sunnyside youth, the Sullivans threw parties. Usually their huge extended family would cram into whatever apartment the Sullivans were then living in, and the cold cuts, whiskey, and beer would flow. Someone would put on an Irish record, and the two girls, Cathy and Pat, both award-winning step dancers, would fly around the packed living room, kicking and leaping. This was in pre-*Riverdance* days, when step dancers were praised for being light on their feet and the form hadn't devolved into mass-culture kitsch. Mary Ellen Maher and I, the two only children in this sea of ever fruitful and constantly multiplying Irish Catholic families, would look on with envy. We loved these parties, as well as going over to the Sullivans' apartment almost every day, because with four kids in their family and all these relatives nearby, there was always something going on, in contrast to the stillness of our own apartments. All the time I was growing up, the Sullivans were like a second, idealized family to me, and Joe and Ellen had been steadfast friends to my mother since my dad died. That's why I insisted that we go to this anniversary party, even though I nervously anticipated that Rich (the Jew) and I (the egghead apostate) and Molly (the Chinese daughter) would constitute the "diversity table" at what would still be an overwhelmingly Irish Catholic gathering.

As I drove over the Verrazano-Narrows Bridge and onto the Brooklyn-Queens Expressway, the skyline of Manhattan rose up on our left. "Look at that," I said to Molly, as I always have as long as we've been making this trip together. "There's New York. It's the most beautiful sight in the world." And how I meant those words. That skyline—the

apotheosis of New York's grace and swagger, creativity and hard labor—
is lovelier to me than the most serene sunset or snowcapped mountain
range. Molly has a picture book called *My New York,* by the folk artist
Kathy Jakobsen, and ever since she could talk, she's been pointing
out the Empire State Building and the Chrysler Building on these car
trips.

Sunnyside, as we approached it, is no one's idea of the most beautiful
sight in the world. In my childhood, its greatest attraction as a neighborhood was that you could see the skyline of New York (we outer-
borough types always call Manhattan "New York") in the distance over
the low gray tenements and factories of Long Island City. Now Long
Island City is sprouting its own undistinguished skyscrapers and the
amazing view is being blocked out. As we drove over the Koskiusko
Bridge, Calvary Cemetery spread out for miles and miles below us. Calvary Cemetery sometimes appears in movies and TV shows, particularly
cop dramas set in New York. It's got great cinematic appeal because it's
such a vast necropolis with the skyline of New York as its backdrop.
When I was in grammar school, my grieving mother used to speed-walk
with me far into Calvary Cemetery at lunchtime, so that we could visit
my grandmother Helen's grave. We'd hurry past the tombstones of Irish
and Italian immigrants who died in the late nineteenth century and past
the clustered mausoleums of the rich. My mother always used to give
me apple juice and a deviled-ham sandwich on these picnics. To this
day, thinking of apple juice and deviled ham together makes me gag—
something about eating in the company of all those piled-up dead. My
dad is buried there now; in the immediate vicinity are the graves of guys
who died on D Day and at the Battle of the Bulge.

St. Raphael's, a little redbrick church with a quaint spire, stands at
the western edge of the cemetery. The center of my life for years and
years, St. Raphael's has become one of the most ethnically diverse
parishes in Queens: all variety of Asian and Hispanic families go to Mass
at the church and send their kids to the school. When I was a student
there, the school population was about as diverse as our green plaid uniforms. Everyone was Irish or Italian or Polish, with a few immigrant
exotics—one French kid, one Romanian, a couple of Dominicans, and
two Scots—sprinkled in at intervals.

We parked and went up to my mom's apartment, which is small and dark, as it always was, even before it became just "my mom's" apartment. It's got the feel of a life in limbo: it needs a paint job, and the chairs and cushions that are falling apart haven't been replaced because, after all, as my mother keeps saying, "I'm going to move soon." My black-and-white baby picture and a publicity photo of me that *Fresh Air* commissioned about a decade ago hang side by side on one wall; photos of Molly now cover the end tables and rabbit-eared TV set. My mom has had her hair inflated at the local beauty parlor she's been going to for half a lifetime, and she's had a nip of brandy. This will be a hard party for her: she and my dad celebrated their fiftieth anniversary, and then they had another year, and then he was gone.

We all got into the car again, and I drove us out Woodhaven Boulevard to the "better" neighborhood Joe and Ellen moved to some years ago. The party was being held in the downstairs room of a big restaurant/catering hall of that indigenous Queens oxymoron: an Irish American restaurant. After we arrived and I eventually made my way over to the steam table, the menu of parties past spread itself out before me: manicotti, fried rice, meatballs, macaroni and cheese. So there, Thomas Wolfe. No matter: the bar, as predicted, was open throughout the event, and the point, as it always was at the Sullivans' parties, was to talk, drink, dance, have fun. Food was just fuel. But my first reaction upon stepping into the room did turn out to be food-related. "They've finally put on a little weight," I thought to myself when I saw Cathy and Pat, whom I hadn't seen since my dad's funeral. They were always reed-thin—Pat, especially, a tall, skinny, black-haired, ivory-skinned beauty whose body type was perfectly in sync with the Twiggy years of our very early girlhood. Even after their accumulated pregnancies, they reverted back to the almost anorectic silhouette of their mother. Next to them, I've always felt fat, even though weight has never been much of an issue for me. Now, at last, they looked more like women than girls. And, indeed, they are women: both of them teachers, both longtime wives and mothers to older kids, some already in college. Together with their parents, Cathy and Pat crowded around Molly, whom they'd never met before, and talked to her sweetly and told her how pretty she looked in her party dress and how very happy they were to see her at last.

When I was trying to get pregnant and stay pregnant, Ellen Sullivan, who had learned of some of my struggle from my mother, wrote to me and told me she was saying a novena for me. That means attending a special Mass the first Friday of every month. Her devotion and concern made me cry. Now she was getting to meet the baby she prayed would come. Except this was a baby whose arrival no one in that room could have anticipated in the olden days of our childhood when all the world was white and Catholic. During the party, Pat, then Cathy, came up to me laughing and quoted something my mother had said to their mother: "Who would have guessed, Ellen, that I would have a Jewish son-in-law and a Chinese granddaughter!" Sounds like my mom all right: the combination of wonderment and bemused acceptance and, underneath it all, the need for reassurance about something else "different" her daughter has done. "Who would have guessed" was probably the thought Cathy and Pat and a lot of their relatives in that room had when they looked at me and my tiny familial band of outsiders. To express the general good-natured surprise through the voice of my mother was a way to make it less judgmental, to keep it, in a manner of speaking, inside the family. But surely I'm selling the Sullivans short. Even if their extended family was still remarkably homogeneous, they must have non-Catholic friends, maybe even a few nonwhite or out-of-the-closet work buddies. The world has changed so much. Even in this Celtic snow globe of a room, well, there's me and Rich and Molly.

Throughout that afternoon, through the terrific step dancing (Cathy, for old times' sake, and a young niece who's now carrying on the tradition) and Clancy Brothers songs, and electric-slide shimmying (the Sullivans knew all the moves and all danced in unison!) and moving speeches, I felt the same old sense of yearning and restlessness. I would love to be part of a family this large and cohesive; that said, I would go nuts if I couldn't go off by myself regularly to read and, instead, had to do something like this almost every weekend—the First Communions, confirmations, birthday parties—the relentless social round of a large Irish Catholic family. No doubt, I idealize this family and underestimate the degree to which the social revolutions of the past thirty years have chipped away at its solidity. Indeed, one of Pat's teenaged daughters sported a tight dress and dyed blond hair. Her quieter older sister looked a bit like Emily Dickinson as we know her from her one authenticated photograph. That sister's eyes were smart, alert, and measuring as she listened to the speeches of her extended family. Both of Pat's daughters live "away" at college—the serious one downtown at NYU, which, I know, caused some consternation among the family. Since men have always benefited more from the Irish Catholic status quo, it's not surprising that these two women of the younger generation, not their brothers, were the ones who visually embodied some degree of departure from the program.

One of the Sullivans' sons—who was a boy of about ten when I'd last seen him—got up to give a testimonial to his parents. Francis is now a lawyer, and he's tall and handsome and at ease in front of an audience. Among other things, he told a story about how his mother, Ellen, once stayed up all night to type a college paper for him that was due the following morning. Then she got herself dressed and traveled the subway into New York that morning to her secretarial job. I was moved by Francis's proud love for his parents and by the way all the Sullivans obviously felt they could depend on one another. I'll always envy their all-for-one, one-for-all togetherness, while knowing that, to mangle Hemingway's famous short-story title, it's a way I'll never be. Large gatherings of people that spout the pronoun "we" most of the time make me edgy.

After the first hour or so, I left Rich and Molly at the diversity table to talk with Jim O'Brien, Cathy's husband. In my senior year at the all-girls Catholic high school we all attended, I was desperate for a date for the prom and Jim agreed to be my "fix-up." (Almost everyone I knew had to be fixed up with a date: one girl in my class was even escorted by her cousin, a priest, who came in his Roman collar and black suit.) Jim and I were not romantically copasetic, but he and Cathy were, and they married shortly after her college graduation. By then, Jim had become a fireman, something he'd always dreamed of being. Now he told me he'd suffered a back injury on the job a few months earlier and was out on disability from his firehouse in lower Manhattan. We talked about work: how lucky we both were to have jobs that, for the most part, we loved, jobs that engaged us and made us feel part of something larger. I told Jim that I thought I had the best job imaginable: telling people about good books and why they should read them. On his "best days,"

Jim gets to save people's lives. No contest, of course, but we need bread *and* roses too.

We were interrupted by the presentation of embossed formal testimonials from the pope, Rudolph Giuliani, and the President and Mrs. Bush. The Sullivans, like most of my own cousins, had forsaken their Democratic roots and were now Republican. Joe and Ellen got up to talk about their lives together and the struggle they had raising four children on one salary in small apartments in Sunnyside. As it goes without saying at an Irish party, there was not a dry eye in the house. Joe mentioned the people who weren't present, in body, in the room with us that day, among them my father. I thought about how my father always sat off to the side at the Sullivans' parties. A nondrinker and a minimal talker, he preferred to stay at home, to smoke and read one of his World War II adventure novels.

The music and dancing resumed, and the deejay, much to Molly's delight, handed out party favors—hats and plastic guitars—to the little kids. That was always one of the most endearing aspects of being with the Sullivans: they loved kids and would never dream of having an adults-only party. By now Molly had started to warm up to all these strangers, and she and I took some turns on the dance floor, performing together her favorite twirl-around-and-fall-down dance. I'm so proud of her and so proud to be her mother. Rich always says she's a big improvement on our gene pool. All the pre-adoption anxieties—about how having a daughter of a different race would make me feel, once again, "odd," or not quite that child's "real mother"—disappeared the minute I held her. No other child could possibly be mine—although not exclusively mine. I erratically beam happy pictures, reassuring thoughts, and words of gratitude to Molly's unknown biological mother and father in China—extended, if invisible, family.

Years earlier, when I was in the thick of my "extreme adventure" to have a child, I begrudged the Sullivan sisters—and all the other fertile friends I had—their children. Now it wasn't an issue: they had their kids, I had mine. That's another warm aspect of this party: the undercurrent of competition that marked my years of growing up with the Sullivans seemed to have disappeared. Who was the smartest in class? Who got the most scholarships to college? Who was the prettiest? Who got a boyfriend first? Who got married and had kids first? Now, who cared? It didn't seem to matter who had what and who did what. We were all just happy to be together in that room again; maybe we'd all lived through enough not to begrudge one another our life victories. "You're writing a book!" Pat Sullivan said to me as she hugged me at the end of the party. "That's so great!" (Apparently, my mother had been talking.) I was touched. Neither writing nor reading had ever been her passion; although she was almost always the smartest girl in our class, she was a math, not an English, whiz. Pat told me that her oldest daughter—the one who looks a little like Emily Dickinson—wanted to be a writer. It figures: the writer is always standing off to the side, observing.

After the party we went back to my mother's apartment and slept, badly, all three of us in my old bed. The next morning Rich and I packed up our car, kissed my mother good-bye, and drove onto the Brooklyn-Queens Expressway. I was behind the wheel as we sped alongside the Brooklyn Heights Promenade and lower Manhattan, once again, rose up at our elbows. "There's New York," I ritually said to Molly. "It's the most beautiful sight in the world." We drove up onto the Verrazano-Narrows Bridge, and Molly and Rich kept looking back at the Statue of Liberty, the World Trade Center, all the other skyscrapers, until we passed the high midpoint of the bridge, nosed down into New Jersey, and the whole skyline disappeared.

*O*n the Thursday after the attack, when classes at Georgetown resumed, I stopped into the office of one of my colleagues, who's also a native New Yorker, to share the shock. I said to her, "All this makes what we do pretty irrelevant, doesn't it?" This colleague is wiser than I. She replied: "No more irrelevant than it ever is. We're always teaching and learning within the shadow of our own mortality." Her remark reminded me of something my father once told me, about how the USS *Schmitt* had a makeshift library on it, spottily stocked with the classics and adventure stories. Distraction, sure, but essential nourishment for the mind and spirit as well. Books are always necessary cargo. So many of us reach for them, irrationally, even in potentially dangerous situations that threaten to wreck our ability to concentrate—as military helicopters whirl above our heads (like they did in our neighborhood in Washington for weeks after the attack) or U-boats silently glide in the waters below us. In the weeks that followed September 11, I and many of my other reader friends coped by reading mysteries, stories that specifically set out to explore, in Raymond Chandler's great phrase, "a world gone wrong." The mystery genre, both its British and American strains, came of age during wartime, and there's something about it that suits tense times— something to do with the way the detective probes deeply into a problem no one else can quite get a handle on, as well as something to do with the mystery novel's often uneasy sense of resolution. The mystery story I thought about most during this period was the one I love the best, *The Maltese Falcon*. A third of the way through that novel, Sam Spade tells a story about a missing-person case he once solved, involving a man named Flitcraft. Flitcraft, a businessman, vanished one afternoon on his way to lunch. Years later Spade found him; here's how he recalls Flitcraft's explanation for his disappearance:

> Going to lunch he passed an office-building that was being put up—just the skeleton. A beam or something fell eight or ten stories down and smacked the sidewalk alongside him. It brushed pretty close to him, but didn't touch him, though a piece of the sidewalk was chipped off and flew up and hit his cheek. . . . He was scared stiff of course, he said, but he was more shocked than really frightened. He felt like somebody had taken the lid off life and let him look at the works.[1]

I mentioned Flitcraft in a piece I did for *Fresh Air* about post–September 11 reading. One astute listener, however, noticed that I ended the anecdote too early and e-mailed to tell me so. Spade does go on to say that, after his life-altering epiphany, Flitcraft eventually got used to beams "not falling" and fell into a routine that re-created the rut of his former life. A lot of us Americans have already gotten used to September 11; we've gotten used to having the works exposed and the lid warped and wobbling. You can read that Flitcraft anecdote a lot of ways. Spade seems to be laughing at the essential ploddingness of human nature; but maybe it also testifies to how resilient people are in their very ordinariness.

Since September 11, I've been in sporadic e-mail contact with Cathy Sullivan. Her husband, the firefighter Jim O'Brien, had not been on duty that morning. (The back injury he told me about at the anniversary party turned out to be his probable salvation.) Jim spent weeks down at Ground Zero looking for his missing "brothers." His best friend, a fellow firefighter, was missing, later confirmed dead, and many of the firefighters he served with and the younger recruits he had trained were lost. Lots of the newsmagazine articles published in the aftermath of September 11 mentioned the prevalence of Irish and Italian names on the lists of the victims: firefighters and police and white-collar banking types who worked in the Towers. So many of the dead were Catholics and outer-borough residents; a lot of them still lived with their parents. Reading *The New York Times*' "Portraits of Grief" page every morning, I often felt like I could have been looking at a program from some mythical reunion of my old St. Raphael's classmates. That trip up to New York on September 8 turned out to be a reconnection with the world I knew as a child—the world that a lot of New Yorkers still lived in—before it vanished for so many.

I've said that I love Pete Hamill's *A Drinking Life*. Obviously aspects of his identity—Irish Catholic, outer-borough type, reader, and writer— speak to my own. But it's a paragraph Hamill wrote about the New York skyline that, for me, constitutes the most magical moment in the whole memoir. He recalls living in Brooklyn as a kid during World War II. On the evening of D Day, he and his neighbors climb the stairs up to the roofs of their tenements. Hamill, who's about eight, keeps asking his mother what they're all doing on the roof, and she keeps telling him to be quiet, to just keep on looking toward Manhattan as the sky gets darker. Here's what Hamill says happened as night fell and darkness enveloped the city:

And then, without warning, the entire skyline of New York erupted into glorious light: dazzling, glittering, throbbing in triumph. And the crowds on the rooftops roared . . . the whole city roaring for light. There it was, gigantic and brilliant, the way they said it used to be: the skyline of New York. Back again. On D Day, at the command of Mayor La Guardia. And it wasn't just the skyline. Over on

the left was the Statue of Liberty, glowing green from dozens of
light beams. . . . The skyline and the statue: in all those years of the
war, in all the years of my *life,* I had never seen either of them at
night. I stood there in the roar, transfixed.[2]

To read that passage these days, to experience that longed-for return
of a missing skyline, well, Hamill makes me imagine what that miracle
would be like. Such is the power of words, of writing, of books. Words
can summon up a skyline from the dark; they can bring back the people
you loved and will always yearn for. They can inspire you with possibilities you otherwise would have never imagined; they can fill your
head with misleading fantasies. They can give you back your seemingly
seamless past and place it right alongside your chaotic present.

"But that only happens in books," my mother, pretty much immune
to the power of the written word, would say.

Exactly. That's why I can't stop reading them.

Acknowledgments

*T*his book would not have been written were it not for the intellectual generosity and sense of adventure possessed by my editor, Kate Medina. In what seems like another lifetime, Kate asked me if I would like to write a book. I said yes, and we were off! But little did I realize that the arrival of my daughter (roughly two weeks after Kate and I made a verbal handshake over the phone) would drain almost all available writing time from my already lively work schedule. Kate has been patient and encouraging throughout the long period it's taken me to write this book, and her literary insights and editorial suggestions have improved it immeasurably. I feel honored to have her as my editor.

Associate editor Robin Rolewicz has been delightful to work with; I've especially appreciated her unwavering mental focus and calm in the face of impending deadlines. Robin's predecessor at Random House, Frankie Jones, also deserves my thanks for her close reading of an early version of the book and her helpful suggestions.

It's a commonplace—and, sadly, often true—assumption that books aren't carefully copyedited anymore. Happily, my manuscript fell into the meticulous hands of Random House associate copy chief Beth Pearson and superhuman copy editor Margaret Wimberger. Never before have I thought twice about whether my father belonged to the Steamfitters' Union or the Plumbers and Steamfitters Union or some variant of either. Truly, any mistakes that stubbornly still remain in this manuscript are my own.

Every writer should be so lucky to have an agent like Stuart Krichevsky. He's funny (really funny), kind, and savvy—and so very smart about literature and the world of ideas that, many times in our conversations, I've wished that we could take a break from talking about my book (yet again) and instead talk about some of the other books that he obviously loves and knows so well. Stuart's assistant, Shana Cohen, is wise beyond her years and has been a much appreciated booster of this book from its earliest stages.

I started listening to *Fresh Air* in my graduate school days in Philadelphia. I remember admiring Terry Gross's intellectual curiosity and breadth of knowledge, worn so much more lightly than the mantle of theory-encrusted erudition I then was struggling to assume. I became the show's book reviewer in 1989, and that job continues to be the highlight of my professional life. Because of the high standards set by Terry and by the show's extraordinary executive producer, Danny Miller (thanks for giving me that second chance, Danny!), I've learned how to be a better critic—to talk about books in a way that, I hope, does justice to them without draining them of their life and artistic sense of play. Phyllis Myers has been my longtime producer and good friend for much of my career at *Fresh Air;* over the years, she's backed me up, corrected me, improved my writing, and saved me from all manner of public humiliation. Before Phyllis, Naomi Person was my producer and remains my friend; Naomi really taught me in a start-from-scratch way how to review books for radio.

My colleagues at Georgetown University have heard about this book ad nauseam, and some of them have even had the dubious pleasure of reading parts of it in an earlier form. I'd like to thank my partner in crime, Carol Kent, along with good friends Norma Tilden, Jeffrey Hammond, Elizabeth Velez, George O'Brien, Rebecca Pope, Denise Brennan, Barbara Feinman Todd, and John Glavin, for their interest over the years. Other friends and family members have been steadfast in their enthusiasm for a book that sometimes seemed destined never to appear. Chief among them are my oldest and dearest friend (and fellow St. Raphael's alum), Mary Ellen Maher-Harkins, as well as Jessica Blake Hawke, Belle Yeselson, Joan and Stan Levin, Maureen McDonough, Christine Hughes, Sarah Hughes, Connie Casey, Elizabeth Judd, Lori Milstein, and David Sahr.

My mother, Jean Corrigan, always has been supportive of this book and my writing—even though books are not her passion. As a mother, she's been an inspiration to me, and she's the most loving grandmother any child could wish for. And my daughter, Molly Yeselson, is, quite simply, the greatest kid in the world and the greatest joy in my life.

Finally, my intrepid husband, Richard Yeselson, read every page of this manuscript at least three times. We are still married. Those two seemingly incompatible facts testify to his intellectual rigor, his loving and active involvement in my work, and his terrific sense of humor.

Recommended Reading

$\mathcal{O}$ne of the pleasures of writing this book has been spending time rereading and thinking about books that I love. Unlike when I was working on my doctoral dissertation, or editing the essays that compose *Mystery & Suspense Writers,* I felt little responsibility here to discuss books or authors I don't like. What follows, then, is a highly subjective list of old and new favorite books. I've talked about many of them in the preceding pages; some have occurred to me as I've been assembling this list.

Female Extreme-Adventure Tales:
Traditional and Feminist

Pride and Prejudice and *Persuasion* by Jane Austen
The Tenant of Wildfell Hall by Anne Brontë
Jane Eyre and *Villette* by Charlotte Brontë
Quartet in Autumn by Barbara Pym
One True Thing and *Black and Blue* by Anna Quindlen

Scoundrel Time by Lillian Hellman
Collected Poems by Stevie Smith
Beloved by Toni Morrison

Catholic Secular-Martyr Tales

Karen and *With Love from Karen* by Marie Killilea
The Night They Burned the Mountain by Dr. Tom Dooley
Charming Billy by Alice McDermott
Final Payments by Mary Gordon
The Beany Malone series by Lenora Mattingly Weber
Mariette in Ecstasy by Ron Hansen

Books About China, Adoption, and Parenthood in General

Operating Instructions: A Journal of My Son's First Year by Anne Lamott
*The Lost Daughters of China: Abandoned Girls, Their Journey to America,
    and the Search for a Missing Past* by Karin Evans
*Wuhu Diary: On Taking My Adopted Daughter Back to Her Hometown
    in China* by Emily Prager
The Exact Same Moon: Fifty Acres and a Family by Jeanne Marie Laskas
Wild Swans: Three Daughters of China by Jung Chang
Little Miss Spider by David Kirk (juvenile)
A Mother for Choco by Keiko Kasza (juvenile)
Happy Adoption Day! by John McCutcheon (juvenile)
Life as We Know It: A Father, a Family, and an Exceptional Child by Michael
    Bérubé

Mystery and Suspense Novels

Gaudy Night and *The Nine Tailors* by Dorothy L. Sayers
A Dark-Adapted Eye by Barbara Vine
Time and Again by Jack Finney
The Inspector Kurt Wallander series by Henning Mankell

The Derek Strange series by George P. Pelecanos
An Unsuitable Job for a Woman by P. D. James
Bucket Nut by Liza Cody
Early Autumn by Robert B. Parker
Death Trick by Richard Stevenson
The V. I. Warshawski series by Sara Paretsky
Fall from Grace by Larry Collins
The Detective Inspector John Rebus series by Ian Rankin
The Mario Balzic series by K. C. Constantine
The Inspector Chen Cao series by Qiu Xiaolong
The Martin Beck series by Maj Sjöwall and Per Wahlöö

Academic Farces (besides the unparalleled *Lucky Jim*,
enshrined under the category "Books I Never
Get Tired of Rereading")

Straight Man by Richard Russo
Publish and Perish and *The Lecturer's Tale* by James Hynes
Small World: An Academic Romance by David Lodge

Literary Criticism That a Nonacademic
Audience Can Enjoy

*The Madwoman in the Attic: The Woman Writer and the Nineteenth-Century
Literary Imagination* by Sandra Gilbert and Susan Gubar
The Girl Sleuth: On the Trail of Nancy Drew, Judy Bolton, and Cherry Ames
by Bobbie Ann Mason
Writing a Woman's Life by Carolyn Heilbrun
Parallel Lives: Five Victorian Marriages by Phyllis Rose

Fiction and Nonfiction That Make a
Reader Believe in Possibility

The collected novels, short stories, and essays of Laurie Colwin
The All of It and *Matters of Chance* by Jeannette Haien

Almost anything by M.F.K. Fisher
News from Nowhere, or An Epoch of Rest: Being Some Chapters from a Utopian Romance by William Morris

Books I Never Get Tired of Rereading

Lucky Jim by Kingsley Amis
Some Tame Gazelle by Barbara Pym
Pride and Prejudice and *Emma* by Jane Austen
Shining Through by Susan Isaacs
David Copperfield, Bleak House, and *Great Expectations* by Charles Dickens
The Age of Innocence by Edith Wharton
The Maltese Falcon by Dashiell Hammett
The Big Sleep by Raymond Chandler
The Great Gatsby by F. Scott Fitzgerald
The Book of Daniel by E. L. Doctorow
Little Women by Louisa May Alcott
The Woman Warrior: Memoirs of a Girlhood Among Ghosts by Maxine Hong Kingston

Biography and Autobiography

Coming of Age in Mississippi: The Classic Autobiography of Growing Up Poor and Black in the Rural South by Anne Moody
Eleanor Roosevelt, Vols. 1 and 2, by Blanche Wiesen Cook
Black Boy (American Hunger) by Richard Wright
Patrimony: A True Story by Philip Roth (plus everything else by him!)
Bronx Primitive: Portraits in a Childhood by Kate Simon
Tender at the Bone and *Comfort Me with Apples* by Ruth Reichl
An Orphan in History: One Man's Triumphant Search for His Jewish Roots by Paul Cowan
Bad Blood: A Memoir by Lorna Sage
Hunger of Memory: The Education of Richard Rodriguez by Richard Rodriguez
Teacher: The One Who Made the Difference by Mark Edmundson
A Drinking Life: A Memoir by Pete Hamill

Jane Austen: A Life by Claire Tomalin
Manhattan, When I Was Young by Mary Cantwell
Minor Characters: A Beat Memoir by Joyce Johnson
Stuffed: Adventures of a Restaurant Family by Patricia Volk
The Autobiography of Alice B. Toklas by Gertrude Stein
Faith, Sex, Mystery by Richard Gilman
The Gatekeeper: A Memoir by Terry Eagleton
The Little Locksmith: A Memoir by Katharine Butler Hathaway

Miscellaneous Fiction and Nonfiction

Dispatches by Michael Herr
Work: A Story of Experience by Louisa May Alcott
The Ragged Trousered Philanthropists by Robert Tressell
The Great Arizona Orphan Abduction by Linda Gordon
Looking for a Ship by John McPhee
The Sportswriter by Richard Ford
Endless Love by Scott Spencer
Cathedral by Raymond Carver
Empire Falls by Richard Russo
Mystery Train: Images of America in Rock 'n' Roll Music by Greil Marcus
Terrible Honesty: Mongrel Manhattan in the 1920s by Ann Douglas
Here Is New York by E. B. White
They Marched into Sunlight: War and Peace, Vietnam and America, October 1967 by David Maraniss
Mason's Retreat by Christopher Tilghman
Arc of Justice: A Saga of Race, Civil Rights, and Murder in the Jazz Age by Kevin Boyle
Bury the Chains: Prophets and Rebels in the Fight to Free an Empire's Slaves by Adam Hochschild

Notes

Introduction

1. Lillian Hellman, *Scoundrel Time* in *Three* (1976; reprint, Boston: Little, Brown, 1979), 612.
2. Richard Wright, *Black Boy (American Hunger)* (reprint, New York: Library of America, 1991), 237–38.

Chapter 1

1. Dashiell Hammett, *The Maltese Falcon* (1930; reprint, New York: Vintage, 1989), 160.
2. Barbara Pym, *Quartet in Autumn* (New York: Harper & Row, 1977), 3.
3. Charlotte Brontë, *Villette* (1853; reprint, London: Penguin Classics, 1979), 97.
4. Ibid.

5. The disaster that, in fact, eventually befell Jane and Cassandra Austen and their mother in the last years of Jane's life. A lot of qualifications must be appended to this thumbnail description of the marriage market as an extreme adventure particularly for nineteenth-century women. I'm ignoring the (in many respects) more dire situation of working-class women—just as most nineteenth-century literature ignored it, because the novels and poems that described this particular adventure were, after all, written by literate middle- and upper-class women. I also don't mean to imply that marriage itself was such a great deliverance. Arguably, in legal terms, it made a woman even more of a dependent by depriving her of her property rights, rights to her own body, privacy, and custody of her children should a separation occur. These objections noted, since marriage was considered by nineteenth-century society as the "natural conclusion" to a young woman's story, not to be chosen in marriage was regarded as a tragic personal misfortune. Think of what being left at the altar did to Dickens's Miss Havisham.

6. Jane Austen, *Pride and Prejudice* (1813; reprint, New York: W. W. Norton, 1966), 162.

7. Ibid., 88.

8. Ibid.

9. Ibid., 234.

10. Charlotte Brontë, *Jane Eyre* (1847; reprint, New York: Norton Critical Editions, 1971), 6.

11. Ibid., 12.

12. Ibid., 14.

13. Ibid., 60.

14. Ibid., 73.

15. Ibid., 93.

16. Ibid., 269.

17. Ibid., 290.

18. Ibid., 322.

19. Brontë, *Villette*, 226.

20. Ibid., 229.

21. Ibid.

22. Ibid., 231.

23. Ibid., 232.
24. Ibid., 231.
25. Ibid.
26. Ibid.
27. Ibid., 232.
28. Ibid.
29. Ibid., 235.
30. Ibid., 235–36.
31. Ibid., 236.
32. Ibid., 596. Actually, Brontë's contemporaries found the ending more cryptic than we do. Lucy's failure to actually pronounce Paul Emanuel lost at sea prompted a few of her female literary correspondents to write to her asking for clarification.
33. Ibid., 237.
34. Ibid.
35. Toni Morrison, *Beloved* (New York: Alfred A. Knopf, 1987), 274.
36. Karin Evans's *The Lost Daughters of China* and Emily Prager's *Wuhu Diary*—both excellent personal accounts about adopting from China and, in Prager's case, returning to China with her five-year-old daughter—weren't published yet in 1999. Neither was *The Exact Same Moon: Fifty Acres and a Family, Washington Post Magazine* columnist Jeanne Marie Laskas's affecting collection of columns about her experiences as the mother of two daughters adopted from China. A flight attendant on the endless "Northworst" flight home from China recommended *Wild Swans* by Jung Chang, praising it as a great memoir about three generations of Chinese women that gives readers a sense of the turmoil of twentieth-century China. She was right. As far as children's adoption books go, Molly is, so far, pretty uninterested in all of them, although she likes to look at the photos in Emily Prager's book. I like the illustrations in *I Love You Like Crazy Cakes,* the bestselling children's book by Rose Lewis about a single mom adopting her daughter from China, but her story isn't like my story, so I find myself "correcting" her text as I read. I like *Happy Adoption Day!* by John McCutcheon and *Little Miss Spider* by David Kirk, which is a spine-tingling tale about adoption (Betty the Beetle rescues Little Miss Spider from the jaws of some hungry birds). But my favorite kids' adoption book—the one

that always makes me tear up—is *A Mother for Choco* by Keiko Kasza (Choco the bird is adopted by Mrs. Bear, who's already a mother to an alligator, a pig, and a hippo). *Choco* addresses, with humor and poignancy, the issue of adoptive parents and children not looking alike—an issue that, obviously, already comes up a lot in my mixed-race family's life.

37. Nell Freudenberger, *Lucky Girls* (New York: Ecco, 2004), 14.

38. Paul Cowan, *An Orphan in History: One Man's Triumphant Search for His Jewish Roots* (New York: Doubleday, 1982), 3.

Chapter 2

1. Vartan Gregorian, *The Road to Home: My Life and Times* (New York: Simon & Schuster, 2003), 257.

2. Kingsley Amis, *Lucky Jim* (London: Penguin, 1954), 61.

3. Ibid., 14–15.

4. Greil Marcus, *Mystery Train: Images of America in Rock 'n' Roll Music* (New York: Dutton, 1975), 125.

5. Dashiell Hammett, *Red Harvest* (1929; reprint, New York: Vintage, 1970), 3.

6. John D. Rosenberg, *The Darkening Glass: A Portrait of Ruskin's Genius* (New York: Columbia University Press, 1961), 178.

7. William Morris, *News from Nowhere, or An Epoch of Rest: Being some chapters from a Utopian Romance,* in *Commonweal,* 10 January–4 October 1890 (reprint, London: Penguin, 1993), 228.

8. "The Gutting of Couffignal," in *The Big Knockover,* ed. Lillian Hellman (New York: Vintage, 1972), 34.

9. One of my favorite, characteristically on-target phrases from Ross Macdonald—this one from *Black Money* (1965; reprint, New York: Vintage, 1996), 88.

10. Raymond Chandler, *The Big Sleep* (1939; reprint, New York: Vintage, 1988), 79.

11. Sue Grafton, *P is for Peril* (New York: Putnam, 2001), 175.

12. Ian Watt, *The Rise of the Novel: Studies in Defoe, Richardson, and Fielding* (Berkeley: University of California Press, 1957), 63.

13. Robert Tressell, *The Ragged Trousered Philanthropists* (1913; reprint, New York: Monthly Review Press, 1962), 434.

14. *Village Voice Literary Supplement,* April 1991, 19–21.

Chapter 3

1. Jane Austen, *Pride and Prejudice* (1813; reprint, New York: W. W. Norton, 1966), 176.

2. Barbara Pym, *Some Tame Gazelle* (1950; reprint, New York: Perennial, 1984), 169.

3. Dorothy Sayers, *Gaudy Night* (1936; reprint, New York: Harper Paperbacks, 1995), 2.

4. Ibid., 5.

5. Ibid., 10.

6. Ibid., 17–18.

7. Virginia Woolf, *A Room of One's Own* (1929; reprint, New York: Harcourt, Brace, 1957), 54.

8. Claire Tomalin, *Jane Austen: A Life* (New York: Alfred A. Knopf, 1997), 255.

9. Allen Ginsberg, "America." ll. 73–74. In *Allen Ginsberg Collected Poems, 1947–1980* (New York: Harper & Row, 1984), 146.

Chaper 4

1. Terry Eagleton, *The Gatekeeper: A Memoir* (New York: St. Martin's, 2002), 104.

2. Rev. Brother Eugene, O.S.F., ed., *The Brooklyn Catholic Speller: Fifth Year* (New York: W. H. Sadler, 1939), 58.

3. Ibid., 48.

4. Ibid., 2.

5. Ibid., 68.

6. Ibid., 80.

7. For a great modern autobiography about wrestling with God, I recommend Richard Gilman's 1986 memoir, *Faith, Sex, Mystery.* Gilman, a theater critic and professor of drama at Yale, had a

conversion experience one summer's day in 1952 while he was browsing in a branch of the New York Public Library. There, in the dusty stacks, he was inexplicably drawn to a large tome, *The Spirit of Medieval Philosophy,* by French philosopher Étienne Gilson. Reading the book started Gilman on the path to becoming a Catholic—a faith he eventually renounced.

8. Charles Dickens, *A Tale of Two Cities* (1854; reprint, New York: Simon & Schuster, 1969), 470.

9. Although its worldview is secular and its range historical as well as autobiographical, *Life as We Know It,* Michael Bérubé's 1996 book about Down syndrome—which his second child was diagnosed with at birth—is an excellent and enlightening modern "inheritor" to the Karen books.

10. Marie Killilea, *Karen* (1952; reprint, Cutchogue, N.Y.: Buccaneer Books, n.d.), 43.

11. Ibid., 45–46.

12. Ibid., 249–50.

13. Marie Killilea, *With Love from Karen* (1963; reprint, Cutchogue, N.Y.: Buccaneer Books, n.d.), 9.

14. Killilea, *Karen,* 42.

15. Ibid., 46.

16. Ibid., 47.

17. Ibid., 75.

18. Ibid., 236.

19. Killilea, *With Love,* 176.

20. Ibid., 225.

21. Ibid., 276.

22. Killilea, *Karen,* 41.

23. Killilea, *With Love,* xx.

24. James T. Fisher, *Dr. America: The Lives of Thomas A. Dooley, 1927–1961: Culture, Politics, and the Cold War* (Amherst: University of Massachusetts Press, 1998).

25. Dr. Thomas Dooley, *The Night They Burned the Mountain* in *Dr. Tom Dooley's Three Great Books, 1956–60* (New York: Farrar, Straus and Cudahy, 1962), 261.

26. Ibid., 334.

27. Ibid., 366.

28. James Monahan, *Before I Sleep . . . The Last Days of Dr. Tom Dooley* (New York: Farrar, Straus and Cudahy, 1961), 10.

29. Lenora Mattingly Weber, *Meet the Malones* (1943; reprint, Calif.: Image Cascade, 1999), 1.

30. Ibid., 23.

31. Ibid., 1, 46.

32. Ibid., 41.

33. Ibid., 51–52.

34. Ibid., 64–65.

35. Ibid., 102–3.

36. Lenora Mattingly Weber, *Beany Malone* (1948; reprint, Calif: Image Cascade, 1999), 186.

37. Ibid., 77.

38. Lenora Mattingly Weber, *Come Back, Wherever You Are* (1969; reprint, Calif.: Image Cascade, 1999), 132.

39. Lenora Mattingly Weber, *Make a Wish for Me* (1956; reprint, Calif.: Image Cascade, 1999), 245.

40. Lenora Mattingly Weber, *Something Borrowed, Something Blue* (1963; reprint, Calif.: Image Cascade, 1999), 93.

41. Weber, *Something Borrowed,* 139.

42. Lenora Mattingly Weber, *Pick a New Dream* (1961; reprint, Calif.: Image Cascade, 1999), 193.

43. Ibid., 250–51.

44. Ibid., 254.

45. Ibid., 258.

46. Ibid., 252.

Epilogue

1. Dashiell Hammett, *The Maltese Falcon* (1930; reprint, New York: Vintage, 1989), 63.

2. Pete Hamill, *A Drinking Life: A Memoir* (Boston: Little, Brown, 1994), 50.